A Piece of Work

A Piece of Work

Playing Shakespeare & Other Stories

Simon Russell Beale

abacus
books

ABACUS

First published in Great Britain in 2024 by Abacus

1 3 5 7 9 10 8 6 4 2

A CIP catalogue record for this book is available from the British Library.

ISBN 978-0-316-72532-3

Typeset in Jenson by M Rules
Printed and bound in Great Britain by
Clays Ltd, Elcograf S.p.A.

Papers used by Abacus are from well-managed forests and other responsible sources.

MIX
Paper | Supporting responsible forestry
FSC® C104740

Abacus
An imprint of
Little, Brown Book Group
Carmelite House
50 Victoria Embankment
London EC4Y 0DZ

An Hachette UK Company
www.hachette.co.uk

www.littlebrown.co.uk

For
Tim, Andy, Katie and Matt
and
Lucy

Contents

Foreword

I was introduced to Shakespeare and his plays when I was very young. There is nothing exceptional about that; most British schoolchildren are required to read his work as part of their early education. Some find the experience tedious, even traumatic, but I, like so many others, fell in love at first sight. The thrill of that initial meeting has never lessened and Shakespeare has become an indispensable part of my life – and my work, of course.

So this book is principally about him; or, rather, it's about my time in his company. Writing about our greatest playwright can sometimes be an exhilarating business. But it can also be treacherous. People hold strong opinions about his life and work, love his plays intensely and, in discussion, ideas can harden and tempers fray. To the outside eye, the endless debate might look courteous, but it can be fierce.

I want to talk about the Shakespearean characters that I have played. There was a time, very recently, when discussion of these characters – thinking about them as if they were distinct, individual human beings – was frowned upon. It had once been a very popular approach. It feels, after all, like a natural, instinctive response to Shakespeare's work. I remember as a schoolboy reading lush and wildly romantic descriptions of his characters by writers from as late as the early twentieth century.

At the time, I particularly enjoyed, for instance, a description of Edmund, the evil brother in *King Lear*, moving through the play like a black panther. I read many other similar, exuberant flights of fancy.

But then, suddenly, this approach became unfashionable. Taste in literary criticism changed; and academics, among others, pointed out that it was almost improper to analyse characters in this way. After all, they are not independent of the poetic form from which they spring. They cannot walk away from our scrutiny and pursue their own lives, as can real, flesh-and-blood human beings.

Since then, the critical consensus has changed again; character analysis is now almost acceptable. Fashion in the world of Shakespeare scholarship is an excitable, inconstant thing. These days, there is a school of Performance Criticism, which looks at the interpretations of individual characters offered by theatre practitioners and judges them to be valid critical comment. Predictably, I welcome this change. It could be argued that it's impossible for an actor, however mistakenly, not to think of the people he or she is asked to play as less than living, breathing men and women. I confess to being guilty of this. Furthermore, having been asked to write about my experiences of performing Shakespeare's work, I decided early on that I am not qualified to talk about the playwright in general or any one of his plays in its entirety. I am not an academic or even a genuine amateur specialist. Nor can I discuss convincingly characters that I have not played myself. So, for instance, you will read very few comments here about *Othello* as a whole or about the title role. Rather, in that instance, I confine myself to Iago, the villain of the piece and the part that I played. It would be presumptuous of me to do otherwise. My knowledge of Shakespeare, though broad enough, has its limitations.

I should also point out that the characters that I write about are my versions of the people that Shakespeare created; and my analyses are circumscribed by the particular nature of the productions in which they appeared. The character sketches that follow are necessarily incomplete. Some may be unrecognisable to my fellow actors.

So my interpretations reflect my individual interests, concerns and prejudices. This is why I have included some more personal reflections too. They may help to clarify the decisions I took. It's a truism that each reader creates their own Shakespeare. I am aware that certain ideas – the pressures of isolation, the loss of identity, the difficulty of finding redemption, the instinct to let things be, the importance of work – recur in my performances; and this recurrence may have more to do with me than Shakespeare. And there are elements in his writing that trouble me – as they trouble many others. I often ignore them because I find them too difficult to finesse. For instance, it will become evident that I worry sometimes that Shakespeare is unthinkingly conservative – politically and socially. Actually, I find it easy enough to accept his political outlook; so perhaps my discomfort is as much to do with an embarrassment about my own instinctive conservatism as anything else. I think I understand his fear of violent revolution and his suspicion of demagoguery. But his thoughts about social tensions – between the sexes, races and classes – are trickier to deal with.

However, it goes without saying that there are a great many things in his writing that I find limitlessly fascinating and that I tend to focus on, both in performance and, here, as a writer. This is why the Shakespeare I know and have lived with is my Shakespeare. In my head, I have transformed his characters into my characters – often, I acknowledge, gliding over some major difficulties. Each actor creates their own Hamlet, Lear, Macbeth. There is no such thing as a correct or complete portrayal of any of these great figures – however brilliant the performer. After nearly half of a millennium of study, this landscape of shifting sands has become a playground. Perhaps it always has been – even when the writer was alive. The range of interesting interpretative possibilities is vast; and what applies to individual characterisation applies to productions too. I recently saw a performance of *As You Like It* in which the majority of the cast were over sixty-five years old. It shouldn't have worked, but it turned out to be an enchanting evening. A play about the difficulties of young love was transformed into something very slightly different – a play about the memory of the difficulties of young love. I think Shakespeare would have been delighted.

This is surely why it's common for many people – including me – to devote a lifetime of work to this one writer. I know that there are obsessive Jane Austen fans, and readers who can't get enough of Charles Dickens or James Joyce. But Shakespeare is, I think, uniquely hospitable. Perhaps because in part we know so little of his biography – enough, but not a lot – his work can be approached in a myriad of different ways and without the constraints and complications imposed by a detailed knowledge of the writer's life. The man himself doesn't get in the way. There is essentially nothing more than the words he wrote; and that's quite enough to be getting on with. He also requires, as a playwright, our participation. Most of his work is there to be performed; and it blossoms with our interaction.

Some readers question whether Shakespeare is as great a writer as he is made out to be, whether his status is a construct that results from unthinking elitism and a history of British exceptionalism. These factors may very well be a component of his pre-eminence, but Shakespeare's writing has retained its grip on readers in a way that other writers, such as Walter Scott or Lord Byron, both lauded in their day, have not. He could not have flourished if he had not been properly great. He responds gleefully to feminist theory, queer theory, environmental concerns, the changing world of identity politics and debates about race.

Discussion of his work has recently centred, not on the minutiae of character development or the intricacies of his verse, but on his possible contribution to contemporary political debate and, excitingly, on his interaction with a larger and more diverse company of practitioners. Shakespeare can take it all on and adapt himself thrillingly to every new demand.

As far as I'm concerned, the greater number of risky and exploratory versions of Shakespeare's plays that we are offered the better. If a particular idea is a disaster, so what? Shakespeare will bounce back as strong as ever. He won't disappear. And a new approach to his work is often exciting and popular – Baz Luhrmann's film *William Shakespeare's Romeo + Juliet* comes to mind. There are many other examples I could list. I'm aware that my own work has almost invariably been in productions that were at the conservative end of the spectrum and with established national companies. But I am proud of all of them and know that they played their part in the ongoing exploration of Shakespeare's plays – as surely as other more experimental work. That's the most important thing – to keep his plays alive. For every individual reader, audience member or practitioner, there is always more to discover.

In the following pages, I mention by name a few of my fellow actors – but only a few. A similar parsimony applies to my naming of the directors, designers, producers, composers and other colleagues that I have worked with over the years. I apologise. I owe all of you, without exception, a huge debt. I must also apologise for the inevitable distortions of my faulty memory. I am sure a few of you will not recognise some of the events as I have described them. I can only say, in the famous words of one of the members of the royal family a couple of years ago, that 'recollections may vary'. I know you will be kind. Theatre people are often mocked. Some of us are over-praised and others are underrated. We are all assumed to be unusually self-obsessed and yet I know many in other professions who are equally egocentric.

I have been surrounded for nearly forty years by many men and women who have been very, very kind. They are also supremely creative, clever and, perhaps above all, fun to be with. One can't wish for more than that.

1

When I was eight, I was sent away to a boarding school in the centre of London. My father, an army doctor, had just been posted to Singapore. Needless to say, this was a very exciting prospect; although, frankly, the excitement felt rather familiar. We were already, even at this early stage, a well-travelled family. I was born in Malaysia, my twin brothers in Hong Kong. We had recently spent a short time on the coast of Libya. Nowhere – even the UK – felt quite like home. Just before moving to Singapore, we were quartered in a surprisingly large and very ugly flat overlooking the River Thames. It felt grand to be living next to the Tate gallery and within walking distance of Westminster Abbey and the Houses of Parliament, but of course it was a temporary arrangement. We were no more than visitors – even, like other army families, vagabonds.

Before Dad left for the Far East, it was decided that, although most of the family would join him in Singapore, I, the eldest boy, should remain in England. I know my mother found this difficult and so, no doubt, did I; but, in fact, I remember feeling more bemused than upset. One autumn morning, in my grandparents' freezing home in South Wales, I was told that my father had flown away and that the rest of the family – Mum and four siblings – was due to take a boat down the coast of Africa, across the Indian Ocean and on to our new home. My mother cried as she said goodbye; and I was left in the care of her parents, my beloved Grandad and Grandma Winter. I did not cry. A short time later, I was to write a letter from school in which I described myself as 'halfway between happy and unhappy'. I was trying to be absolutely accurate.

Despite the confusion that I felt when I finally arrived at my new school, I enjoyed, before that, a couple of very happy months in Wales. The plan hatched by my parents was that I should stay with my grandparents for the length of a school term before travelling down to London. I lived, during that time, in their small, semi-detached house in Newport – a city that has never enjoyed a noticeably sympathetic press, but that I loved. My mother's family were all teachers. My grandfather worked as an academic engineer – the principal of Newport Technological College, no less – but, in his youth, had flirted with the possibility of becoming an artist. He had a beehive in the garden and produced his own honey. Grandma was a teacher, as was her sister, my great-aunt, Vi, who lived, at this stage of her life, in the same modest home as Grandma and Grandad. Auntie Vi had a rather hairy chin and too few remaining teeth. She ate tinned grapefruit for breakfast and enjoyed the occasional square of very dark, bitter chocolate. My grandmother, was, in my eyes, simply perfect. She tried to teach me my multiplication tables, which I never mastered, and she was determined to tidy up my handwriting, so that it was well-formed and legible. We would share the postcards that Mum sent regularly as she and the family travelled around the globe. A year later, during my first holiday in Singapore, Mum gave me a scrapbook, which was stuffed with mementoes of her epic journey – pictures of unbearably exciting and exotic places such as Durban, Colombo and Calcutta. I still have it, very battered now, and I treasure it. I suspect that it would be the first thing I would try to save if my house burned down.

The scrapbook contains a picture of the boat that carried my family to Singapore. To my adult eyes, it looks tiny and rather frail; but it obviously did its job well enough. My mother and siblings arrived safely in their new home, greeted by my father, who was waiting for them on the quayside. In my child's mind, I travelled along with them. That was one of Grandma's skills – the skill of a teacher, I suppose. In that small house, heated intermittently with coal fires, squatting by the mud-choked River Usk, she conjured up for me visions of the spice markets of Sri Lanka and the rubber plantations of Malaysia, the deafening noise of Bombay and the empty expanse of South Africa. She told me, to my delight, that a writer had once described my birthplace – the island of Penang – as 'the pearl of the orient'. The ship stopped there before the last leg of her voyage.

I celebrated Christmas that year in Wales – and marked too my eighth birthday, which followed soon after. One memorable treat during that festive period was a visit to the local amateur dramatic society to watch my cousin Anne play a leading role in *Our Town* by Thornton Wilder. I thought she was beautiful; and the play itself, surprisingly perhaps, for a family that didn't go to the theatre regularly, was mesmerising. I was still rather a novice when it came to live performance. My piano teacher, an elderly lady called Mrs Ritchie, who lived in a tiny flat in Pimlico, London, with her equally musical daughter, Connie, had taken me, a year before, to a performance of *Don Giovanni* at the Coliseum. I found it tough – Mozart operas, beautiful though they are, do go on a bit – and, while I was thrilled by Mrs Ritchie's kindness, I was a little bored. I was more excited by the delicious tomato sandwiches she made. The tomatoes were sprinkled with lemon and sugar – an unbeatable combination.

The school in London that had been chosen for me was a choir school. For the next six years, I was to sing every day in St Paul's

Cathedral – as my father had done before me. We had all grown up with stories of his time there – the bomb that fell on the cathedral during the Second World War and that destroyed the high altar; he and his friends playing football on the flat roof of the choir school, where the boys could hear the loud, comforting hum of the telephone exchange nearby; singing for the king and queen as the country celebrated victory. Actually, he and the rest of the choir didn't spend all of their time in London, since they were evacuated to Truro in the early days of hostilities. The rivalry with the local Cornish boy trebles was apparently undisguised and I sense that my father was relieved when the choir was posted back to London. He told me only recently that just after their return, they were taken up to the dome on VE day to watch the searchlights swinging in triumph over a devastated city.

My mother gave me two presents before she left for Singapore – a small brown plastic record player and an LP of choral music, sung by the choir of St Paul's. They were a good choice – the record player was portable, for a start – and they also served as a gentle indication, or prediction, that music was to continue to play a fundamentally important part in my life. In fact, it had done so since the day I was born. There was no way I could have avoided this, even if I had wanted to. Dad has sung all his adult life – and sung to a high standard, too. At home, classical music was all around us. My siblings are all musical and know their Bach from their Handel and, if asked, could probably remember some of the Gilbert and Sullivan that Dad performed in his younger days. My twin brothers even appeared on stage with him at the Garrison Theatre in Singapore in a handful of performances of *The Mikado*. So they know that particular score very well indeed. When we caught a piece of music on the radio, Dad would ask me to guess who wrote it and, if I failed at that, then at least to have a stab at an approximate date of composition and the nationality of the composer. It's a habit that has been hard to break and I do it even now – although, mercifully for those around me, only in my head. Living abroad for so much of our childhood, we saw very little television – except, every four years, the Olympics, which were compulsory viewing – and our knowledge of popular culture was very limited. We missed all the TV programmes that our friends would talk about back in school; and we were ignorant of any new music that they might be listening to. However, I should mention in passing that my siblings are all good at sport – rugby, competitive swimming, hockey. That set of skills has passed me by.

Unsurprisingly, the musical training offered up at St Paul's was intensive, demanding and unrelenting. But, as I suspect is often the case with children, many lessons were absorbed without us realising it. I don't remember learning to sight-read music, but I must have done so at some point. And, since all the choristers had to play the piano and one other instrument and since daily practice was unavoidable, it was expected that we would leave with a pretty high degree of musical skill. In fact, as my headmaster told me in my final year, it was expected that we should all win music scholarships to our senior schools. In his mind, that was the least we could do.

I have never regretted all this. I don't regret the fact that, for a few hours each day, we were treated as professionals. The pressures of musical life in a major cathedral demanded that. I don't regret being forced to play the piano – my stumbling career with the oboe is another matter – because piano playing has been a limitless source of pleasure and a therapy all my life. What I do regret, however, is never being quite good or confident enough either as a performer or as a theorist to make full use of the opportunities I was given. I suspect that I do not possess an innate musical talent, although I was superbly trained and can sometimes look and sound convincing. For many years now, I have known and worked with great musicians. At university, for instance, I knew, alongside some fearsome academics, four singers who went on to enjoy major operatic careers and a couple of important composers. One of my close friends became the leader of a professional big band. So I know what the real thing looks like.

When I was in my forties, I decided to teach myself the rules of harmony and counterpoint. This was a feeble attempt, I realise, to wipe out the humiliating memory of the catastrophic grade I took away from my A-level music exams. I got a D. Among the many books I bought about the subject, there was one small hardback that was written early in the last century. Halfway through, having covered the basics, the author announces, rather imperiously I think, that any student who lacks an instinctive understanding and a discerning ear would probably be wasting their time in going any further. As I read, I felt that it was me in particular that he was talking to and that I was being put firmly in my place.

I wonder sometimes whether the musical training I received as a boy was as much to do with the eye as the ear. It's a particular legacy. The school's emphasis on sight-reading means that I still ask for any music that I have to perform professionally to be written down rather than putting everyone through the more laborious process of teaching me aurally. The huge amount of music that a cathedral choir has to rehearse and sing on a regular basis means that the ability to pick up a score and perform immediately is as important as skills that depend more on a good ear – such as memorising or improvisation. After all, during rehearsals at school, time was short and precious. When we made a mistake as we sang, we used to raise our right hand, which signalled to the conductor that we recognised our error, would not repeat it and that therefore there was no need to stop and go back to sort out the problem. This behavioural twitch was drilled into us at a very early age and became second nature. I still find myself putting up my hand when I make a mistake in rehearsal, even if now it's not so much music I'm dealing with but words. And if you watch adult choirs in rehearsal, there will often be hands flying up from singers who went through the same training as I did. Most of them, like me, are probably unaware of what they are doing.

The regime was tough, but it would be wrong to give the impression that it was joyless. After all, the results were often thrilling. There are not many small boys who get the chance to sing Bach's *St Matthew's Passion* and Handel's *Messiah* every year; or who join an orchestra – a proper, grown-up orchestra, for goodness' sake – for a series of Haydn masses used as part of the liturgy during Lent. Very few boys get to sing masterpieces by Monteverdi in front of the lord mayor at the Mansion House in the City of London or join the choirs of Westminster Abbey – our great rival – and the Chapel Royal for a giant annual celebration of music on St Cecilia's day.

And, of course, there were classes in other subjects than music – other things to study and to think about. Our headmaster, who was predictably stern but genuinely kindly, took the occasional lesson. Sometimes he taught history. I remember a term spent on the action-packed story of the British in India – an odd and uncomfortable idea now. And he taught us about English literature. Every week he would read to the whole school of thirty-eight children – usually adventure stories or Arthurian legend – and, more significantly, he changed the course of my life by introducing me to William Shakespeare.

St Paul's Cathedral Choir School was housed in a small, concrete building attached to a ruined Christopher Wren tower at the east end of the cathedral. It was very stylish. A plaque by the front door informed visitors that it had won some significant architectural award. The choirboys moved there from the building that Dad had known during the war. The new premises enclosed a large rehearsal space, a small playground (no football on the roof for us), a tiny swimming pool, a chapel and a library. It was in the latter that I first read Shakespeare out loud; and it must have been a memorable moment for me because the details are still clear – where I was sitting, the sun blasting through the large windows and, above all, what I read.

My family was not particularly literary; but my parents always encouraged my reading. By the time I became a teenager and had fallen under the spell of the books that I studied at school, all my time at home was spent devouring any author that I could lay my hands on. I didn't stop. When we lived in Germany, Dad's final foreign posting, we used to enjoy long, magical holidays that took us right across the continent. They have become a fundamental component of my family's mythology. We'd hitch a caravan to the back of the car and drive to southern Italy or northern Spain, spend some time there on a beach and then drive slowly back, stopping off at places that looked interesting. We saw Rome, Florence, Pisa, Venice, Salzburg, Avignon, Paris. When Mum was pregnant with my youngest brother, we spent a swelteringly hot day visiting Pompeii and Vesuvius. And I took my books with me everywhere we went. One year it was all the Brontës, the next Solzhenitsyn. There is a picture of me, lying on the sand in the Amalfi sun, reading, of all things, the latter's *Cancer Ward*.

In the years before that, it was C. S. Lewis, of course, and, above all, a writer called Jean Plaidy. She's largely forgotten now and I think most of her books are out of print; but she wrote a huge number of historical novels, not exactly fictional and definitely not swashbuckling, but rigorously and perhaps rather primly based on fact. There must be thousands of men and women of my age who learned their European history through her writing. The worlds she conjured up were unashamedly romantic, but she didn't shy away from hinting delicately at more complicated and unpleasant situations. One of her most popular books, *Murder Most Royal*, dealt in part with accusations of incest that were levelled against Anne Boleyn and her brother.

This storyline must have been part of the blurb on the back of the paperback because one day, as I was reading the book in the waiting room of my mother's surgery, the practice nurse spotted it and rushed into Mum's room to alert her. My mother apparently looked nonplussed – she was probably rather busy – and then shrugged.

So I was probably ready for my first look at Shakespeare.

On that day in the library, the headmaster asked me to read aloud a speech from *Julius Caesar*. In those days, this was a very popular play to give young children to study. I can't think why. Perhaps it was because it contains no overt references to the complexities of love or sex. It may be because the language is easier than many of Shakespeare's plays and the plot is simple and fast moving; but I would have thought the details of Roman politics would be considered a little dry for young minds. Despite having only a desultory interest in the story of the play, my vanity was tickled by being asked to perform. I was eager to show off, I suppose. But something else happened as I started to read. The speech was a famous one – not that I knew that at the time – about the carnage that was likely after the murder of Julius Caesar. Mark Antony is speaking over the corpse of the dictator, whose body has been punctured multiple times and whose clothes are presumably soaked in his blood. Antony promises to unleash 'the dogs of war', a familiar phrase, but still an extraordinary and ignoble image to come across for the first time. His pain and anger, both apparently genuine, compel him to predict a universal bloodbath – a prediction that, of course, turns out to be pretty accurate.

The pictures that Shakespeare paints are terrifying; and so is Antony's state of mind. He is both fevered and in icy control of his feelings. That contradiction is what this long argument in verse gives us – a tension that is also a sustained display of power. Our headmaster hadn't told us anything about verse structure – stresses, rhythm, line length and so on. He let the words speak for themselves and, even without instruction, I felt a thrill in my stomach as I spoke, like the low hum of an expensive car. During my career on stage, I have played a few characters that wield great personal and political power – not many, but a few – and the excitement I have felt when those characters swing into full-bodied oratorical life has its roots in that day in the library.

There must have been many other occasions at choir school when we read Shakespeare, but I don't recall them. At some point, we put on a small production of *A Midsummer Night's Dream*, in which I played Hippolyta, Queen of the Amazons and the wife of Theseus. My paternal grandmother made my costume. I thought it was beautiful – a dress of ivory silk with a length of gold cloth wrapped around it like a toga. It represented quite an effort on her part. But then there was always something dogged about Grandma Beale. Since my parents were living abroad, she would come every fortnight from Romford in Essex to take me out for tea after evensong. Since this was the only time we were allowed to meet with friends or family and we had to be back at school within two hours, the teas we took, at the Golden Egg round the corner or, later, when I was more grown-up, the Strand Palace Hotel, were mildly stressful. They certainly must have been for Grandma; but she was loyal, loving and dutiful, and she never let me down.

Like any responsible, grown-up actor, I did some research about Hippolyta, of course. I found out that the Amazons were fighters and that each warrior was thought to have cut off a breast in order to make it easier to draw a bow. This was intriguing, if gruesome; but unfortunately it was of little use to me. My Hippolyta was sedate, humourless and irredeemably middle class. She had beautiful hand gestures, though. I was very proud of a half-circle that I traced in the air at the mention of the moon, described as like 'a silver bow/New-bent in heaven' at the beginning of the play. And I loved being on stage.

It was a seductive, perhaps, some would say, a dangerous, moment; but at choir school I don't think I was often the centre of attention. I never sang a solo during my time at St Paul's; or, rather, I might once have been given the chance to perform a very small passage by myself, but it was a disaster. My voice was not considered good enough and our head of music clearly had doubts about both my musicality and my self-confidence. Curiously, my father was never given a solo either – so perhaps my incompetence was inherited. I did, however, enjoy one moment in the spotlight, although under rather strange circumstances. One Christmas, the BBC World Service decided to record a series of interviews with people who had to work through the holiday period. In the group of those they talked to, they wanted to include a chorister. I presume that, for many listeners, it was intriguing – even mildly inhumane – that we were kept in school over Christmas, although it seemed perfectly normal to us. Since I was the only boy in the school who lived abroad and the programme was being made by the World Service, I was chosen for the interview. I must have been about nine years old.

I was very nervous about the whole thing. My interlocutor was kindly, but my voice shook. I answered accurately and at length. When I was asked to describe a typical day in school, I began to go through every detail of the week, Monday to Sunday, minute by minute, until I had to be stopped. I had only got to Tuesday morning and felt that I had failed to provide all the necessary information. I finished the interview by singing a Christmas carol, but I started too high and had to begin again. The final broadcast was heavily edited.

I didn't hear the programme at the time it was aired, but a copy was sent to my parents in Singapore. When I arrived for the holidays, Dad proposed that we should listen to it. I was appalled and decided to run away from home. I got a few yards down the drive, but then Mum came out to apologise and take me back to the house. The interview was never mentioned again.

Many years later, when I was working at the National Theatre in London, I received a small parcel at the stage door. Inside was a letter from the producer who had talked to me as a boy. He wrote that he had been tidying his office and had found a unedited copy of my interview. He thought I might like to have it. It was a very kind gesture and I was rather touched by his generosity. I also thought that it would be fascinating to hear how I spoke as a boy. So I found an old machine in the sound department of the theatre and popped in the cassette. I'm sorry to say that it was horrible. I sounded like Princess Elizabeth speaking on the radio during the war. Nothing wrong with that, I suppose, but I found it difficult that my voice was so clipped and so high; and I could clearly hear my nerves. I listened for a couple of minutes and then switched it off. I've kept the tape – it's sitting in a cupboard somewhere – but I have never played it all the way through.

My little sister, Lucy, died while I was still a chorister. She was four years old. She had suffered all her life from a congenital heart defect. This was why the family travelled by boat to Singapore rather than by air. She was always a small child with translucent skin, large eyes and a faintly blue complexion; and she was much loved. Her death was as devastating as might be expected. Ten years after she died, I was being driven by my mother to Swindon station to catch a train. At that time, I was thinking of doing a doctorate at the University of London and my mother asked me to tell her about the subject of my thesis. I replied, without thinking, that I wanted to study how death, and especially the death of children, was portrayed in Victorian literature. After a long and heavy silence, my mother quietly apologised to me for not talking more over the years about Lucy's death. She had wanted to, she said, but she 'didn't have the words'.

A couple of years after Lucy's death, my youngest brother, Matthew, was born. He never knew Lucy.

Two Malcontents

Cassius

Shakespeare often addresses questions of class and class conflict in his work. But it can sometimes seem that his interest is cursory and superficial. So many of his plays deal principally with kings and queens, generals and statesmen, and he is always exercised by the concerns that weigh down these impressive figures. Working people, especially in the Roman plays and in his great English history cycle, are often portrayed as fickle, violent and stupid. His writing became more nuanced as he got older, perhaps, but in his early work he seems wary of mob rule and mistrustful of political populism. This is why he is considered by many to be a conservative writer, eager to uphold the values of an established order and terrified of the consequences of its dissolution; it is also why I have heard him quoted, approvingly, but out of context, at Tory party conferences. He seems to work well in that environment. Actually it is difficult to argue against his political conservatism. He seems to assume that those in power should remain in power – a king, once anointed, should remain a king – although the value of this principle is a tricky thing for him to argue if the rulers, anointed or otherwise, behave badly. Of course, we will never know what he himself really thought – he's not that kind of writer – but he does seem to like the company of the rich and famous. Furthermore, although he wrote about the working class, he, unlike some of his contemporaries, doesn't seem particularly interested in middle-class characters. *The Merry Wives of Windsor* is an exception, but, charming work though it is, nobody would claim that it is one of his best.

Sometimes, though, when he feels the need to look more closely at issues of class and the exercise of power, he can play a subtler game. Or, rather, he allows his actors to do so. We can, if we wish, refract his writing through the lens of our own contemporary class consciousness. It may result in distortion, but such distortion is an inevitable component of any actor's interpretation. And, anyway, it's fun. I sensed this when I was asked to do *Julius Caesar* three decades after I first read it at school. This is a play that dramatises a famous political assassination, of course. It's possibly the most famous murder in Western history; and, since the principal victim is a potential tyrant, any telling of the tale has to confront the issue of republicanism. This must have been a sensitive topic in an England where an autocratic ruler was coming to the end of her life and the future – especially since she refused to nominate an heir – looked uncertain. Shakespeare shows a degree of courage in choosing this story; and he wouldn't be the great writer that he is if he was unwilling to argue the case for a republic (and the necessity, in certain circumstances, of political murder) and to do it with conviction. It is also a play that is intriguingly ambiguous about the motives and characters of the assassins. Simply put, it is impossible to know whether the playwright admires or despises them. Or rather, they are both admirable and despicable, just as Julius Caesar himself is both magnificent and dangerous. There are also significant and subtle differences between the conspirators who are, after all, ostensibly of the same class and would be expected to believe the same things. Such distinctions are not seen so clearly in Shakespeare's earlier history plays – like *Richard III*, for instance. In that play, the principal actors all sound similar; and they believe in the same things. Many of them are members of the same family, after all. One senses that they would all behave as ruthlessly as Richard if only they had his wit and speed of thought – and could get away with it.

*

When the director, Deborah Warner, invited me to be in *Julius Caesar* in 2005, I wasn't asked to play Mark Antony. I wasn't to repeat my experience at school, it seemed. Antony went to Ralph Fiennes. Ralph and I had first met years before when we were both at the Royal Shakespeare Company. Even then he was a star – extremely good looking and blessed with an impeccable technique. He also loved and understood the repertoire. He went on to enjoy an astonishing career in film, but he has never lost his interest in the hardest and most demanding writing for the stage – Shakespeare, Ibsen, Shaw, even T. S. Eliot. While Ralph started his time in Stratford playing leading men, I was judged by the same company to be a comic actor. I first heard Ralph's name when one of the directors, Adrian Noble, decided, after putting me through a long audition process, not to give me an important and serious role – Henry VI – in the massive sequence of early history plays that he was to direct as part of the upcoming season. He had just seen a marvellous young actor at the National Theatre, he said. His name was Ralph Fiennes and the role of Henry was to be given to him. As a consolation, Adrian kindly offered me the chance to do three Restoration fops in a row. My heart sank; but, against all expectations, it proved to be a fascinating year. For a short period, I became a sort of super-specialist in seventeenth-century comedy, which was of little use in later life or, indeed, in my career, but intriguing enough at the time. Ralph triumphed as Henry.

As for Deborah's production, I was too young for Caesar. Brutus, the chief conspirator and the troubled centre of the play, was not on offer. The director wanted to give me Cassius, Brutus's principal collaborator. This was surprising. I had some inevitable preconceptions about the character. I understood that he was clever, sly and acid tongued. More significantly, I thought to myself as Deborah talked about the part, wasn't he supposed to be thin? Caesar describes him as having 'a lean and hungry look' and, a little later, expresses a wish that 'he were fatter'. Given the fact that I am visibly overweight, I worried that people would laugh. Deborah promised that she would ensure that they wouldn't. The 'lean and hungry look' became solely about Cassius's psychological make-up and had nothing to do with his physical appearance. I don't quite know how she managed it, but, to her lasting credit, there was no laughter.

Weight is also, as it happens, an issue in *Hamlet*. As he is fighting his last duel, the dashing young prince is described as fat by his mother – 'He's fat and scant of breath'. *Hamlet* was written in the same year as *Julius Caesar*. For many years, editors and commentators bent over backwards to argue that Hamlet's mother could not possibly mean that her son was plump. Hamlet, surely, is slim and athletic (and, since he's Danish, probably fair-haired). He couldn't possibly be overweight. When he describes the prince as 'fat', Shakespeare must mean 'sweaty' or 'out of condition'. On the other hand, in *Julius Caesar*, 'fat' clearly means 'fat'. Since only months separate the composition of the two plays, one would think that the word 'fat' might mean the same thing in both cases. But for many, this was inconceivable. Things have changed now; Hamlet's appearance is less of an issue. But it was an issue – albeit a minor one – when I played him. A local newspaper in the West Country headed a review of our production with an elaborate pun: 'Tubby or not tubby, fat is the question'. It probably wouldn't be acceptable now, but at least it was clever and the review itself was positive, so I couldn't object too strongly. Anyway, by that time, I was used to people writing about my weight. An actor's size and shape are a part of what people see on the stage and maybe I was fair game.

I have an image of Shakespeare watching his leading actor, Richard Burbage, on stage as Hamlet. Burbage has been playing the part on and off for a few years now and the slim young man for whom the playwright wrote Hamlet is approaching middle age and developing a bit of a paunch. During the last scene of the play, when the prince is fighting Laertes and has presumably discarded his doublet and is wearing just the bare minimum, Shakespeare realises that Burbage's gain in weight is glaringly obvious and has to be acknowledged. So he scribbles the line, 'He's fat and scant of breath', hands it to the actor playing Gertrude and in it goes. Who knows, but perhaps Shakespeare really did work like that?

Deborah Warner wanted to present *Julius Caesar* as absolutely contemporary. The story of Caesar's murder never loses its relevance, so this seemed appropriate. The designs for the early scenes in Rome were sleek and monumental – Fascist architecture, in essence. Once the civil war was underway after the murder of Caesar, the stage was stripped bare, revealing pipes and wiring and large expanses of bare concrete. When Anton Lesser, who played Brutus, sat alone in that vast space, dressed in his combat fatigues, he looked like the photographs we had all seen of soldiers fighting the endless, exhausting wars in the Middle East. The designer dressed the senators of Rome in suits. The crowd has an important role in *Julius Caesar*, and Deborah crammed the stage with a hundred people – some professional actors, others local amateurs. In this, she was following in the footsteps of famous nineteenth-century producers who thrilled London audiences with huge, meticulously researched versions of *Julius Caesar* – and other Shakespeare plays – which involved very large numbers of people. After a run at the Barbican in London, we were due to tour the show on the continent and couldn't take with us many of the actors involved in the crowd scenes. So in Paris, Madrid and Luxembourg we used local performers. In Luxembourg, it felt as if half the population of the country had joined us on stage. A couple of assistant directors were employed to deal with the extras, but it was Deborah herself who managed to inspire a fierce loyalty and absolute commitment in all of us – a very impressive achievement.

I had met Deborah long before this, but I didn't know her

well. I first heard of her when I was a student. I was up in Edinburgh performing as part of the annual festival. I was probably in something unwatchable. I can't remember what exactly – which I'm sure is a good thing. As a young actor, I went to the Edinburgh festival four years in a row. The year that I first became aware of Deborah might have been the same year that I played a pantomime dame in a student show – an experience for both me and the audience that will never, I hope, be repeated. All the theatre practitioners used to gather in the Traverse Theatre bar – just as comedians went to another watering-hole and musicians went somewhere else again. That year, everyone in the student community was talking in hushed voices about a production of *King Lear* by a new young director who used a text that was uncut and deployed a fiercely brutal aesthetic. I didn't manage to see the show, but the director's name – Deborah Warner – stuck in my head. In 1988, during my first season at the Royal Shakespeare Company, I went along to see her version of *King John* in a tiny theatre called the Other Place in Stratford. The building was essentially a tin hut that was unbearably hot in the summer and freezing cold in the winter. It was in the dog days of July or August when I saw the play and I was very uncomfortable, though probably not as uncomfortable as the actors, who were all wearing big, heavy costumes and, as far as I could see, a lot of fur. However, the production was sensational. I was bowled over by it. Deborah had by then established herself as one of our most important young directors. Along with so much else, she developed a brilliant creative partnership with the equally dazzling actor Fiona Shaw. Not long after my first season in Stratford, I saw Fiona in a performance of *Electra* directed by Deborah. It was a masterclass in the control of suppressed fury. It was as if Fiona began the play in a frame of mind that most actors achieve only at the end of a long tragic story. She started at an agonising emotional pitch and then climbed still higher. I anticipated that Deborah would ask for the same mental and physical energy in *Julius Caesar*. I was not disappointed; and she was, to my delight, at her most imaginative and magisterial.

Julius Caesar is the story of very public events – an assassination and the unrest that follows – and it charts the lives of men and women who are used to performing in the public arena. That is why it is always so interesting to see them, as we sometimes do, in private. But, unlike his portraits of some of the other characters in the play, Shakespeare gives us almost no information about Cassius's private life. An actor has to ferret around for tiny details and make those details count. In contrast, we know that Antony is a party animal with, presumably, a busy sex life; and we know too that Caesar and Brutus are married. We meet their wives and see both couples at home. For all we know (and despite the evidence of history), Cassius might as well be single. We have no idea where he lives or with whom he might sleep. The canvas is left almost blank.

I had to find a place to start. It is always worth registering what other people say about the character one is playing, even if their analysis is untrustworthy; and so it proved in this case. Early in the story, Caesar paints a portrait of Cassius, whom he mistrusts, as secretive, perhaps even a loner. That seemed to be something worth exploring. It also appears that the other characters have as little information about Cassius as the reader or audience member. For a public figure, he seems to be a very private man. The question is why?

When Cassius takes Brutus aside to persuade him to join the conspiracy to kill Caesar, he speaks very, very carefully. It makes for a brilliant, disturbing moment early in the play. This is when I assumed that the skilled manipulator that I had heard about would be most clearly evident. He is, as expected, sharp witted and fast thinking. He certainly talks a great deal. But he seemed to me to be rather needy. He tries too hard.

For instance, the stories he tells about his relationship with Caesar, and which are there to make the leader look weak, are as much to do with boosting Cassius's worth in Brutus's eyes as anything else. What I read were the words of a man who is tentative, even frightened. He is not sure that he will succeed in convincing Brutus and he would be in great danger if he failed. He knows that he is, to say the least, on shaky ground. This is understandable, since Cassius's proposals are treasonous. But I wondered if something else was going on. He flatters Brutus shamelessly, reminding his colleague not only of his personal qualities but also of his famous ancestors. Cassius points out that Brutus is a great man and from a great family. Perhaps, I thought, Cassius is neither.

And then Cassius mentions their fathers and how they had both told stories of the great days of old Rome. A whole world opened up. Did Cassius and Brutus know each other as boys? Did they go to the same school? And, most importantly, does Brutus make Cassius feel inadequate because, even if they had enjoyed a similar education, the former was born into the topmost rung of the ruling class and the latter wasn't? I know that this might look like an inappropriately contemporary reading, but if the answer to this last question was yes, then I had found a motive for Cassius's behaviour.

I pushed this idea of Cassius as an insecure man as far as it would go. In my mind, he was the scholarship boy who went to a fancy public school and didn't have an easy time there. Brutus's family had gone to the same school for generations. I probably went further than the playwright's words could bear. I acknowledge this. My approach ignored the details of Roman history and Elizabethan society. For instance, many in Shakespeare's first audiences would have known that the historical Cassius was married to Brutus's sister and indeed, in the play, Brutus refers to Cassius as 'brother'. So they were, in a way, related and were, from childhood, part of the same social milieu. But Shakespeare skates over this fact of a familial connection pretty quickly. It doesn't seem to interest him very much. So I ignored it.

More significantly, I had read too many commentaries on the play that assumed that Cassius is a nasty and unlikeable man. In the same commentaries, Brutus is seen as an honourable dupe, who, in his heart, doesn't really want to kill Caesar or, at the very least, needs some encouragement. By extension, since Brutus is a fundamentally decent man, the republicanism that Cassius espouses is essentially an absurd and wicked fantasy, and any attempt to establish a republic – especially through violence – is bound to fail. Seen in this light, Julius Caesar should, on balance, remain in power. He may be untrustworthy, but it is probably wise not to rock the boat. The good and the bad are clearly delineated and mutually exclusive. Brutus is good and Cassius is bad. But, I thought, Shakespeare is surely a better writer than that.

When I started out as an actor, I was given a rule of thumb, which has since proved very useful: never take a character's self-evaluation at face value and, as I have already hinted, always question what others think about him or her, even when what they say might be useful. A good exercise is to write down everything that a character says about themselves and then what others say about them. It can reveal surprising things. Cassius thinks of himself (and others think of him) as Machiavellian; but, although he is a good talker and incisive in debate, he is, despite himself, in awe of Brutus, follows his recommendations too often and consequently makes too many mistakes. The murder of Caesar is, to be honest, a muddle and the fallout is appalling. Politics is an inexact science and Cassius is not light-footed enough to deal with that. He fails spectacularly. And, as for Brutus, his much-praised honour – something of which he himself is very proud – is arguably tarnished very early on, as Mark Antony makes painfully clear.

So, in resisting the idea of the arch-manipulator, my Cassius turned out to be a committed and sincere republican – in public and in private. He never lies about that. He trusts in the idea of a Rome free of Caesar. He loves the old, established principles of Roman government, which he genuinely believes are now under threat. As a result of his upbringing, however, he is also a nervous and unsteady operator.

This combination of sincerity and insecurity reveals itself elsewhere. I discovered that, in scene after scene, Cassius keeps threatening to kill himself. He says that he could not live in a world where Caesar is king. At first glance, this could look like posturing; but I preferred the idea that such thoughts are genuine. Cassius's behaviour is the result of his passionately held beliefs. He is not, politically, a cynic. He might loathe Caesar as a man, he might resent his behaviour towards him, but it is more important, surely, that, for him, the whole idea of autocracy is abhorrent. This is what makes his last days so moving to watch. The grim knowledge that he has betrayed his own ideals and that the whole honourable enterprise has failed is devastating. Brutus, over his friend's dead body, calls him 'The last of all the Romans' – as Cassius was described by contemporary Roman writers. Brutus also says that 'It is impossible that ever Rome/ Should breed [his] fellow.' It is a compliment, I assume; and maybe Brutus, whatever anyone else might think, is right.

The details Shakespeare provides about Cassius's private life are tiny, almost imperceptible. But they are used to impressive effect. It's a technique that Shakespeare employed throughout his writing – introducing something that appears to be insignificant but that packs an emotional punch. On the day he dies, Cassius tells us that it is his birthday – with no further comment. This could be simply a statement of fact with no emotional significance; and it is certainly best played that way. But it also feels to me like a man looking back, affectionately and sadly, to his childhood, to the father whom he admired, to his mother and his family, to his life at school. He might even be thinking of Brutus, a man whom he has looked up to since they were boys together and whom he once admired and loved without qualification.

In his last moments, around the time that he mentions his birthday, Cassius describes a colleague as his 'best friend'. It is not Brutus, as one might expect, but somebody called Titinius, about whom we know next to nothing. Without warning, another private world opens up. Cassius is not a dry stick. Perhaps he is not a natural loner. It appears that he needs people to love, and, in the case of Brutus, to love and respect. In our production of *Julius Caesar,* Cassius and Titinius, in the moment before their deaths, kissed – not a farewell peck on the cheek, but properly, passionately, like lovers. Again, it might not be what the playwright intended, but it made sense to us.

It is always fascinating and instructive to look at the source material that Shakespeare used for his plays. In the case of *Julius Caesar,* he read a translation of a Classical text – Plutarch's *Lives of the Noble Grecians and Romanes.* Plutarch is crisp and sharp in his judgements. He doesn't seem to trust the motives of the figures he writes about. Shakespeare is more generous. He doesn't presume to understand the full picture. In omitting certain things that Plutarch mentions – Cassius has a son, for instance, and apparently owned a pride of pet lions – and touching only lightly on others, Shakespeare allows more room for doubt. Into that space, actors, readers and audience can crawl and do their work. That, I suppose, sums up the essential difference between a historian and a great playwright.

Malvolio

Malvolio in *Twelfth Night* is a man who comes up directly against class prejudice. This is undeniable. In fact, whereas with *Julius Caesar,* I constructed an argument about class from a small number of clues – and those clues could, in any case, be read in an entirely different way – it is absolutely clear that Malvolio can be seen as fighting against the restrictions imposed on his class. He suffers in part because he insists on acting above his station. *Twelfth Night* is essentially a story about aristocrats and Malvolio is a domestic servant in a very grand house. Many in the play think he should know and keep to his place. Sir Toby Belch, who loathes Malvolio, says as much. Malvolio is also a prude and a killjoy, but that's another matter. The point is, when it comes to the final punishment meted out to him, his tormentors – his employers and their friends – think he is asking for it and deserves what he gets; and his punishment is as much to do with his presumption as with his puritanism.

Twelfth Night has been described as Shakespeare's last romantic comedy. Later in his career, he would write other plays with happy endings – a crude definition of comedy – but these works are either darkly problematic and, indeed, have been called his 'problem' plays, or have a magical or supernatural component. This sounds like hair splitting, but Shakespeare's early comedies are securely grounded in the real world and even extraordinary events can be explained away quite rationally. They are also, if one overlooks the odd bit of unpleasantness, sunny. His later plays are, quite definitely, not sunny. In part because it is a work of Shakespeare's maturity, *Twelfth Night* is often thought of as having an autumnal quality, as being almost Chekhovian. To any actor who is asked to play Malvolio, that description can only appear reductive. Autumnal is the last word that comes to mind. Perhaps wintry would be more accurate.

As it happens, there is a rumble of military conflict in the background of *Twelfth Night* – not a particularly Chekhovian ingredient, even if one takes into account *The Three Sisters*. One of the characters in Shakespeare's play has been involved with skirmishes off the coast of Illyria. This is barely explored in the text, although it would be interesting to see a production in which this threat – this shadow in the background – is more clearly acknowledged. Most skate over it, as the writer does. Similarly, Viola, the young woman at the centre of the story, arrives in Illyria after a shipwreck that leaves her stranded, homeless and alone. From a contemporary perspective, she is a refugee – an idea that might be a productive one to explore. It's worth remembering that *Twelfth Night* need not be simply – and comfortably – melancholic.

A link with Chekhov was acknowledged by Sam Mendes when he directed the play in 2002. He put it on as part of a final season in the theatre that he had run so triumphantly for ten years – the Donmar Warehouse in London. He decided to cast the same group of actors in both *Twelfth Night* and *Uncle Vanya* – a Chekhov masterpiece. Both plays are concerned, among other things, with the pain of unrequited love and with the joy of love discovered and reciprocated. There is a rueful quality about both of them that suited Sam's gesture of farewell. One night, the last night, as I remember, he invited a host of directors, designers and actors, all of whom had worked at the Donmar over the past decade, to see our version of *Twelfth Night*. As the cast began to get ready for the show, Sam came to the dressing room to wish us luck and then disappeared to greet his guests. Five minutes later, he rushed back to apologise. The audience would be friendly, he said, of course they would, but among them were many, many actors who had performed the play in the past – a gaggle of great Malvolios, great Violas, great Olivias. Now he was asking us to present our version of the play. He was sorry to put us under that sort of pressure. He was looking sheepish. He could clearly read the terror on our faces and so he quickly left. In fact, it turned out to be a joyous occasion. At the end, we didn't take a curtain call – it seemed inappropriate somehow – but instead went to sit in the auditorium to listen to Sam and his colleagues say their final goodbyes from the stage. The whole evening was transformed into a celebration of their achievements.

Sam and I had, by this time, done a handful of shows

together – all written by Shakespeare. We never used to talk much about the work before we started rehearsals. He would sometimes ring me to let me know about a piece of casting or a design idea, but that was merely a courtesy or a chance to gossip. He was quite happy to make early decisions without my input. On this occasion, though, we did meet for a drink to discuss some thoughts that he had had about Malvolio. There is a very famous scene in *Twelfth Night* that Shakespeare sets in a garden. Malvolio is a steward and runs the household of a rather imperious lady called Olivia. He is a stickler for correct form and encourages sober behaviour. He is self-important and humourless. However, it is well known by everyone who lives in the house that he is in love with his mistress. A plan is hatched to humiliate him. A letter is written that appears to be from Olivia. In fact, it has been penned by her maid, Maria, who claims, rather improbably, to be able to imitate her mistress's handwriting. In the letter, the writer declares her love for her steward. The letter is dropped in the garden where Malvolio is sure to find it. He does so and predictably believes every word. And so his downfall begins.

Sam didn't want to set this scene in a garden. He thought that Malvolio should discover the letter in his bedroom – his private space. It was an idea rich in possibilities. As with Cassius, we know nothing of Malvolio's background – and, up until this point, nothing of his personal life. But a scene in his bedroom might allow us a glimpse behind the professional mask. So I decided to run with Sam's idea.

Once the decision to change the location of the scene had been made, the next step was essentially a question of design – principally, the look of Malvolio's sleeping arrangements. We plumped for a single bed, indicating that, at night, the man expects to be alone. He is probably lonely. The bed had a grim iron bedstead and a single pillow; and the bedclothes were crisp, professionally laundered cotton sheets and itchy woollen blankets, as you might have seen years ago in an English prep school. Perhaps Malvolio has never really grown up. There was nothing else in the room, because he doesn't own anything else. Perhaps he has no spare money – or is saving for his retirement.

I left that first meeting with Sam after about an hour; and then rushed back almost immediately to the hotel where we had had our conversation. The image of a bedroom had sparked off a whole series of thoughts. I asked Sam, who was still in the bar finishing his drink and paying the bill, whether he thought Malvolio should have a secret vice – a small bottle of vodka under his pillow, perhaps, or a pornographic magazine or, best of all, a paper bag of mint humbugs. Over the course of another hour, all were rejected. Other characters in the play drink heavily, so the vodka didn't work. Malvolio should remain sober. The pornography wasn't right, because, for all his many faults, Malvolio is not a sexual hypocrite. The thought of mint humbugs really excited me, but they too were dropped in the end. I rather missed them; although, thinking about it, it might have been impossible to deliver any of Shakespeare's lines with a large sweet in my mouth.

In the show, Malvolio entered the bedroom and then lay down on the bed to take a nap. A little later, he spotted the letter on the floor, slipped under the door as it were, picked it up and read it. The fact that he was in a private space meant that the way he talked, as he imagined both marrying Olivia and climbing to the top of the social ladder, flaunting his power and exacting his revenge on the likes of Sir Toby Belch, had a rapt, masturbatory quality – appropriate for someone described elsewhere as 'sick of self-love'. This might not have been so easy or such fun to play in a garden. In this new setting, Malvolio's dreams could really fly. There was even a suggestion of orgasm. He doesn't know, poor man, that he is being spied on.

From that point in his story, things got more difficult for me. The first problem arose in the next scene in which Malvolio appears. In the letter, Olivia had asked him to throw off his customary sober uniform and put on more attractive clothes – including, so she specifies, yellow stockings with cross-gartering. She also asked him to smile. This is something that he finds difficult and uncomfortable. Malvolio dresses as he is commanded and then, smiling, appears in front of Olivia. Since she knows nothing of the letter, she is understandably horrified.

Off the top of my head, I can't think of any other scene in Shakespeare that is quite so reliant for its impact on the clothes that one of the characters wears. If the costumes are Elizabethan or Jacobean it's easy enough; wearing stockings of various colours was not unusual for men at that time. Presumably, too, cross-gartering was not that uncommon. But if the production is set in any other period or style, then things become difficult. The costumes that we wore in our production were beautiful – very simple and elegant and with no reference to any specific period. They liberated the actors and allowed the play to sing. It was a successful and much-admired design. So, in writing this, I am quite emphatically not criticising those directors and designers who eschew period costuming. Over the years, many of Shakespeare's plays, including *Twelfth Night*, have been liberated and revivified through a whole, wide range of design ideas. That is not the issue. I just didn't know what to do with this one scene.

I ended up with a strange combination of clothes that aimed to be sexually provocative. They were also quite clearly an outfit that Malvolio had never worn before. He looked ridiculous – as, of course, he should. But something made me uncomfortable. He is not a stupid man. Gripped by a powerful combination of lust and ambition, he behaves foolishly – we can all agree on that – but I didn't believe that he would compromise his dignity so comprehensively as my Malvolio did. Indeed, perhaps he should behave even more pompously than he usually does. Perhaps his version of flirtation should be as stiff and clumsy as one might expect from a man who has never before had to employ any techniques of seduction.

Another minor problem that I came up against is the fact that the letter refers to 'your' yellow stockings, just as, later, Malvolio refers to 'my' yellow stockings. So he has a pair in his wardrobe and has probably worn them on previous occasions. So it can't be that great a surprise that he later appears in them.

(Many months after the run of our show, I found out that cross-gartering was considered old-fashioned at the time *Twelfth Night* was written. It occurred to me that the trick played on Malvolio might be that of getting him to dress not only in a style and a colour that Olivia dislikes – her maid tells us that she hates yellow – but also in clothes of a previous generation. In contemporary terms, it would be like someone dressing up in the things that Edward VIII might have worn on the golf course – plus fours, long woollen socks, etc. In other words, Malvolio quite definitely wouldn't look sexy and, furthermore, Olivia might be reminded of her recently dead father, whom her steward had once served. It would then be no wonder that she is upset. Unfortunately, it's an idea that probably wouldn't work on stage. There are too many things that an audience couldn't be expected to know and would, somehow, have to be told – and, anyway, the scene might become unpleasant rather than amusing. An older man behaving inappropriately to a much younger woman is dodgy enough, without it being heavily emphasised or laced with a whiff of incest. Still, it was an interesting line of thought.)

Many will see my concerns as a case of a workman blaming his tools. And they could be right. I can't blame my costume for my discomfort. To be frank, I really wasn't very good in this scene and that had to do with other, more important things. Principally, I made the grave mistake of trying to be funny, burdened by the idea that Malvolio is essentially a comic character, even a clown. But he is more than that. If I had trusted the situation, the risks that Malvolio is taking, the results would have been more convincing. Actors will tell you that comedy works only if the performers believe absolutely in their character's predicament and do not signal to the audience that laughs are expected. There is a famous story of two actors – a husband-and-wife team – who worked extensively in the West End during the middle years of the last century. They appeared once in a play that required the wife, at one point, to ask for a cup of tea. In the early days of the run, it always seemed to get a laugh. But over time, the laugh died away. The request for the cup of tea was greeted with stony silence. The wife asked her husband for advice. 'Ask for the cup of tea and not for the laugh,' he told her.

I'm not sure it's quite as simple as that, though. The principle of playing the truth of any situation is a good one, of course, and ignoring that was clearly the mistake I made when I played Malvolio; but great comic actors bring something else to their work. It's difficult to define what that something is. People talk of particular actors having 'funny bones'. Where those 'funny bones' come from is a mystery. Perhaps comics are deeply puzzled by the world around them. Perhaps their sense of the absurd is an attempt to resolve this anxiety. I don't know. But I do know that two actors can play the same scene with equal skill and sincerity and one will be funny and the other not. Nor has it necessarily anything to do with the quality of the script. It is said that the great comic Tony Hancock could make any line funny when he wanted to. Watch an actor like Mark Addy, for instance – an actor who can also break your heart, as he did in *The Full Monty* – and, should he wish it, you will see this indefinable comic magic in action.

After the scene with the yellow stockings, the next time we see Malvolio, he has been locked up in a dark cell. In our production, as a further humiliation, he wore a straitjacket. He is visited by another character who pretends to be a priest and who insists that the prisoner has lost his mind. Malvolio fiercely contests this, but he is in such distress that it feels as if he is unsure whether he is mad or not. In effect, he is tortured. This is thought by others in the story to be a just punishment for his presumption, although even Toby Belch worries that things might have gone too far. It is a horrible scene. It is also, in terms of Malvolio's journey, a big leap. We have come a long way from watching the repressed, puritanical steward trying to seduce his mistress.

It feels to me as if there is something missing. Shouldn't Shakespeare have written a scene in which, at the height of his pomp and inflated with new social and sexual confidence, Malvolio is told to his face that he has been duped? Shouldn't we be able to see how he reacts as the full significance of his humiliation hits him? I realise that Shakespeare is dealing with multiple plot lines and has a lot on his plate, but isn't it important for the audience to see a scene like that?

It's clear that, sometimes, the things that Shakespeare omits, or at which he only hints, leave a useful space for actors, readers and audience to fill. For instance, halfway through *Hamlet*, the prince is exiled to England by an exasperated king. He leaves the stage for quite a long time. This may be in order to give the actor playing him a rest. After all, he's been working very hard up to this point. But there's something more important going on here. When Hamlet returns, he is a different man. He seems calmer, even more forgiving. He has accepted the inevitability of his own death. But, despite the information Hamlet gives us about his time away, we will never know for certain how or why this transformation has happened.

There is something wonderful about this mystery and the questions that arise in its wake; because, when he returns to the play, Hamlet has, in a sense, shut himself off from the world around him. It seems almost presumptuous to look for answers. Hamlet's thoughts and feelings are now a very private matter. It is telling that he no longer confides in the audience. There are no further soliloquies. This is not the case with Malvolio. His humiliation and his anguish are there for all to see and I think that we need to know more fully how this situation came to pass and what Malvolio feels about it. In this case, for me, too much is left unsaid.

Malvolio is finally released from his cell. He has lost his job, of course, and has to leave the household. His parting words are explosive. Turning on all those who have destroyed him, he says:

'I'll be revenged on the whole pack of you!'

When I played Malvolio, I was asked what form I thought this revenge might take. I'm not sure. I don't know precisely what a man like Malvolio would do after he has been brought so low. Perhaps he sells his story to the tabloids. As I say, I don't know. But I do think that it's a serious threat. Class war has been openly declared. If Malvolio has anything to do with it, other people – and, in particular, all those privileged, self-satisfied people for whom he has worked – will suffer as he has suffered.

Just after he reads the fateful letter, Malvolio says very simply that he is 'happy'. It's as if happiness is a new sensation for him, as if he knows that he has never been happy before. For all his self-importance, Malvolio is a vulnerable man and easy prey for Sir Toby and his gang. At the end of the play, it feels probable that he will never be happy again. That, in itself, is a terrible punishment.

It's difficult to know how Shakespeare's audience would have reacted to Malvolio's last moments. Would they have delighted in his promise of revenge? Would they have cheered him on? Or, rather, did they consider his social pretensions to be offensive and therefore his punishment to be just? After all, he is a terrible killjoy and a bore. Of course, there would have been a range of responses, just as with a modern audience; but, since Malvolio's fate remains unchallenged by anyone else on stage, I have a niggling worry that the playwright himself was probably happy that the established hierarchy remains unchallenged. It's a minor worry, I know, but it won't go away.

Sam's production was beautiful and much admired. After

London, we went on to New York with both *Twelfth Night* and *Uncle Vanya*. Sam won three Olivier Awards that year – an extraordinary and probably unique achievement – and, one night in Brooklyn, members of the cast presented them to him, one after the other, at the curtain call. It was an evening to remember.

I have seen very few *Twelfth Nights* on stage; but I have heard stories about individual performances – especially of Malvolio. One of the most famous readings of the part over the last few years was given by Sir Donald Sinden. I got to know Donald a little in the years before he died in 2014 and was on stage when once, during a recital, he gave a stand-alone performance of the famous letter scene. It was shameless – that night Donald improvised a great deal – and it was very, very funny. The audience was spellbound. Aside from his work as an actor, Donald was known as one the best raconteurs in the business and his stories were honed to perfection. Someone told me that, when he prepared a script or even just something to amuse his friends, he used to score, from one to ten, the laughs that he expected to get; and he always got them, just as he had planned. However unlikely this might be, I really want to believe it. Watching him do this must have been like following a great clown, a great craftsman, developing a physical routine – only, this time, with words.

However, his letter scene in *Twelfth Night* was celebrated for a piece of physical 'business'. Malvolio, fussy and self-important, was standing in the garden – as is traditional – and was surrounded by trees and box hedges. In front of him was a sundial. Malvolio checked the time on the sundial. He frowned; and then took out a fob watch from his waistcoat pocket. He looked at the watch and frowned again. He then stepped forward and moved the sundial.

This short routine encapsulated perfectly the essential elements of the character. I would have loved to have used it myself, when I played Malvolio; but, of course, many of the audience would have recognised it and known it had been stolen. And, anyway, the scene in our production was no longer set in a garden. Perhaps, many years hence, another actor will be able to revive it. It would be a shame to let it go to waste.

2

As my headmaster had ordered, I won a music scholarship to Clifton College, a public school in Bristol. My life at St Paul's came to an end. My voice broke and I went off to the West Country. Two of my brothers – the twins – were already there, although in the junior part of the school. I was lonely during my first term, which is unsurprising. I sometimes went to see them in their boarding house, but they were always and predictably busy and probably didn't want to be bothered with a dull and subdued older brother. My sister, Katie, was at a neighbouring school up the road and, rather than sitting alone in my room, I would go to hang around with her or watch her swim – she was a wonderful competitive swimmer – pounding up and down the pool, practising the butterfly. It was always an awesome display.

One day, as I was sitting at my desk ploughing through some work, a fellow pupil came into the room, gave his name, sat down beside me and began to chat. I can't think what made him do it – I don't think we had ever met before then – but from that moment, and for the next four years, we were inseparable. His name was Chris Breen. I still joke that we had, and still have, nothing in common; but somehow that never mattered. He has remained a friend for life, despite his moving to the States. I was no longer lonely.

I suppose that many people might assume that Clifton would embody all the clichés of an English public school – a small world that was sport obsessed, culturally philistine, politically self-satisfied. But it didn't, at least from my perspective. The people I met at Clifton were liberal and rather open-minded. For a start, my being gay didn't seem to bother anyone. Sport was important, but then why shouldn't it be? Many enjoyed it, of course, but nobody considered being good at games an essential skill for any of the pupils. When it came to my having to play sport, I was left alone – except for a single, disastrous attempt at hockey and a short spell with the school swimming team. Perhaps they all thought that, when the time for playing games came around each week, I was off somewhere practising the piano and that was considered exercise enough. Alongside sport, music and drama were taken very seriously. Inter-house competition in both disciplines was fierce; and, from early on, I was required to contribute.

I was the only music scholar in my house and, even in my first years, had to organise our entries into the schoolwide singing and instrumental competitions. There was nobody else around to do it, so it wasn't really a vote of confidence. Among other things, I arranged a slow movement from a Beethoven piano sonata for the few instrumentalists that I had available in the house. I grew to loathe the piece, which I also had to learn for a grade eight exam; and I've had a problem with Beethoven's piano works ever since. This is heresy, I know, and ironic too, since I've grown to love all his other music – his symphonies and concertos and chamber work – and love it unreservedly, but that's how it is. Our head of music – a man of dark charisma called David Pettit – once expressed his regret at having to introduce us to Beethoven when we were too young to appreciate him. My English teacher said much the same about Jane Austen, though, despite being a teenage boy, I rather enjoyed reading her.

Later, I trained and conducted a large group of boys in a

rough-edged rendition of a Schumann song and, most satisfyingly, sang in the house quartet. I had, of course, no good or even competent singers to choose from for this – except my two brothers, who joined the upper school a year after me and who gamely agreed to help me out. All our voices had broken by this time and a fourth singer was persuaded to take the top part. We won the competition at our first attempt and won again in the years that followed. Since I regarded this as a personal triumph and the direct result of my brilliance, it was mildly irritating that my brothers won yet again a year after I left the school – a salutary reminder that none of us is indispensable.

My brothers tell me that I was very bossy – especially with them. I think they're being kind. I was often insufferable. When I was a senior boy, I was asked to direct the house play. I chose a short version of *The Revenger's Tragedy*, which was thought at that time to be by a writer called Cyril Tourneur, but which is now credited to Thomas Middleton. It is a play about violence and aristocratic depravity that I clearly found very exciting. There were three female roles. I decided that I would act one of the women – the most exciting of the trio – and I insisted that my brothers should take on the other two – a mother and her daughter. The latter was, predictably, innocent and chaste. For her, I chose my brother Andrew. I dressed him in white, which seemed appropriately virginal. Given that he was by then regularly playing rugby for the first XV and was a big boy, it was hardly flattering. He remembers putting a streak of dark make-up down the middle of his already-hairy chest to give the impression of a cleavage; and, more significantly, spotting a group of girls from the neighbouring high school sniggering from the front rows of the auditorium. I can only offer him a sincere and belated apology.

I was busy but, when it came to my music, fundamentally lazy. The senior music scholar during my time at Clifton was a violinist called Peter who went on to become a professional player. Below me in the pecking order, there was a dazzling organist (and classicist) who sailed into Oxford University after his time at school. He has since become a superb writer and an expert on the Middle East. I was stuck in the middle and my speciality was considered to be singing; but even that became questionable when a boy arrived a year after me who was blessed with an astonishing voice. He was called Chris Purves and, even as a young teenager, he could produce a gorgeous, creamy bass-baritone. I was comprehensively overshadowed. It all seemed so easy for him. I'm sure it wasn't; it just looked like that. And nobody can have an operatic career like his and, among many other triumphs, go to Glyndebourne to perform a wonderful Falstaff in Verdi's opera – as Chris did later in his life – without some serious work.

My head of music had to take me aside many times to remind me of my responsibilities as a scholar and point out that I was spending rather too much time in the school theatre. The seeds of this interest in drama had been planted early, of course, at my previous school, but here in Bristol there was a proper theatre building and some rudimentary technical support. At some point during my first year, I was lying on my bed reading a very exciting novel about Catherine the Great when I was interrupted, presumably at the moment when our heroine first sets eyes on the handsome Potemkin or something equally thrilling, by two senior boys. They were both scary and, to my eyes, terribly sophisticated. They told me that our housemaster had decided that, despite my being a new boy, I should be put in charge of the costumes for the house play. At the time, I couldn't think why I had been chosen, since I have never had any perceptible visual skills and the design of the house play was considered to be a very important job. It was also time consuming. The play that had been chosen required a large number of period costumes that we had to borrow from the Bristol Old

Vic theatre; but I somehow managed to collect together what I needed and, more surprisingly, found the confidence to tell senior boys what they had to wear. In retrospect, I think the housemaster was aiming for this – building my confidence through contact with older pupils – more than worrying too much about the final results.

At another level altogether was the annual school play; and this is where a very great teacher – Brian Worthington – enters my story. He was our head of English and an imposing, even intimidating, individual. He had studied at Cambridge University as a young man and, while there, had come under the influence of the critic F. R. Leavis; and that influence permeated every detail of Mr Worthington's teaching. The study of literature was a very serious activity. Judgement was severe – Victorian poetry and the novels of Thomas Hardy, for instance, were beneath consideration – and any analysis of a piece of writing was expected to be rigorous and unsentimental. An emotional response was discouraged, although it was assumed that we loved the works that we were studying. It sounds strict, even limiting, and in many ways it was; but it was thrilling. And, above all, it was important.

In those days, if one wanted to try for Oxford or Cambridge, one had to stay on at school for an extra term of tuition and exams. This was known as the 'Oxbridge term' or the 'seventh term'. Naturally, it was a hectic time for the students, although it was liberating to concentrate only on a subject that one found genuinely fascinating. I had, over the previous two years, taken a couple of science A levels. I assumed that I would one day become a doctor, like my parents. Studying biology and physics hadn't been a great success and it was good to let them go. It seems astonishing to think of it now, but F. R. Leavis and his wife Queenie – another major literary critic – were invited to meet the Oxbridge English students and to take some of the lessons. This increased the pressure on the students somewhat;

and it was made very clear how lucky we were – which I suppose was fair enough. Dr Leavis had died by the time I took my Cambridge exams, but Queenie, who was to die herself not long after, came down to Bristol to see us. I argued with her about the novels of Henry James – only a few of which I had actually read. She trounced me. Mr Worthington invited her to come to our school play, which he directed and in which I played King Lear. I was to meet Q. D. Leavis once again, when she invited me for tea during my first weeks at university. She was, by then, very frail. I don't think she could remember my name. She called me 'King Lear'.

Mr Worthington had little time for professional theatre practitioners – he had no time at all for the Royal Shakespeare Company, for instance – although he himself was a fine actor and, much to my surprise, told my parents at a meeting after my O levels that I might consider acting as a career. Perhaps, I thought then, he doesn't despise theatre as wholeheartedly as it seems. As well as performing himself, he was also in charge of many of the school productions; and he asked me, not long after my arrival at Clifton, to take a role in his next play – *Othello*. He wanted me to play Desdemona, despite the fact that, as he wrote to me after it was all over, he could have used girls from a neighbouring school. He knew that I could sing, which was important, since Desdemona sings a beautiful song on the night of her death; but he obviously had no idea about whether I could act. So it was a risk.

I was not a beauty, to be honest, which was a handicap. I'm not sure that it was helpful that I had to wear a wig that doubled the size of my head, but my costume was pretty and understated enough. I sometimes dropped into the school library to look at a book that had pictures in it of a famous production of *Othello* from the National Theatre, far away in London, and I would dream that I might somehow transform myself into Maggie Smith, whose imperious, beautiful face kept staring back at me.

A wife of one of the teachers told me that if I tucked my thumbs back into my palms, my rather square hands would look more delicate. I didn't want to point out that it also looked as if I had only eight fingers in total and that I felt like a lemur. Another woman helped with my make-up, a principal feature of which was a large pair of false eyelashes. During one performance, these stuck my eyelids together and I had to play the scene of Desdemona's death without being able to see properly. I was given sticks of heavy, oily foundation to play with; and I was told to put red dots in the corner of my eyes to make them glitter under the lights. It was my first experience of the 'smell of greasepaint' that so many have eulogised and that has long since disappeared – along with the make-up box that actors used to carry with them as a badge of office, like doctors with their bags. Modern theatre lighting doesn't require actors to paint their faces as heavily as they once did. An inevitable loss; although, equally inevitably, many miss it.

Desdemona was my first experience of playing a full-bodied, full-length Shakespearean role. We must have cut some of the text, but essentially we did the play in its entirety – just as any professional group might have done. I can't pretend that we aimed at any complexity or subtlety, although Mr Worthington insisted, characteristically, on absolute clarity. We knew exactly what we were saying. But I didn't at that time have the tools to question the assumption that Desdemona was docile, even passive. My reading of the part was conventional – the default reading, really. There wasn't the need or inclination to dig deeper. It was not long after that I realised that this young, aristocratic Venetian woman displays an exceptional courage and single-mindedness in her choice to marry, in secret, a man of whom her father and, indeed, the state was bound to disapprove. Nor did I appreciate that the real heroine of the story is another woman – Iago's wife, Emilia, who breaks her silence at the end of the play and risks her life to tell the truth about her husband.

That realisation, too, came later, when I was asked, as an adult, to play Iago, the play's manipulative monster, at the National Theatre in London. But by then it was too late to change my performance at school.

There were other school plays; and a lot more music. Once it had broken, my singing voice developed into a light tenor, although I always had a problem with my upper range. Actually, I didn't have an upper range. Perhaps I was a baritone all along. I suspect that if I had pursued a career as a singer, which I thought about at one point in my early twenties, I would have ended up in the sort of repertoire that I was already performing at school. I don't think I would have sung Verdi or Wagner. For me, it was going to be, for the most part, earlier music. Our chaplain at Clifton, a man called David Stancliffe, who went on to become bishop of Salisbury, was an amateur enthusiast of historically informed performances. A revolution in the playing of early music had started decades before my time at school; but, as choristers, we were largely unaware of it. If it came up in conversation, it was regarded with the same defensive suspicion as vegetarianism or environmentalism. It looked like both a fad and hard work, even though we admitted that the results might be worth listening to. Mr Stancliffe organised concerts with singers and instrumentalists that he assembled himself and that shared his interests; and he asked me to join them.

The results of Mr Stancliffe's hard work were not perfect, by any means, but they fascinated me. Here was a wholly new sound-world. And then, one day, I listened to a recording of Handel's *Messiah* – a piece that I knew very well indeed – played and sung by a group of early music specialists. It was radically different from the type of performance I had grown up with. The *tempi* were fearsome – some sections were played very fast indeed. The chorus was correspondingly virtuosic and the soloists light and agile. The strings were without vibrato, and the wind and brass were often harsh and peremptory. It didn't feel smooth or clotted or sanctimonious. I was hooked; and have been ever since.

This new world was exciting not only because the energy was infectious, but also because it brought to life the historical context in which the music was composed. When, for instance, I later heard a four-part mass by William Byrd sung with only one voice for each line, as if it were in secret, it immediately conjured up the world of clandestine Catholic worship in Elizabethan England; and a performance of Beethoven's *Eroica* symphony on period instruments will remind any listener of the explosive, abrasive effect it had on the first audience.

It was during my Oxbridge term that Mr Worthington decided to put on a production of *King Lear*. He asked me to play the king. I tentatively pointed out that I had important exams to work for and that I might not have the time to do the play justice, and that, anyway, King Lear is eighty years old. Even by the unexacting standards of school productions, it might seem absurd that I should play him. Mr Worthington brushed aside my objections and, needless to say, he was right to do so. *King Lear* was a turning point for me. It opened up new future possibilities and also served as a luxurious farewell to my time at school.

I was now concentrating solely on my study of English literature. Everything else – even, for a short time, music – was of secondary importance. My flirtation with the idea of studying medicine had died a natural death. I must make it clear that my ambition to practise as a doctor was not the result of any parental pressure. My parents remained resolutely disinterested when it came to my choice of career, although I suspect that they were unsurprised, perhaps even relieved, when I declared my interest in reading English at university. After all, my understanding of science was pretty ropey and I probably would have made an equally ropey doctor.

King Lear was part of a new excitement. It is such a big

play – arguably the biggest, greatest play that Shakespeare ever wrote – and the sense of cosmic disorder, the intensity of human despair and the remorseless storyline had a profound appeal to a group of teenage boys, even if the specific problems of old age were something I couldn't be expected to understand. The whole production was a big and solemn undertaking; and when I came on at the end of the play, carrying the dead body of my daughter, I was aware, for the first time, of how lucky I was in being asked to embody, however inadequately, a profundity of thought and feeling so much deeper than my own.

It was probably a bore to watch, I know. I can't pretend that there was any evidence on the stage of great talent or skill. But, after it was all over, Dad wrote me a letter – a rare event at that time – to congratulate me. So he must have been proud.

I had a privileged childhood. There is no doubt about that. My parents worked hard to give me and my siblings the best start that they could. I know that they themselves did not enjoy the same luck as their children did, happy though they may have been. Dad scrabbled around for any bursary or scholarship that he could find to get him through his medical training. Mum had to fight hard to become a doctor. Her school was fiercely resistant to the idea and offered no help at all; and, of course, women were still a rarity at medical school. Mum had to cope with predictable, and wearying, discrimination. With young children, including a daughter who was desperately ill all her short life, my parents never had a lot of spare cash to throw around. It was helpful that my time at choir school was free and, as my parents travelled around the world, the army helped out financially with our later education in England. When they were posted to Libya – a time that I barely remember – the family ate nothing but tomatoes for weeks on end. They were very cheap, after all; and luckily they were delicious.

What my parents never lost – and the gift they gave their

children – was a sense of adventure. After medical school, they could have stayed in England; and originally planned to do so. But they didn't. They decided to fly off and see the world. Dad once told me that, during his National Service, he, along with his colleagues, was asked to attend a meeting to discuss their future. By this time, he had qualified as a doctor and had recently become engaged. My mother had also qualified – with, as it happens, more impressive grades than Dad. The officer who took the meeting – a heavy drinker apparently – presented the group of young men in front of him with various options. One of them was to travel to Malaysia. The only hand that went up at that prospect was Dad's. Presumably, he then had to go and tell his fiancée about what he had done. She surely must have been somewhat taken aback, but she eventually agreed with his decision. So general practice in England was forgotten and, not long after, the two of them – Mum now pregnant with me – flew out to Penang, half a world away from Romford and Newport. It must have taken a lot of courage and some serious imagination. That attitude, that willingness to try something new, never changed. They offered all their children a fine example of curiosity and generosity of spirit, and an upbringing that was unquestionably stimulating and always exciting.

The Face of Evil

Iago

In the play named after him, Othello is a general, working for the Venetian republic. He has a junior officer serving under him called Iago. Iago is, quite simply, the nastiest character that Shakespeare ever wrote. He has no redeeming qualities; or, at least, none that I can see. I played him in a production by Sam Mendes for the National Theatre, London, in 1997; and I played him for a whole year. There were times that living with such an unpleasant man became burdensome – even depressing. I once described the experience as like walking around with a dense ball of basalt in my stomach. I suppose one shouldn't expect anything else when one's object of study is the personification of unmitigated evil. And, in fact, over the long period of performance, many of the cast experienced moments when they felt overwhelmed. *Othello* may be a masterpiece, but it's very bleak.

Although we rehearsed the play in London, we started our run in Salzburg, as part of a festival organised by the great director Peter Stein. He was a hero of Sam's, as it happened, responsible for a host of influential productions over many years. We had been invited to show our work to an audience brought up in a Germanic tradition of Shakespeare productions – very different and more self-consciously experimental than the British. Sam had decided, rather unusually for him, to set his *Othello* in an essentially naturalistic environment. He thought it suited this most domestic of Shakespeare's tragedies. There was a nod to *film noir*, but the feel of the production was of post-imperial British colonial life. The Venice of the play was infected with the insecurity of a fading world power. It was, naturally, a gorgeous design. But some of our Austrian audience must have thought it looked old-fashioned. At a forum during the festival, Peter Stein, in the course of interviewing Sam, described the show's design as 'a bit retro'. Sam shot back: 'More retro-chic, I think, Peter.'

After a run in London, we took our show around the world. This long tour was one of the most exhilarating and exhausting experiences of my life. We travelled to Asia, Australia, New Zealand and, finally, the USA. It is impossible for me to describe all the wonders that we saw and the warm hospitality that we enjoyed. I spent most of my days with Maureen Beattie, who was playing Emilia, Iago's wife. I would force her to get up early – too early, usually, after a long show the night before – and off we would go to explore the Five Grand Palaces of Seoul or the Forbidden City in Beijing or Sydney Harbour. We travelled as lightly as possible and had only a few clothes with us, including one coat each. Hers was maroon and mine blue. We had our photograph taken in each new location, wearing the same coats each time, and when we came to go through them all at home, it looked as if we had simply gone down to an old-fashioned local photographic studio and stood in front of a rolling series of backgrounds provided by the store.

There were moments on our journey when I felt as tired as I have ever been. We stopped over in San Francisco for a couple of nights on our trip from Adelaide to New York and I couldn't lift my arms properly from the effects of jet lag. Maureen and I went for brunch in the Castro district of the city one morning and, as we were eating, I watched her head drop slowly into a bowl of Caesar salad. It was the first time that I had seen anything like it. It's the sort of thing that one sees in films or on stage, but that one trusts would never happen in real life. I was understandably worried. She seemed content enough, though. She just needed to sleep.

This tiredness and the unrelenting schedule had an effect on the show, of course. We had received very good reviews everywhere we went, until we arrived in New Zealand. The local press clearly didn't like our work and this negative reaction forced us to recognise that our standards might have slipped. We sent an urgent message to Sam and asked him to fly straight out to Wellington to help us out. At that time, he was rather busy in New York with his new production of *Cabaret* and he gently, but firmly, pointed out that it would be a waste of time and money for him to fly across the Pacific for just a couple of hours' work with us. Instead, having watched a video of our latest performance, he sent some notes.

I mention this because his notes were unexpected and

surprisingly effective. They were simply a series of questions aimed at each and every character. They didn't directly concern the text or the storyline of the play. Rather, they were about the totality of the lives that our characters led. The one that I remember – from a few that were aimed at me – was, 'At what time in the day does Iago have his first drink?' I decided that the answer was eleven o'clock in the morning. From now on, Iago, rather than being a man who likes the odd shot of whisky, was someone with a problem – a high-functioning alcoholic. It was a new thought that, despite not changing anything specific, recharged my performance. I know that these questions had the same impact on other cast members. Since the play is, for the most part, on a domestic scale, tiny, apparently irrelevant, details count. Sam said later that he had heard of this question technique from another director, but I like to credit him with the idea.

When we finally arrived in New York – our last date – we did a dress rehearsal in the new space. This was the usual procedure. In every new venue, we would have to run through the play – though, in most cases, the director was not present. This time he was; and, afterwards, he gathered us together to share some thoughts. He kept everyone for a few minutes, dismissed us and then, to my surprise, asked me and Maureen to stay behind. The next half hour was tough. He obviously wasn't happy with my performance and had decided to go back to basics. Essentially, this meant clarifying the nature of Iago and Emilia's marriage. We had discussed all this during the first rehearsal period, but Sam felt that there was something missing. He and Maureen, whose performance he had no problem with, were there to help me out.

Maureen and I had invented a whole backstory that took into account the specific environment in which our particular production was set. This story was not grounded in Shakespeare's text. Our idea was that Emilia had been working as a civilian in an army camp – possibly in the NAAFI – when she caught Iago's eye. At that time in his life, he would have been regarded as a good catch – a young soldier with ambition and prospects. She didn't fall in love with him, but they married. They never had children. Their relationship at the time of the play is distant and Iago can be aggressive, although, in my mind, he never physically harms her. He wouldn't want to waste the effort. For the most part, he ignores her.

This was important for us, because one of the spurs for Iago's extreme behaviour may be the state of his marriage. The same could be said of Emilia, of course. And it means that there is a poetic justice in Emilia being the person who uncovers the truth and implicates her husband at the end of the play. She deserves her revenge.

Reading the source material that Shakespeare used for *Othello* is instructive on this point. In *Gli Hecatommithi* by Cinthio, there is a short story which the playwright must have studied. The plot is, in broad outline, that of *Othello*; but there are differences. In Cinthio, Emilia and Iago have a child – a little girl; and Iago is a good father. He is also rather dashing. Shakespeare quite deliberately gets rid of the child. He wants the marriage to be childless. If, let us suppose, the Iago and Emilia of the play wanted children but were unable to have them, or if some other conflict about children had arisen between them, then one can imagine the marriage becoming unbearable. And this may go some way to explain why Iago acts as he does. In our New York meeting, Sam wanted to delineate the substance of this conflict and settle some of the details.

The motives for Iago's behaviour are famously difficult to pin down. An unhappy marriage could very well be one of them, although this is never mentioned explicitly in the text. Furthermore, his ultimate aim is also unclear. He says that he hates Othello. He clearly resents the fact that his boss has passed him over for promotion. And it seems, in response, he is looking to destroy the relationship between Othello and his new bride, Desdemona. But at the beginning of the play, Iago doesn't appear to be aiming at much more than being an irritant. He hasn't yet, for instance, come up with the idea of accusing Desdemona of adultery with Cassio, Othello's aide-de-camp. At the start of the story, he wakes Desdemona's father in the middle of the night to tell him that his daughter has left the house and married Othello in secret. Since Othello is black and a foreigner, Brabantio, Desdemona's father, is horrified. He is easy prey for Iago, who lards his conversation with foul, racist imagery. Given that this abusive language is something that Iago employs only with those who will respond as he wishes, we can assume, perhaps, that Shakespeare's audience felt that such attitudes were unacceptable. Certainly, in this context, they could have read Iago's selective racism as a clear sign of his fundamentally unpleasant and aggressive nature. He encourages Brabantio to go to the duke and to ask the latter to declare that the marriage of Othello and Desdemona is invalid. It is significant, though, that Iago doesn't trust that this tactic will work. He says clearly that he understands Othello to be a fine general and, since Venice is currently at war with the Ottoman Empire, is too valuable an asset to lose.

Iago knows his limitations, it seems. He has no power or real influence in Venice. Shakespeare starts his narrative in a large, cosmopolitan city with a complex and exclusive political establishment, and only later moves to a small military outpost in Cyprus. Giuseppe Verdi, when he came to write his extraordinary opera based on *Othello*, cut the early scenes in Venice, despite the fact that, in other respects, he followed Shakespeare's play very closely. This excision certainly makes for a tighter structure – and a shorter work – but it misses an important point. Iago's malice can have an effect only in a small environment. He can juggle a handful of people, but is incapable of more complicated manipulation. He fails in Venice. This is why I never thought of him as a sort of criminal mastermind. He is too small a figure for that to be an accurate description.

Iago also doesn't know how the story will end. He has to improvise. When he starts out, I cannot think that he predicts the deaths of three people – Othello, Desdemona and Emilia, his wife – although that becomes increasingly likely as things develop. He just wants to create unhappiness; but, to his delight, he succeeds in doing so much more than that. In fact, he succeeds beyond his wildest dreams.

When, in the early nineteenth century, the critic Samuel Taylor Coleridge wrote about Iago, he came up with a phrase that has since exercised a huge influence on readers and performers. In talking about Iago's soliloquies, he said that the character displayed the 'motive-hunting of a motiveless malignity'. It's the sort of statement that I used to dismiss – too neat, too glib, too alliterative and a cop-out to boot – but, needless to say, it's actually brilliant and very useful. Many disagree with Coleridge, however. When I talked to the actor Antony Sher, he insisted that Iago's principal motive for the horror he unleashes has to be his professional disappointment. It's certainly true that Iago mentions this many times; and he despises the man who gets the job he wanted – Cassio. The latter has many qualities that Iago seems to lack. Cassio is urbane, well-educated, good looking, honourable and talented. He is also, in Iago's eyes, perfect casting for the imagined role of Desdemona's lover.

However, I think Coleridge may be right. Iago gives reasons other than professional frustration for his behaviour. One of them, as I have already mentioned, is his hatred for Othello and for Cassio. Another is his contempt for Desdemona – and, indeed, for all women. Another again is his suspicion that Emilia has had an affair with the general, which is, frankly, hard to believe. I'm not sure that Iago believes it himself. So he has too many grievances to settle convincingly on one alone. Consequently, when he talks to the audience about his motives, it's as if he is lying; and as if he doesn't care that he's lying. What is interesting for me about this deceit is that, from the perspective of theatrical convention, it is an abuse of trust. An audience should be able to expect that when characters talk to them directly they are telling the truth – at least, as the characters themselves see it. This is the case in every other Shakespearean example that I can think of. But I sense, in Iago's case, it is not.

This is why Iago is so dangerous. His moral compass is profoundly defective. He is, in other ways, a very ordinary man. It could be that Othello is quite right to refuse him promotion. In our production, Iago was seen working at a desk, shuffling papers. There was no indication, whatever he might say to the contrary, that he was a brilliant soldier. He's dull company – 'honest Iago', Othello calls him, which is damning with faint praise. Maybe he's even a pub bore. His use of language, except when talking about sex or employing his extensive racist vocabulary, is workmanlike and dull. It's no accident that his principal victim, Othello, is one of the most dazzling wordsmiths in the repertoire. He's a great man with a great mind. One of the sadnesses of the story is that Othello is destroyed by mediocrity.

Iago might, in many ways, be a very ordinary man, but his capacity for hatred is all-powerful and all-encompassing. Deep in the grain of his soul is a rooted lovelessness. In Verdi's opera, Iago is given an aria in which he says that he believes in a cruel God. This has no equivalent in Shakespeare's text. I don't think the playwright would be able to say whether the God that Iago believes in is cruel or loving – either is a dreadful thought – or whether Iago is, in fact, an atheist. The important thing is that there is no love, from whatever source, in Iago's life.

I will go further and say that if, as theologians say, hell is the state of being cut off from the love of God, then Iago is in hell;

and I will go further still to say that he is, unconsciously, on a suicide mission. His life is unbearable. His destructive plot is, or becomes, a last roll of the dice.

In the fourth act of the play, there is a scene between Iago and Othello at the end of which the latter suffers a seizure. By this point, Othello believes every word that Iago says. In Othello's mind, Desdemona is unquestionably guilty of adultery. The writing here is technically dazzling. It's as if the two characters are completing each other's thoughts, sharing each other's sentences, metamorphosing into the same organism. It's the moment of Iago's greatest triumph. Another human being is, at last, feeling and thinking exactly as he does. Othello is suffering as Iago suffers. Perhaps the thought of Iago's suffering is too fanciful, but a man whose understanding of the world around him is so bleak cannot be happy. The only satisfaction Iago could possibly look for is in the knowledge that someone else sees the world as he does – a type of vindication, in essence. And, here in this scene, Othello provides it. To top it all, Othello ends up physically incapacitated and at Iago's mercy.

Iago's villainy is exposed, of course – by his wife, of all people; and he is arrested. Othello confronts him and accuses him of being a 'demi-devil', which is apt. He then asks Iago to explain why he acted as he did. Iago replies:

> *'Demand me nothing. What you know, you know.*
> *From this time forth I never will speak word.'*

I cannot be the only person who finds these last words terrifying. Iago is about to be imprisoned and tortured. He will die alone. He is probably anticipating all that. But he will never speak again. This is a man whom we have seen unable to stop talking – the part is arguably the longest in Shakespeare – but he now chooses silence. Iago was once described by my great teacher at university, Eric Griffiths, as Hamlet's 'malign step-brother'.

Hamlet is another man who cannot stop talking, although he speaks with more grace than Iago; and he also famously ends his life with the words: 'The rest is silence.' As he says this, Hamlet signals that he is ready for death. I think Iago, too, is prepared to die. More, he wants to die. It's what he's unconsciously been working towards this whole time.

And, finally, what does Iago mean when he tells Othello that he knows what he knows? At the simplest level, it could be a reaffirmation of Desdemona's adultery. But that idea has been emphatically thrown out by all the characters left on stage. Othello must know that. Rather, Iago's simple statement has a power that is simply indefinable. Maybe he is reminding Othello of the destructive power that they unleashed together and the exhilaration they both felt. It's impossible to know; but I feel that, in this moment, some hidden secret shared by the two men is acknowledged and indulged – at least by Iago.

The first fan letter I ever wrote was to an actor whom I had just watched playing Iago. Not long after I joined the Royal Shakespeare Company, I was taken to see Ian McKellen in a production of *Othello* at the Other Place in Stratford. The whole thing was marvellous – Ian, in particular. I ran back to my digs, determined to write to him and tell him how excited I had been by his performance. The only paper that I could find was a pack of small cards that were pink and bordered with spring flowers. Goodness knows whether I had bought them myself – it seems unlikely – or whether somebody else had left them in my house. I nevertheless used one of the cards to write a gushing message for Ian, raced back to the theatre and dropped it at the stage door. I wonder whether Ian ever got it and what he thought. I'm sure he appreciated the gesture – maybe even the design of the notepaper.

Richard III

There is a clutch of famous villains in the Shakespeare canon; and the most well-known of them is Richard III. This is, in part, because it is a spectacular role that has inspired a long history of great performances. But it is also because the version of Richard that Shakespeare presents – a murderous king who bears little or no resemblance to the historical figure on which he is based – has provoked, through the years, fierce controversy. Before I started rehearsals for *Richard III* in Stratford in 1992, I received letters begging me not to play a role that perpetuated such a glaring injustice. Later, when I visited Bosworth Field and stood on the spot where Richard is thought to have died, I noticed bunches of fresh white roses that had been left by people still appalled by the playwright's treatment of their king. The idea of Richard as tyrant was current in the sixteenth century, as it happens. Presumably the new Tudor dynasty was not unhappy with that and were quietly delighted that Shakespeare added his voice to this new version of recent history. Because it's Shakespeare's propaganda that has real power and the longest reach.

All I can say to the people who mourn the historical Richard is that, frankly, it is too good a part to turn down. Vanity and ambition are not valid excuses, I know, but at least, in mitigation, I can point out the irony that very few would be interested in Richard if it hadn't been for Shakespeare's play. Without it, he would have sunk into obscurity – like his brother, Edward IV. There would have been much less excitement generated by the discovery of his bones a few years ago in a Leicester car park than there was; and no film would have been made about the discovery, either.

Richard III was the second play that Sam Mendes and I worked on together. The first had been *Troilus and Cressida*, a difficult play, stuffed with tangled verse and angry, cynical characters. In some ways, *Richard III* was a simpler challenge than *Troilus*. It was written in the first years of Shakespeare's career and it has the energy and employs the bold colours that one might expect from a young writer. The verse is, for the most part, regular. The political landscape is pretty clear, although some of the historical details are difficult to follow. It's a play about the internecine struggles of a single ruling family and, since this part of the story can get complicated, we thought it wise to have a family tree handy in the rehearsal room. Unlike the earlier history plays, it is absolutely dominated by its central character. It's as if all the political and emotional complexities, the shifting allegiances, of a long civil war have become concentrated in the figure of a single man. And what a man Richard is – as compelling as Tamburlaine or Faustus or the other characters who had dominated the Elizabethan stage in previous years. Was the young playwright still unable to shake off the influence of his great predecessor, Christopher Marlowe, who specialised in ruthless, power-hungry, over-reaching men? Perhaps.

Once the show was up and running, we enjoyed a short spell in Stratford and then took our production around the UK. The Royal Shakespeare Company called it a small-scale tour. We visited towns that had no permanent theatre; and so the crew had to build, from scratch, an auditorium in each venue. For them, it was very hard work. This tour lasted for a period of twelve weeks, at the end of which we would go to London and then on to Tokyo and Rotterdam.

After the first show in London, which seemed to have gone well enough, I was taking a shower and looking forward to a celebratory dinner at the Ivy with Meg, my agent, when I felt a sharp pain in my back that then shot down my left leg. I ignored it, assuming that it was nothing that a couple of Martinis wouldn't cure; but a few hours later I was crawling out of the restaurant on my hands and knees to take a taxi to a local hospital. Meg sat with me in the casualty department, holding my hand, until four in the morning. It felt, even at the time, beyond the call of duty.

The problem was clearly a slipped disc; but I refused to believe it. I was convinced that everything would be fine after a course of light acupuncture and some gentle massage. The show was cancelled for a few days, but I went back to give one more performance. This was painful for me and, I guess, infuriating for my fellow actors, since I could barely move around the stage. In the final fight with Henry Tudor, the Earl of Richmond, which, in normal circumstances, involved the two of us slugging away at each other with heavy broadswords, I simply fell down and died, before my opponent could attack me. I can't imagine what the audience thought – that Richard had simply, and uncharacteristically, given up, I suppose. My performance was fuelled by a barely hidden rage, though, which I had never felt before, so perhaps it still had some impact.

One of my medical brothers, a radiologist, insisted that I had a scan. My doctor read it and pronounced sternly that I needed an operation at once. I took his advice, of course; and there then followed a miserable few months. I was taken aback at how angry I felt about my injury. If I had been asked before it happened, I would have predicted that I would just shrug my shoulders and wait patiently until I could get back on stage. But, to my surprise, I was furious. Part of the problem was that, once the surgery had been successfully carried out, the pain magically disappeared. So, in my head, I was perfectly fit and able to act again. There was a payphone at the end of the ward where I was convalescing and every day I would hobble down the corridor and ring Sam to assure him that I was ready to return to the show. I know he found this difficult and he was forced, in the end, to ask me to stop the phone calls. He told me – and this was very hard to hear – that another actor, my friend Ciarán Hinds, would take over the part and go on to Tokyo and Rotterdam.

I did return to the show a little later in the run. I had to wear a corset to support my back.

Before we started work on the play, Sam had warned me that Richard was a physically demanding role – a 'ball-breaker', he called it. So I should have been more careful. I knew full well that, in the past, other Richards had hurt themselves. I suspect that this high rate of injury may be because Richard is, famously, disabled. According to the script, he has some curvature of the spine and a withered arm. Shakespeare also added a limp, which was presumably a result of the problems with Richard's back. Nowadays, it is considered appropriate that disabled actors play the part, but back then it was usual for an able-bodied performer to take on the role. As a result, he or she would put their body under some pressure.

Richard is one of the few roles that I have played where decisions about a character's appearance have to be made in the very early days of the rehearsal process. After all, how he looks and the nature of his disability determine not only how he moves but also how he sees himself. So there are physical and psychological questions to be answered. I was keen, from the beginning, that he should be a fighter and, more than that, known to be as athletic a fighter as those around him. *Richard III* is the last in a series of plays about the Wars of the Roses and, in them, we see Richard as a young man and follow him as he grows up. Throughout his story, he is admired by everyone for his achievements on the battlefield.

Antony Sher had played Richard not long before me, in a performance that was universally admired. Unfortunately, I never saw the show, but I read a great deal about it. He equipped his king with a pair of crutches and he flew athletically around the stage. This was quite clearly a 'bottled spider' – as another character in the play describes him. I couldn't compete with that degree of physical virtuosity and scoured the text for other descriptions of Richard. I came across 'bunch-backed toad'. An image of decayed power came into my head. I decided that Richard should look like a long-retired American football player, a mass of muscle that has gone to seed. He became a hulking and threatening presence; and one that, despite his decay, you would not want to meet down a dark alley or, indeed, in battle.

In addition to this, Sam decided that Richard should have a walking stick. I'm looking at it now. I kept it as a memento after the run had ended and it now leans against my study wall. The stick is very frail and it used to bend into a semi-circle when I leaned on it. Charlie Chaplin carried something similar. I didn't look as tiny as Chaplin when I played Richard; but, of course, a tension between bulk and delicacy, violence and wit, is what Sam was aiming for.

This contradictory combination is what makes Richard such a powerful figure, both for the other characters on stage and for the audience. Everyone knows that he is an unpleasant man; but he somehow gets away with it. His hypocrisy is brazen and his lust for power is crystal clear; but he is witty and, one suspects, good company – unlike my Iago, for instance. The people around him feel compelled to insult him, often to his face, and yet are unable to thwart him. He is irresistible – to them and to those watching him in the theatre. Academics tell us that this persona owes a great deal to the Vice figure of earlier English drama. Shakespeare would have grown up with Vice characters, who were both evil and spellbinding and who, particularly through their soliloquies, had a direct contact with the audience.

While I was rehearsing for *Richard III*, another director, Roger Michell, gave me a tip about soliloquies. 'When you have to speak directly to the audience,' he said, 'always give them a role.' It's a simple and brilliant idea. As an example: I said earlier that Iago lies to his audience. If that is true, then he would, presumably, think of them as a pack of gullible idiots. For Hamlet, the only people he can really trust are his friends in the audience; he believes that, whatever happens and whatever he chooses to do, they will understand him. In Richard's case, he behaves like the leader of the gang. Any challenge that the audience might throw down – seducing a woman over the corpse of a man that he's just killed, let's say, or seizing the crown – he will accept. And he will triumph – to his and the gang's delight.

There is a problem with Richard's charm, though. In essence, it's a moral issue; and it's a familiar one. It's evident in many fictional characters; and, though this might be hard to prove, I think Shakespeare was aware of some difficulty that had to be acknowledged. He knew that, however attractive Richard might be, he is, in the final analysis, a killer. It is fascinating to trace how the playwright, through the span of his career, dealt with the portrayal of evil on stage. Aaron, the villain in *Titus Andronicus,* a very early work, has great charisma. He is effortlessly sexy. Indeed, he is the lover of a powerful woman and fathers a child with her. He has supreme confidence and an easy manner. He shows all the qualities that we associate with Marlovian heroes. The birth of his child elicits some tenderness from him, but Aaron does not change in any significant way through the play and he dies unrepentant. Richard, likewise, has charm, and although he is not exactly sexy, he has the confidence, despite the odds stacked against him, to seduce a woman in front of our eyes. He, too, has charisma.

But there is a shift in *Richard III.* Just after he is crowned king, Richard orders the murder of two young princes. They are children and pose no real threat to him. It could be argued that they might serve as a rallying point for future traitors, but nobody else in the play seems to hold that opinion. Up until that point, any killing in which Richard has been involved is silently excused as having some political value. After all, murdering rivals seems to be part of any ambitious man's armoury. But infanticide is a different matter. Tyrrel, the man who organises the killings, calls it a 'most arch deed of piteous massacre'. Ironically, the killers themselves weep 'like to children' as they murder the boys. They all three know that it's an inexcusable sin; and I felt that Richard knows it too.

I wanted to mark this moment as a turning point for the new king. One day I happened to be watching an episode of *Coronation Street*. I can't think why, since I don't follow that particular soap opera. One of the actors had just died and so, of course, the character he played had to die too. As a mark of respect, the producers decided not to have any music playing as the credits rolled at the end of the programme. During these final, silent moments, the actress playing his fictional wife – Jean Alexander – sat at a kitchen table and slowly opened a small package that she had received from the hospital where her fictional husband had died. It was wrapped in brown paper and contained small objects – his pair of spectacles, his handkerchief. It was very moving.

I thought that this idea could work in *Richard III*; and, quite ruthlessly, I stole it. In our production, when Tyrrel came to see the king in order to confirm that the boys were dead, he was carrying a small brown-paper parcel tied up with string. He gave this to Richard, who opened it. Inside were the boys' pyjamas. Richard looked at them carefully for a long time, raised them to his nose and sniffed them (I imagined they smelled of talcum powder) and then gently laid them aside. He looked unconcerned; but he was, for the first time in his life, deeply disturbed.

It occurred to me that Richard might never get over this. The murder of his nephews is something that even he cannot rationalise. Not only is it a sin in itself, it is also a clear abuse of family loyalty; and the idea of family is, ironically, important for Richard. It's certainly important for Shakespeare. In the prequels to *Richard III*, young Richard clearly adores his father and is loved by him in return. Until things turn sour, he seems to love his brothers. His mother is a different matter; but then, by the time we meet her properly and see her with her son, both now unable to hide their mutual contempt, the idea of family loyalty has become a preposterous fantasy.

This one major and abusive scene between them comes at a particularly delicate moment. Just before we see mother and son together, we watch a powerful display of grief from four women – a long, incantatory passage of anger and pain. They are all mourning the loss, at Richard's hands, of family members. It is a savage reminder for the audience of the price that other people have to pay in order to maintain the new king's grip on power. Richard is, unusually, nowhere to be seen; and his absence is significant. He has yet to be confronted directly with another person's grief. When he finally appears, his mother denounces him. She is absolutely unforgiving. He is dismissive, but perhaps his apparent indifference – and his irritability – masks unacknowledged hurt.

The confrontation between mother and son is transitory, but leads on to the greatest confrontation in the play – that between Richard and Queen Elizabeth, the wife of Edward IV and the mother of the two young princes. This long scene, in which the demands and value of family loyalty play such a large part, is the mirror image of another encounter earlier in the story – the famous seduction of Lady Anne over the corpse of King Henry VI. In the earlier scene, we see Richard toying gleefully with a vulnerable young woman. Although he is not yet a king, he is at the height of his powers. His success with Anne confounds all expectations, as Richard knows. After she leaves, having agreed to consider his proposal of marriage, he turns to the audience – his gang – and delivers a blistering speech. It's a poisonous mixture of delight in his own abilities and contempt for those around him. He anticipates the audience's approval and assumes that he wins it.

Things are very different with Elizabeth. Richard is tired and embattled. He has been so for quite a time now. At his coronation, I decided that Richard would choose to dispense with his stick. He thought it made him look weak. He also wore a huge, heavy blue cloak which dragged on the floor behind him. Just before he reached the throne, he tripped and fell. He had to bawl to his ally, the Duke of Buckingham, to help him up. He was humiliated at the moment of his greatest triumph; and it's been downhill from then on. It's as if kingship is much less fun than he thought it would be; and he desperately needs to succeed with the dowager queen Elizabeth. Earlier, the happy outcome with Anne was a bonus – and only half-expected. Now, he must succeed, or, as he sees it, the country will collapse into a bloody chaos. His plan is to persuade Elizabeth that peace in England is possible only if he marries her young daughter, the sister of the two murdered princes. Civil war, says Richard, cannot be avoided except by this marriage. He then repeats the thought with one small, but important, change. Civil war, he says, *will* not be avoided except by this marriage. Richard cannot, at this point, entertain the idea of failure. But it is clear that the proposed marriage is an outrageous and repulsive idea, and one that Elizabeth dismisses out of hand.

Richard, of course, assumes that he will win his sister-in-law over by employing tried and tested methods. But one of the fascinating things that occurred to us as we worked on the scene in rehearsal was that Richard, perhaps for the first time in his life, might find himself speaking with complete honesty. It's possible that he does not employ his old techniques. What if there was little or no evidence of the trickster we had all come to know and love? What if there was no delight in the game? After all, the stakes are quite simply too high. Lies will no longer work. In addition, Elizabeth forces him to recognise the pain he has caused:

> *'The children live whose fathers thou hast slaughtered . . .*
> *The parents live whose children thou hast butchered . . .'*

In our production, this was the first time that Richard had to face the human consequences of his actions. He was forced to consider the families he has destroyed. And he had no answer or excuse. He simply remained silent.

He fails with Elizabeth. I enjoyed the idea that Richard fails only when he speaks the truth. He recognises this irony too, I think – even if he would never articulate it – and, when the scene ends and Elizabeth leaves the stage, Richard turns to the audience not, as after the seduction of Anne, with a long, confident speech, but a single, feeble line about his opponent:

'Relenting fool, and shallow, changing woman.'

We don't believe it; and neither, in his heart of hearts, does he. He has lost his powers of seduction. He is no longer attractive to those around him, or, one suspects, to the audience. Here is some resolution of the moral paradox. Richard has not, as yet, paid the price for his misdeeds – that, maybe, comes later – but he has certainly lost his charm. The magic has gone.

Richard enjoys his food. There are many references to this in the play. On the night before the final, fatal battle, he refuses to eat. Although they make no mention of this change in the king's behaviour, it must be obvious to those around him that, if Richard has lost his appetite, then the situation must be desperate. I discovered this nugget only late in the run and so could make no use of it; but, talking later to an academic friend in Stratford, he told me that he had recently seen a production in France in which Richard gorged himself throughout four acts and then stopped, to everyone's horror, only in the fifth. What a wonderful idea, I thought, and a missed opportunity.

3

When I first arrived in Cambridge to start my degree course, the town looked stunning. King's Parade, the main university thoroughfare, was cobbled. Its brightly coloured shopfronts gleamed in the autumn sun. The merchandise in the windows seemed appropriately quaint and old fashioned. There were even horses in the street. It was exactly how I had imagined it.

But it was all fake. During my first term, they were filming *Chariots of Fire* in the town. When I returned after Christmas, the fibreglass cobbles had disappeared, although the shops, with their lick of fresh paint, still looked inviting. They now sold stuff that people actually wanted to buy – takeaway pizza slices, Union Jack keyrings and teddy bears wearing college scarves and bobble hats. There were no longer horses trotting down the street. The film crew had long gone.

Despite this unanticipated transformation, it was still, for me, a spellbinding place, and remained so for the three short years that I studied there. I did all the things that students are supposed to do, like drinking far too much and eating a huge number of late-night kebabs. Daily life was, for much of the time, mundane, but a sense of the long history of the university was inescapable. I took a ridiculous pride in the fact that my college had been founded in the fourteenth century. Thirty-five years after my graduation, I was invited to the funeral of Stephen Hawking, which was held at a church in the centre of town. While his extraordinary scientific achievements were acknowledged, the academic posts he had held and the books he had written recognised, he was buried simply as a fellow of Gonville and Caius College. That was all the information that was printed on the front of the order of service. It was a proud gesture from a small community of scholars reclaiming one of their own and a reminder of their long history. Perhaps some might think this sentimental, but it was unquestionably effective.

Cambridge University is famous for many things. Some of them have been world changing – clarifying the structure of the atom, discovering the circulation of the blood, setting out the principles of gravity, for instance. Of arguably less importance is the fact that, over the last hundred years, it has nurtured many important figures in British theatre. The long list of names is well-known. I knew students who were determined to follow in their illustrious footsteps and considered their time at the university as a first step on that journey. Their academic work was of secondary importance. This is curious, because, during my time at university, undergraduate interest in theatre was tolerated by our teachers, but, apart from a few notable exceptions, not actively encouraged. After all, it took up a lot of our time and they understandably considered that our academic work should be our principal concern. It was what we were there for, after all. There was enthusiasm in some academic quarters for theatre and most people were kindly about the whole thing, but it wasn't considered a particularly serious activity. The study of drama was part of the English degree I was taking, of course, but that was because the plays we looked at were often judged to be great literature. More practical considerations of theatre-making were fun, but no more.

Maybe things are different now. Even then, our teachers knew very well that a number of their students would go on to enjoy careers in theatre and film. A few might become famous or celebrated. My teacher Eric Griffiths seemed positive about my interest in drama. He was recognised as the most exciting lecturer in the English faculty and I wrote to him in my final year to ask him to take me on as a pupil. This was not considered the 'done thing', but I was unaware of that. Eric didn't seem to mind and agreed to teach me about Victorian poetry. His written comments on my work were not so much simple notes but rather essays in reply. Here, evidently, was a very serious teacher. My hours spent with him were inspirational. In fact, they rather turned my head. After I completed my degree, there was a short period when I toyed with the idea of working as a postgraduate student. He told me very firmly that this was an absurd idea and that I should go off and become an actor. Ignoring his wise advice, I decided to train as a singer; but that's another story.

At Cambridge, I didn't devote as much time to theatre as many of my friends. I still performed quite a bit, but not nearly as much as they did; and, to be honest, some of my work on stage was pretty feeble. Most of my working day – nearly every afternoon, in fact, and many evenings – was taken up with music. I was reading English but had also been awarded a choral exhibition, which required me to sing regularly in the college chapel. In the afternoon, when others might have been rehearsing plays, our college choir would gather for a run-through of the music for that evening's service. There was then a short break – in which I invariably went to the bar and drank a glass of white wine and ate a Kit Kat, a surprisingly good combination – and, after half-an-hour, we returned to the chapel for evensong.

The college choir was an eccentric group – particularly with regard to the music we made. It was all male, but we didn't have boy trebles. There were sixteen singers, so we often produced a hefty sound, especially for a chapel that was comparatively small. We performed a wide range of music, from Dufay to Rossini – all adapted for our limited resources. I don't remember many people coming to worship. This may have been for confessional reasons, although I can't help thinking that the large amount of noise we produced might have discouraged people who were looking for a more contemplative experience. The year that I arrived in Cambridge was also the first year that my college admitted women. This was a welcome development and one that I, deprived of female friends throughout my schooling, delighted in. Sadly, it was only after I left that women were invited to join the choir and provide a soprano line. Since then, it has become one of the finest choirs in Cambridge.

The standard of musicianship in the choir was very high, even if the final results were sometimes a little rough round the edges. We were all involved in the extensive music-making that was such an important part of university life. And there were unexpected and exciting discoveries. My close friend and fellow choral exhibitioner, Michael, was an expert classical musician, but his real love was jazz, about which I knew nothing. He introduced me gently but insistently to a new world. I remember clearly sitting in his room and listening to Billie Holiday for the first time. It was like nothing I had heard before – a sharper pain and a fiercer anger than I was used to.

There were song recitals and operatic performances and impressive choral events. I joined the University Chamber Choir, which was led by a frightening and brilliant man called Richard Marlow, who, much to my surprise, was sympathetic about my theatrical activities and allowed me to skip the occasional rehearsal. He ran a truly wonderful group, responsible for, among other things, an unforgettable performance of Bach's Mass in B minor in Trinity College chapel. Every summer, we would gather on the river for an al fresco concert, sitting together in punts as we sang, watching the sun set. It would have been absurd, if it hadn't been so beautiful.

There was also a wild visit to Puglia – during one of our holidays, of course – where we were asked to provide the chorus for a couple of operas. It was 1981, the year of the wedding of Prince Charles and Lady Diana Spencer, and the bride's picture was on every magazine in town, even there in deepest southern Italy. The director kindly gave us the day off to watch the event, although, to be honest, the schedule was not heavy and we hardly needed more free time. All members of the team were offered an alcoholic lunch every day and a long siesta. Our singing was acceptable, but our Italian was apparently dreadful. As we were rehearsing a scene in which the men of the choir were trying to impersonate a group of drunken bandits, one of the assistant directors said wearily that we sounded like working-class Milanese, whom he said speak the language as if it was spoken by Englishmen.

Most of the theatre that I was involved in was not of the highest standard. But I was surrounded by some major talents. Emma Thompson, Stephen Fry, Hugh Laurie and Tilda Swinton were all fellow undergraduates. Except for Tilda, I knew none of them well. I shared a stage with Stephen in a production of *Volpone*, in which he dazzled as the title character, and met the other two a couple of times, but that was about it.

I got to know Tilda, though. I had never met anyone like her before. She was very, very clever and astonishingly beautiful. She knew lots of things that were new to me. She owned a car – or, at least, had access to one – which was rare for an undergraduate at that time. We once took a trip to London together, where she seemed to know the best shops to visit and the most stylish bargains to look for. At one point, in a store off Bond Street, she picked out a dress that looked to me like a hessian sack. I couldn't understand what she liked about it. I need hardly say that she slipped it on and it looked tremendous. She didn't buy it, as I recall. We went off to a small restaurant nearby and ate unfamiliar seafood for lunch.

At that time, Cambridge seemed a long way from London. The train journey between the two cities always felt interminable. As a student, I was shut off from the outside world and, even within Cambridge itself, I never travelled more than a few hundred yards from my rooms because everything I needed or wanted seemed to be on my doorstep. Even contact with home was rare. We didn't have mobile phones and, since there was only one payphone in college and I'm not sure that I could tell you where exactly it was located, all communication was in writing. Mum wrote letters, but I'm pretty certain that I never replied. Once, to my surprise and delight, she sent a parcel of newly bought underpants crammed together with a packet of Jaffa Cakes – the perfect gift for a student.

Tilda was also politically informed and confident in her ability to defend her corner. Margaret Thatcher had just started her first term as prime minister. The mining industry was in turmoil. The battle against the horrors of apartheid was in its final agonies. So there was a great deal for my contemporaries to argue over and to fight for. Our efforts were undoubtedly often weak and self-important – like those of so many young people before and since – but they were well-intentioned. I watched from the sidelines most of the time, because I was woefully ignorant about the issues. It's something of which I'm not proud. But theatre was part of the fight and I was getting to know a little about that. We all followed the work of companies such as 7:84 and playwrights such as Athol Fugard – artists on the political frontline.

As at many universities, the theatre scene was dominated by a small number of students. Some of the biggest talents – Emma, Stephen, Hugh – were part of the Footlights, the famous revue group that, in my time, triumphed at the Edinburgh festival. When it came to straight theatre, Tilda was without question the leading actress, although there were others who had a high profile. She, predictably, worked many times with the pre-eminent undergraduate director – Steve Unwin. They were an impressive team. Their work together was always clean and clear – and precociously assured. I thought of Steve as a new Peter Brook and I wasn't alone. He had an unusual authority for an undergraduate; and I dreamed helplessly that I might join his group of actors that was clearly destined to change the world. I spent my three years at Cambridge praying that one day I would get a message from Steve asking me to join him in a new production. It did happen eventually, but only in my last term. He cast me as Lafew, an ostensibly wise old counsellor, in *All's Well that Ends Well*.

Steve was a natural teacher and I don't think I'm exaggerating when I say that he taught me more about acting than anyone else I've known. He was no older than I was, but he knew what he was talking about and I suppose that I was eager to learn. At that time, my thoughts about theatre – if I had any – were incoherent and much of the work that I had done up to that point was simply a type of showing off. Steve changed that. He demanded simplicity and – dare I say it? – truth. Preconceptions and easy answers were unacceptable – an attitude of mind that I've tried to exercise ever since.

There is a character in *All's Well that Ends Well* called Parolles. He is an extraordinary figure – of the type that people in Shakespeare's time would have called a braggart. He lies compulsively about everything, but principally about his imagined military career. Inevitably, he is caught out and humiliated. The actor playing him in our student production was called Andrew Normington. He was a tall, delicate man of impressive sensitivity – not predictable casting for a character who has to appear to be a bluff soldier. Andrew and Steve turned this conventional figure inside out – or so it seemed. I had assumed that Parolles knows all along that he is a liar; but Andrew played a man who believes every word he says at the time that he says it. I am sure that actors before and since have presented Parolles in this way, but it was new to me. This version of the braggart did not shy away from the fact that Parolles is often infuriating, but he nevertheless elicited the audience's sympathy. In a way, he was an innocent. It was as if he were not responsible for his falsehoods, as if he needed to lie in order to define his place in a world that would otherwise ignore him. And so his downfall was heartbreaking. He has to start all over again – 'Simply the thing I am/Shall make me live', he says. Steve was, among other things, teaching me to question everything, to take nothing for granted.

Towards the end of *All's Well that Ends Well*, there is a scene where the inevitable clown (Lavatch), Parolles and Lafew all meet. Lafew is an elder statesman and a pompous, even faintly ridiculous, man. Parolles has been exposed as a liar and a fantasist and has now to rebuild his life. The clown is a familiar Shakesperean figure – wisecracking and truth-telling. It's as if all three fools in the story are together – for the first and only time. Parolles begs Lafew for a job. The latter thinks for a moment and then says:

> '. . . *though you are a fool and a knave you shall eat. Go to; follow.*'

It's a very kind gesture; and Andrew Normington's bemused and chastened Parolles deserved it.

At university, I spent more time reading Shakespeare than acting in his plays; and I read a great deal. I had to. I wish that I could pretend that I didn't work hard, that I was one of those students (and I knew plenty) who sailed effortlessly through to their final exams. But, sadly, that wouldn't be accurate. I spent most mornings in the college library, churning out essay after essay. Looking back, my efforts were more about constructing an argument – any argument would do – than about the value or impact of the work that I was asked to study. Method was more important than substance. I couldn't engage with a bigger picture. Inevitably, some of my essays were more successful than others. Buried in a cardboard box at home, I still have a piece that I submitted in my final year. I can't, off the top of my head, remember about what. I do remember that it was written in pencil – which was very rude, even contemptuous. It might have been about medieval literature – *Sir Gawain and the Green Knight* or something – which was one of the specialities I had chosen to study. The essay was returned without comment, except for a hastily scrawled and infuriated message from my teacher on the last page: 'This is rubbish.'

As it happens, the English faculty at that time was debating, often heatedly, changes in the principles on which it based its teaching. A few years previously, a new way of thinking had arrived in Cambridge from the Continent. It was called Structuralism. I don't know that I understood it then and it would be foolish of me to attempt an explanation now; but the two ideas that I took from it were, firstly, that language is essentially an arbitrarily constructed set of signs and, secondly, that the assignment of value to any piece of writing beyond its function in a particular time and place was redundant. There was no such thing as a central canon of literary work. I found the new methods of analysis that I was reading about tremendously exciting, even if most of its complexities passed me by and even if the final destination of any argument seemed faintly disappointing. It felt iconoclastic; and it infuriated a great number of people, which intrigued me.

I didn't attend many lectures. The building where they were given always felt a long way from my college and the walk across the river, especially on a bitingly cold winter day, seemed an unnecessary effort. But I did take lessons nearer home, many of which I attended with my friend Barry Isaacson. We were taught together by a fellow of our college called Jeremy Prynne. I had heard that he was a poet, but I didn't read his poems, which was careless of me. Not that this would have worried Mr Prynne. I found out only much later that his work is much admired and very difficult. He always wore a black suit with an orange tie and had extremely large feet. During our lessons, which sometimes lasted for hours, he paced up and down the room without stopping. Barry and I sat crammed together on a small sofa as Mr Prynne constructed terrifyingly complex arguments from close analysis of tiny bits of text. As it happens, Barry was besotted with the movies, an area of study that, like theatre and jazz, was on the extreme borders of the curricula. It was another new world for me; and Barry was yet another great teacher. His enthusiasm has never left him. He would later move to Los Angeles and enjoy a brilliant career in Hollywood.

I remember very clearly one essay that I wrote. It was about *Macbeth*. As I sat in the library one morning, I suddenly felt that the argument that I was pursuing might be of some real value. It didn't feel workaday and plodding, like so much of my other work. I had known and loved *Macbeth* since school – one of the soliloquies was the first Shakespearean speech that I learned by heart – and had always thought it was, in some way, qualitatively different from all the other tragedies that Shakespeare wrote. This has something to do with the fact that Macbeth's original mistake is, in truth, a crime, which leads to a particular type of punishment and a particular type of pain. I became so excited as I wrote my essay that I had to take a short break. I left the library and went downstairs to get a coffee; and I stayed there for an hour, just thinking. I applied some of the ideas that I had then when I came to play Macbeth years later. It didn't quite work, but I still believe that the arguments have weight. More importantly, I discovered that intellectual endeavour can sometimes be an intense emotional activity. I might not have discovered the electron or the laws of gravity, but it felt just as exciting to me.

Love and Marriage

Macbeth

At around the time I wrote my university essay on *Macbeth*, of which I was so proud, I went to see a play by Athol Fugard in a neighbouring college. It laboured under a very long title – *Statements After an Arrest Under the Immorality Act* – and it starred Tilda Swinton. It told the story of an affair between a black man and a white woman in apartheid South Africa. One day, as they are making love, police break into her apartment, arrest the man and take him away. Inevitably, he will be charged, found guilty and punished. The woman is left on stage, naked, despairing and alone.

What I remember most clearly about that afternoon is the speech that the woman gives in the moments after the arrest of her lover. My memory is doubtless faulty and I haven't read the play since that performance, but I believe I still have her words in my head. As she stood, absolutely still, she insisted that she would remain motionless for as long as possible, because the moment she moved – even a single muscle – then the full horror of her predicament and the predicament of her lover would become clear. As time started to roll forward, the pain and the sense of loss, for both of them, would become unavoidable.

It struck me as an extraordinary idea, and it resonated with the thoughts I had had about Macbeth. I had an image, which I couldn't shake out of my mind, of the king, in his last days, sitting in a chair, absolutely immobile. I thought of him, at this point in his life, able to live only in the present – the past and the future are both too disturbing. So long as he doesn't move, then Macbeth feels that he will somehow survive. Perhaps his famous meditation on tomorrow and the following day being essentially the same as today is a neat expression of this sense of stasis. I brought all these thoughts with me when I agreed to play Macbeth at the Almeida Theatre, directed by John Caird, in 2004. I don't think they helped particularly, though I believed in their value. I still do. But maybe I should have stuck to my rule, which I am forever mouthing off about, of ridding myself of preconceptions before the start of rehearsal.

Our show was not particularly well received; or rather, in that coy phrase, it had mixed notices. I was proud of a great deal of it – and very proud of the work that my colleagues did – but the reaction of some of the critics was demoralising. One's immediate reaction, in the face of adverse criticism, is an urge to stop doing whatever it is that is judged to be objectionable. But, of course, with a play, when the length of a run in the theatre has been decided long before the reviews come out, that is not possible. The worst bit about it is the sense of being personally responsible for the failure of the show, of one's own work not being good enough, and of letting other people down.

In Chekhov's play *The Seagull*, there is a scene in which a young woman called Nina, who is trying to earn a living as an actress, talks to her childhood friend, Konstantin. She is not enjoying huge success and much of her work is, one suspects, mediocre. I played Konstantin for the Royal Shakespeare Company very early in my career, in 1990, with the astonishing Amanda Root as Nina. Every night, I would listen to a line from her that made my blood run cold. I know that it has the same effect on every actor who hears it. Talking about her life in the theatre, Nina says, in Michael Frayn's translation: 'You don't understand what it's like when you feel you're acting badly.' She's absolutely right – it's a terrible state of mind, and almost impossible for non-actors to comprehend.

I believe that my acting wasn't all bad in *Macbeth*; but, on balance, I failed. I know, at least, that I had thought my decisions through. John and I had a series of meetings at his house in north London before rehearsals started. It was a chance to thrash out some ideas. I told him of the thoughts I had had about the play at university – including my interest in Macbeth's physical and mental immobility at the end of his story. We talked about the design and the soundscape. I was keen on using the call of birds – ravens and owls – since they are mentioned so often in the text. I liked the prospect of using the sound of bells, too. I also wondered if we could do the play with as little blood as possible. I had seen so many productions where blood was everywhere – the kingdom of Scotland as an abattoir – that I thought we might do something different. That was a daft idea and didn't survive our first meetings. One can't escape the fact that the sight of blood is an important component of the drama.

In passing, I told him of a visit I had recently paid to the Folger Shakespeare Library in Washington, DC. The custodians there had taken a great deal of trouble to put together a selection of exhibits that they thought might interest me. Knowing that I was about to do *Macbeth*, they showed me an edition of *Holinshed's Chronicles* of British history – a major source for Shakespeare's play – in which there was an illustration of Macbeth's famous meeting with the witches – or the Weird Sisters, as the playwright prefers to call them. The three women look very grand, which surprised me. None looked young, although it was difficult to tell. We have become used to the idea that the witches are part of an alternative counterculture, figures from the fringes of society. I thought how terrifying it might be for Macbeth if the opposite was the case. What if they reek of the establishment? Seeing them would make Macbeth feel very uncomfortable. I don't believe he thinks of himself as a player at the centre of political power, but rather assumes he is a tolerated outsider, useful as a military commander, but no more. At the beginning of the play, he is socially awkward, unlike his smooth fellow-soldier,

Banquo. He is taciturn, perhaps even sullen in company. I sense that he doesn't feel at ease in the presence of the king, the princes and their courtiers. So, for him to be confronted by three aristocratic, ancient women, speaking in dangerous riddles, might be very disturbing. We decided that, in our production, the Weird Sisters would be very old and of very high status.

John Caird had directed me in *Hamlet* in 2000 and I trusted him completely. I knew him to be a man of great intelligence and sensitivity. He has, among many other things, an endearing habit of seeing the best in all the characters he is asked to direct. It's a good place to start – especially with a man like Macbeth; because the first and fundamental question to ask about Macbeth – or, rather, the question to which everybody wants an answer – is whether he is, in essence, good or bad. Was he born to be a murderer? I know it has crossed his mind, but is murder something that he would ever think of carrying out? Is it a fantasy and no more? The difficulty in finding an answer to these questions lies in the fact that, at least at the beginning of the play, Macbeth is something of an enigma. Actually, perhaps it's not a difficulty to surmount, but rather a gift from the playwright that should be embraced. Macbeth gives very little away. It's as if he is, somehow, morally neutral – a *tabula rasa*. What he feels, and what he thinks, are hidden from most of those around him – even his wife. Maybe he is a profound thinker; or maybe he doesn't feel, or think, much at all. Indeed, it could be said that the activation of a dormant moral sensitivity and the discovery of a new expressiveness in Macbeth is at the heart of the play. That is one of the things that makes it so surprising and unusual.

Macbeth is a professional soldier, so he is used to killing people, but only as part of his job. The first time we see him is with Banquo, returning home after a bloody, but successful, battle. They are neither of them elated, it seems, merely exhausted. There is no sense of triumph. Macbeth says, rather laconically, that the day has been 'foul and fair' and no more than that. Killing for these two is an everyday activity. They then meet the Weird Sisters, who hint at a great future for both men; and their minds begin to spin.

The women tell Macbeth that he will, one day, be king. Banquo is told that, although he will not be crowned himself, he will be the progenitor of a long line of kings. So one of the most important distinctions between the two men boils down to the question of children. We find out later that Banquo has a son and that Macbeth has no issue. From the beginning to the end, children haunt this play. Shakespeare wrote often about parents and their offspring – particularly fathers and daughters – but never quite like this. Children are in every dark corner of *Macbeth*. We see living children, hear of dead children, watch a child being murdered, a baby appears as part of a terrifying image at one point, and children play their part in a disturbing vision summoned up by the Weird Sisters. On top of this, if the Macbeths' marriage is childless, then at the centre of the story is a dull ache that won't go away. As in *Othello*, Shakespeare sees a marriage without children as, in some sense, a failure. We don't think like that now, of course, but I'm pretty sure that's how this writer saw it.

It's a truism that we know only a few details of Shakespeare's life and that we know absolutely nothing of what he actually thought or felt. However, I'm sure that I'm not the only person who feels that Shakespeare's opinion that children validate a relationship in some fundamental way is something he held in his own life. It was not simply a narrative option in his writing. He really felt it. I can provide no evidence or support for this idea, beyond the fact that we know he had two daughters, but lost a son; and that he returns compulsively to the issue of children – and the loss of children – throughout the long span of his work.

(I have a sense, incidentally, that Shakespeare experienced sexual jealousy and that he also suffered from insomnia. Again, I can provide no proof for this. It's just that he keeps coming back to these subjects. Funnily enough, although jealousy does not play a part in *Macbeth*, sleeplessness does. Once he decides to kill the king, it's as if Macbeth never sleeps again.)

In an early conversation with her husband, when they discuss the possibility of murder, Lady Macbeth reminds him that she has had a child:

> '. . . *I have given suck, and know*
> *How tender 'tis to love the babe that milks me.*'

Some years ago, this passage gave rise to a satirical essay by an academic who took aim at those readers who wanted to know more about this baby – and, indeed, about any other babies that Lady Macbeth might have had. These readers were foolish, so the academic said, because, as he saw it, the concerns were impossible to resolve and irrelevant to boot. He was wrong. If the two actors playing Macbeth and his wife don't face up to the issue of children and the role they play in their marriage, then they might as well go home. We don't know very much about how plays were rehearsed in Shakespeare's time, but I guarantee that the first actor who played Lady Macbeth asked his resident playwright a few pertinent and insistent questions about the baby. It would have been irresponsible not to.

For a start, is the child alive or dead? Boy or girl? Is or was Macbeth the father? In order to fill the gaps, it's probably wise for the actors to construct some sort of history. Emma Fielding, who played Lady Macbeth in our production, and I settled for the simplest option. Macbeth and his wife had one child, who died young. Other people might very well come up with different scenarios, of course. But it's good to get the details sorted out, whatever they might be, because the really important thing about Lady Macbeth's mention of the child during a heated discussion with her husband is why and when it happens.

Macbeth says very little in this major confrontation with his wife. The audience has come to expect that. He never seems to talk much to anybody; but, just before her entrance, he delivers the most extraordinary and lengthy soliloquy. Up to this point, we have not heard him talk like this. Here a new poetic voice is in evidence. His monologue begins with an argument about crime and punishment. He would be willing to commit murder, he says, if he could get away with it, both here on earth and in 'the life to come'. There's nothing exceptional about this train of thought. I guess that most criminals probably think the same. But then his speech expands, blows up like a balloon, as he visualises a day of divine judgement. The images he conjures up are so wild and extreme that it was always difficult for me to get a grip on them. At the centre of this tangle is this:

> '*. . . pity, like a naked new-born babe,*
> *Striding the blast, or heaven's cherubin, horsed*
> *Upon the sightless couriers of the air,*
> *Shall blow the horrid deed in every eye . . .*'

It's terrifying – particularly the baby. I suppose one could look through the apocalyptic lexicon and quickly find angels and horses – even blind horses – but what about the tiny (or huge) naked child riding the wind? The speech moves relentlessly towards this explosive revelation of the subconscious; and, although he is appalled, it occurred to me that Macbeth might also revel in it. Indeed, perhaps his repressed and dulled personality finds a thrilling new focus and a degree of liberation in both the thought of murder and a new, wildly expressive language. The last lines of the speech have an hallucinogenic quality; but, as with any drug, there is, after the pleasure of the first hit, the possibility of addiction. Macbeth, in my mind, becomes an addict.

And, of course, in order to articulate his new terror and his new excitement, it's inevitable that he should conjure up the idea of a baby – and a monstrous baby to boot. Nor is it a coincidence that, a few seconds later, his wife, as the killer blow in their argument, should herself mention their dead child. When we played this scene, Emma and I always felt that the child's death is a trauma, perhaps from many years back, that they have never talked about, but which is always present. So much of the subtext of their dialogue is about their failure to have a living child. She has earlier 'unsexed' herself (no more motherhood for her), proclaims herself to be more of a man than he is (a hint at his impotence, perhaps), accuses him of a lack of real masculinity (including, by implication, his inability to produce live offspring) and implies that murder – and a crown – are the only possible compensations she will accept. Macbeth, after that onslaught, has no option but to kill the king; he may even know that it is the only way to maintain the stability of their marriage. It might be a simplistic or offensive reading, but this is why I've always interpreted his decision to kill Duncan as a perverse act of love.

When I said that the thought of murder is, in some sense, a liberation for Macbeth, I hinted at the next step in his journey – the cost of that liberation. As far I can see, any feeling of a new freedom is, for Macbeth, a momentary delusion. The new thoughts he has, the new poetic voice that he discovers, might feel like a release, but they are, in fact, a trap. This is, in part, because they are incommunicable, even to his wife. Macbeth says as much. At one point in the play, he spins out a lyrical description of night falling; again he uses a register that we have never heard him use before. Lady Macbeth is uncomprehending and her husband recognises this: 'Thou marvell'st at my words', he says. What is interesting about this interaction could be that it is not the substance of Macbeth's speech that surprises his wife – there is, after all, nothing unusual about nightfall – or, indeed, the possibility of future criminality but, rather, the elaborate way he is speaking, the uncharacteristic style of framing his thoughts.

Macbeth ends up living only in his own head. He slowly collapses into himself. Husband and wife drift apart and the outside world becomes for him no more and no less than a threat. The expression of his internal life changes into a compulsion; and something that starts as pleasurable or liberating turns slowly into a terrifying restriction. This is his punishment. Excitement becomes guilt; and then guilt is transformed over time into a paranoid isolation.

My undergraduate essay started at this point. I was trying to locate the reasons why I felt that *Macbeth* was qualitatively different from Shakespeare's other tragedies. Because the hero's original sin is not a mistake or carelessness or weakness, but a crime, his suffering is not a sudden realisation of wrongdoing, but a slow living death. He is not surprised by his guilt. His journey starts with an absolute understanding of what he has done and develops from there; and he knows that the price he has to pay is living with this. It's interesting that, by the end of the play, Macbeth simultaneously wants to die and to live; and his perspective has shrunk to an existence only in the present. The past is too painful to think about – a dead child, a once-loved wife who is now slipping into insanity, a murdered king; and the future is also unbearable – no heir and a poisoned legacy. That is why it feels as if he wants to kill all the children in Scotland. If he can't have a future, then neither can anyone else. That's one of the few powers he must feel is left to him.

Among the children Macbeth wishes to kill are those of a fellow thane called Macduff. We see this on stage – representative, perhaps, of more general slaughter. Macbeth has commissioned a squad of killers to carry out the murders. They are joined, unexpectedly, by another man, who remains nameless. It seemed obvious to me that this has to be the king himself; or rather, it seemed too good an opportunity to miss. In our production, this stranger stood silently and watched. My Macbeth needed to see the death of a child with his own eyes – another private thrill for him, perhaps, but also a symptom of the bleak curiosity of a man who has lost, and perhaps never knew, his own child. As Macduff will later point out, in one of the saddest moments in the play, Macbeth 'has no children'. The world of parental love is beyond him.

Macbeth's last speech, when he is fighting for his life against Macduff, ends like this:

> *'... damned be him, that first cries, "Hold, enough."'*

I changed the punctuation of this line. I put a full-stop after 'Hold'. The single word, 'enough', stood by itself. It signalled an end to Macbeth's struggle to make sense of his life, a recognition that it had become drained of meaning. It's not the done thing to fiddle around in this way with the text, but I thought it was worth the risk.

Perhaps this suffering is what makes him a sympathetic character. Unlike Othello and King Lear, Macbeth knows from the very beginning that he has done wrong. He spends the rest of his life trying to compensate for this and, simultaneously, to secure his position as king. There is a moment, just after he has taken the crown, when Macbeth meets a suspicious Banquo. The latter has decided to go riding with his son, Fleance. Macbeth is already planning to kill them both. He asks his friend whether he is taking his son with him:

> *'Goes Fleance with you?'*

Clearly, in order to facilitate their murder that night, the new king wants to know where both Banquo and his son will be. But it crossed my mind that, even if only for a fleeting moment, Macbeth might consider separating Banquo from his son – keeping the son at home while the father goes riding. Perhaps Macbeth could then kill his friend and adopt his boy – a substitute for the dead child. Macbeth could go on to make him his heir. I know this all sounds a stretch – and it is – but, for Macbeth, it would surely be a way of making things better. It would wipe out the memory of the murder and restore stability. After all, why would Macbeth want to perpetuate his own and his country's misery?

When I did *Hamlet* for John, he had a similar thought about Claudius, the King of Denmark and Hamlet's stepfather. Claudius has murdered his brother, Hamlet's father, in order to seize the crown and marry his brother's wife, Hamlet's mother. Young Hamlet has been called back from his studies at a German university to spend time at the Danish court – and Claudius wants him to stay. It doesn't really make much sense. Why not leave Hamlet where he is? After all, he seems happy enough as a student. Claudius may want to keep his stepson close to him, rather than in Germany, in order to prevent him becoming a focus for political discontent; but John and I thought there might another more personal reason. In his first speech to Hamlet, Claudius offers himself as a new father figure. This is usually seen as hypocritical or sly. But maybe the new king, having won his brother's crown and his brother's wife, feels the need to win his brother's son as well; and adopt him as his own. He genuinely wants a son. In other words, the offer to Hamlet is heartfelt. If the young man agrees, the inconvenient fact of the murder of the old king can be brushed under the carpet and things can settle down. It was an intriguing and subtle idea.

In plays, such as *Macbeth,* that deal with so many characters in extreme situations, it is worth holding on to these small touches of honesty. After all, people can do something wicked and, almost simultaneously, display genuine emotion or ordinary human decency, can't they? There was a moment I remember from our production that shows what I mean. Lady Macbeth, just before she ends her own life, is seen sleepwalking. She talks in her sleep, too. At the end of the scene, she says:

'Come, come, come, come, give me your hand. What's done, cannot be undone. To bed, to bed, to bed.'

One would assume that Lady Macbeth, in her dream, is talking to her husband. But Emma Fielding, who, in our production, played Lady Macbeth as a fundamentally decent woman who makes a terrible mistake, took a different route. As she left the stage, she held out her hand as if to a child and led the invisible toddler back to bed. Our last sight of her is as a mother. It was heartbreaking.

I would like to play Macbeth again. It's one of the very few parts I want to revisit. I wonder whether he could be presented as a much older man than usual, a man nearing retirement, as it were. The murder of the king is his last chance to make something of his life, which, although a success on paper, he finds unsatisfactory. I picture him as looking like one of those terrifying generals we used to see on the television during the Gulf wars. You never know, it might happen.

Benedick

The first time Nick Hytner directed me in a Shakespeare play was in *Much Ado About Nothing* in 2007. It was during his already-legendary time as director of the National Theatre in London. We had first met years before, in Stratford. I was sitting one day in my house opposite the theatre – I must have had the day off – when there was a knock on the front door. It was Nick. I knew he was deep in rehearsal for his production of *King Lear* with, at its heart, the astonishing John Wood playing the central role. That day, Nick had been planning to take his show out of the rehearsal room and into the theatre, with full set, costumes, lighting, sound; but his schedule had ground to a halt. He and his team had designed a huge, hollow cube that stood in the centre of the stage. This was supposed to spin at various points during the play – a significant technical challenge; and on this particular day it wasn't working. While the crew tried to fix the problem, Nick had some time off and decided to ask me – someone he barely knew – out to lunch. We jumped into his car and drove to a nearby village to eat. Nick must have felt very frustrated with all the delays in the theatre, but there are worse places to while away some time than in a restaurant in deepest Warwickshire. We enjoyed a therapeutic couple of hours and, by the time we got back to town, the technical hitch had been sorted out.

My friendship with Nick is one of the most important in my professional and personal life. After our lunch in Stratford, we would meet regularly to eat, go to the theatre or watch a film. For the first few years, he didn't seem interested in using me as an actor. I assumed that he didn't rate me very highly, but he assures me that this was not the case. Whatever the reason, it was not until he took over the National Theatre, in 2003, that he cast me in a play. *The Alchemist* by Ben Jonson was our first venture together, *Much Ado About Nothing* our second. Gratifyingly, there were many more to come.

I had heard that Nick could be rather fierce. It was evident to everyone that he was very clever and that he did not suffer fools. In the early years of our friendship, I would quite consciously put my brain into top gear before I met him, because I realised that, if I were to enjoy myself, I would have to concentrate and think more quickly and more clearly than I usually did. His eyes – large, clear and ice blue – were famous. They would sometimes fix you in a stare that gave the impression that he was waiting for you to say something interesting or, at the very least, relevant. Actually, as he admitted to me many years later, he was often thinking about something entirely different, even as he was looking at you. I suppose multitasking is the curse of being a director, and especially of being the artistic director of the National Theatre.

I say all this because Nick is, in reality, one of the kindest, most sensitive and most generous men I have ever met. His triumphant reign at the National would have been much less successful if he had not been kind, sensitive and, especially, generous. And, certainly, *Much Ado About Nothing* wouldn't have been the glorious experience it was.

It is a golden play. I think it is the most human-sized of Shakespeare's comedies. Its central plot has been described as like *Othello*, but with a happy ending. A young man, Claudio, and a young woman, Hero, fall in love and agree to get married. On the day of the wedding, to the great surprise of her family and friends, Claudio humiliates and rejects his bride at the altar, claiming furiously that she has slept with another man. It is an absurd and cruel accusation, the result of a malicious plot devised by an unhappy, disgruntled and envious man, Don John. Hero is taken home by her family, where they pretend that she has died from grief. Claudio hears of this and then finds out that he has been misled by Don John. He is devastated. The depth of his remorse encourages Hero's family to tell him that she is not dead, but alive and still, astonishingly, willing to marry him. And so, despite the nagging suspicion that the marriage of Hero and Claudio can't possibly survive after such a disastrous start, the story ends happily.

It's true that the play explores jealousy, as *Othello* does; but the differences are more telling than the similarities. The plot to discredit the young Hero is malicious, of course, and things darken noticeably for a short while; but the villain, Don John, hasn't anything like the weight, either in terms of his part in the story or individual psychological complexity, that Iago has. Neither, for that matter, is Claudio like Othello. The latter is a mature man of overwhelming talent, the former a callow boy. So, in the comedy, Shakespeare keeps it as light as he can, as the title of the play suggests. Even at the darkest moments – and things do get rather unpleasant – the audience never really loses hope that all will turn out for the best.

However, the major difference between *Othello* and *Much Ado About Nothing* has to do with the subplot. *Othello* barely has a subplot; in the case of *Much Ado About Nothing*, the subplot is the chief glory of the play. It features a woman, a cousin of Hero, called Beatrice; and Claudio's friend and fellow soldier, Benedick. After a great deal of elaborate and hurtful bickering, these two very clever people end up together. It's often said that the Macbeths are the only happily married couple in Shakespeare. I'm not sure that's true – *The Merry Wives of Windsor* comes to mind – but I do know for certain that the one couple that will unquestionably go on to enjoy a wonderful life together after the play is over is Beatrice and Benedick. Perhaps that is why I consider it to be a golden play; at the end of the story, genuine happiness is somehow assured – at least for these two.

Nick asked me to play Benedick; and offered Beatrice to Zoë Wanamaker. This was something of a surprise to both of us. Frankly, we both considered ourselves too old – twenty years too old, in fact. The two characters are normally played by much younger actors; and, consequently, their fractious relationship is often not that far removed from the more staid and conventional courtship of Hero and Claudio. They are, all four of them, young people looking for the type of love that young people look for. Making Beatrice and Benedick much older allowed for a more complicated and difficult history between the two of them; and, in addition, their possible romance had the flavour of being a last chance. Actually, using a much older couple is not a totally new idea. Other directors have gone down the same path. So I make no claims for it being a radical thought. But it's rare enough; which is a shame, because it works.

The story is set in Sicily, at the house of an aristocratic family. Our designer, Vicki Mortimer, came up with a soft vision of lemon trees and grapevines, of the sun cutting through slatted blinds. At the beginning of the play, the lights came up on the family – Hero, her father and Beatrice – sitting around a large table, outside on the verandah, enjoying a long, lazy breakfast. Nick said later that it looked like his dream holiday. A group of soldiers arrive, returning home after a fighting a small war. Even this war feels light-hearted and rather fun. Nobody seems to have got hurt. The conflict probably entails boys running over the Sicilian hills with the occasional light skirmish. It's all very easy and romantic.

When Vicki showed her model of the set to the cast, the most memorable feature was a garden, at the centre of which was a large ornamental pool. Nick announced to everyone that this pool would be deep. In fact, it would be deep enough for someone to jump in and become completely submerged. It was, predictably, irresistible. There is a scene, halfway through the play, when Benedick is trying to hide from three of his friends. They are talking about Beatrice and about how glaringly obvious it is that, despite her protestations to the contrary, she is in love with Benedick. Since he, in his heart of hearts, feels the same about her, he wants to hear every word of their conversation; but he doesn't want to be seen. As the scene progresses and his friends move about the garden, Benedick tries out different hiding places; but none of them is satisfactory. Finally, he is forced to jump into the pool.

This was, by a long way, the most physically satisfying moment I have ever enjoyed on stage. When I was young and my family lived in the Far East, and we children spent all our days swimming, my siblings and I sometimes liked to jump into a swimming pool by doing a 'bomb'; and, now, here, in the middle of the Olivier stage, I leapt, tucked my knees up to my chest and 'bombed' the pool. It was like being a ten-year-old again. There was the most enormous splash, a laugh from the audience that seemed to go on for ever, and I lay hidden from them in the water. A clever piece of technical wizardry meant that I could keep breathing while it looked from the outside as if I was under the water for an impossibly long time. It was surprisingly comfortable, especially since the pool had been gently heated.

The three friends of Benedick continued to talk for a short time, perfectly aware that he was lying in the pool. They pretended not to notice and then left the stage. After a beat, my head emerged from the water. Fellow cast members said that, with my hair flat against my head, I looked like a seal. I then delivered a soliloquy, gently paddling round the pool. Some actors will tell you that they go through their lines while relaxing in the bath. Words somehow come more easily when you are immersed in warm water. It's a useful thing for an actor to know. And here was I, doing exactly that, but in front of a thousand people.

I have to confess that, during this soliloquy, I played fast and loose with the punctuation – as I did in the final scene of *Macbeth*. All my more purist principles were thrown out of the window. At one point, speaking of Beatrice's feelings for him, Benedick says this:

> *'Love me? Why, it must be requited.'*

This is how it is punctuated in any edition of the play that you might care to look at. I changed it – just a little:

> *'Love me? Why? It must be requited.'*

As with my messing around with *Macbeth*, I have no excuse for being so cavalier with the text except that the line – that 'Why?', in particular – got a very big laugh. It was a ruthless choice – the laugh was too good to miss – but it was also an indication that Benedick might not be as self-confident as he looks, which was useful. He is astonished that Beatrice might love him. If pushed, I could argue that Shakespeare and his contemporaries used punctuation in a different way and with different aims than we do. If you look at a printed text from his lifetime, you will see that commas, full stops, semi-colons and the rest of the armoury are more of a guide to breathing – they indicate the length of each gap, in effect – than a clarification of sentence structure. Those rules came later. However, that argument doesn't really convince when it comes to question marks. I could also argue that it was not my idea in the first place. Some of the cast thought it was, but in fact it was taken from someone else's performance. I think Derek Jacobi, one of the greatest Benedicks of the last fifty years, did the same thing as I did. I'm pretty sure Roger Allam did too. I wasn't alone. But I (and they) have no argument that would convince the puritans. However, the laugh was great.

The speech in the pool was one highlight, but there were many others. One was Mark Addy and Trevor Peacock as Dogberry and Verges, the local constables, bumbling their way to solving the mystery that caused chaos at Hero's wedding. They alchemised two famously tricky parts into theatrical gold. Another was Andrew Woodall's sour and taciturn Don John. But, for me and many others, the principal glory of the play is the fierce and funny relationship between Beatrice and Benedick. As with the Macbeths, it's important for these two characters to construct a clear past history. There are many more pertinent clues in this play than in *Macbeth*. When we first meet them, it is clear that they know each other, and have known each other for some time. 'I know you of old', Beatrice says to Benedick at one point. However, their relationship is now, to say the least, combative; their conversation is not much more than the trading of insults. Since they are both quick witted, these insults are often sharp and hurtful; but it's obvious, to the audience and to their friends on stage, that they are playing, perhaps unconsciously, a different game.

Beatrice is damning in her judgement of Benedick. In her eyes, his friendships with other men are shallow and without value. She points out that he seems to find a new best friend every few months. As for women, he cannot be trusted. Indeed, she implies that she and Benedick had an unsatisfactory affair some time ago. Talking of her own heart, she says that, once before, Benedick 'won it of [her] with false dice' and that now she has 'lost it'. She presumably fell in love.

I think we can trust this to be accurate. It seems that Benedick treated her badly – or irresponsibly. When it comes to Benedick, the picture that is built up through the play is of a type of man that I suspect is familiar to all of us. That is what I mean when I say that *Much Ado About Nothing* is a very human comedy. All the characters, not just Benedick, seem familiar. Benedick himself enjoys no profound friendships; and he is wary of any romantic commitment. Maybe he has casual sex when he can find it. Perhaps he pays for it on occasion. He is an enthusiastic drinker and genuinely good company. He is not a great soldier and he hates the idea of duelling. He's a lazy man, both physically and emotionally, and, despite being clever enough, any profound thoughts or feelings that he might have are deeply buried.

But he turns out, to his own surprise, to be the bravest man in Shakespeare. His sense of justice and his love for Beatrice compel him, despite the opposition of his male friends, to support a wronged woman. The conservative world of the play is one where the sexes are rigidly separated; so Benedick is taking quite a risk in behaving as he does. Oddly, by the end of the run, I realised that the cast had divided, quite unconsciously, into two distinct groups, determined by sex. There was a group of boys and a group of girls. It was rather sweet and old fashioned. We were mirroring the story that we had rehearsed and played.

When it came to relations between the sexes in conservative societies, I had some help from home. Two of my closest friends, my neighbours Judy and Mimmo, used to run a hairdressing business. They are a married couple. She is English, but he comes from a small town in southern Italy. One day,

I was sitting in their salon, talking about the new play that I was rehearsing. I told them that it was set in Sicily and that the world it portrayed seemed to be one where men and women were strictly segregated. Mimmo went on to describe a holiday tradition that his friends and family used to observe when he was a teenager. I can't remember what festival it was, probably some *carnevale,* but it was clearly a time for celebration. The young men of the town would go from house to house, in disguise, and dance indoors with the local girls. Proper courtship was always a possibility. In each house, the women would sit in a row on chairs that they had set up against the wall. A record would be put on the record player. The boys would then have to pluck up the courage to ask a girl to dance – by silently pointing at her. Presumably, the girls, too, needed some courage to accept. This was all under the severe gaze of older chaperones. There is a masked ball in *Much Ado About Nothing.* When I told Nick about what Mimmo had said, he ran with the idea and the scene staged itself.

Immediately after Hero is humiliated at her wedding, Beatrice and Benedick are left alone in the church. She insists that Benedick should challenge his friend, Claudio, to a duel, and then kill him. Benedick agrees. This is not something that he finds easy. Nobody would. And, as the playwright has already pointed out, Benedick really doesn't like duelling. He certainly doesn't want to kill anyone. Nor is it easy for him to eschew male company from that moment, as he will have to do, and side unreservedly with the women; but, unexpectedly, he takes on the challenge. The principal motor for this change of heart is, of course, love. For it is at this point in the play that Beatrice and Benedick, those two bickering, aggressive figures, finally reveal their feelings for each other; and it is breathtaking. I know *Romeo and Juliet* is marvellous and often quoted, but I think that this love scene in *Much Ado About Nothing* is the best that Shakespeare ever wrote.

It is wonderful for many reasons. Among them is the fact that it is so surprising. The first declaration from Benedick spills out of him as if resistance is now futile. It's not even in response to a direct cue. It comes out of the blue:

> *'I do love nothing in the world so well as you. Is not that strange?'*

A few lines later she responds in kind and the exchange continues:

> *Beatrice: I was about to protest I loved you.*
> *Benedick: And do it with all thy heart.*
> *Beatrice: I love you with so much of my heart that none is left to protest.*

Most of this little conversation is monosyllabic. This is significant, because whenever Shakespeare aims for the hardest-hitting emotional impact, this is what he does. He falls back on single-syllable words. One sees it again and again in his writing. It's as if he's saying that there are moments in life when there's nowhere left to hide; any elaborate argument is otiose. So you might as well say what you really think as simply as possible.

One other point: this declaration of mutual love happens when they're talking about something else, something much more important, when there is a major problem elsewhere that needs to be resolved – and resolved as soon as possible. The real pressure behind the scene comes from that, not from their feelings for each other. Again, that feels true to ordinary life. After all, Beatrice and Benedick are not part of the principal plot – quite literally. Their lives are of only peripheral interest to those around them. They provide the material for an amusing practical joke, that's all. But here and now, for a few seconds, to their own surprise, they are at the centre of their shared universe.

A little later, Benedick goes to see Beatrice, who is looking after her cousin, Hero. He asks her how she is; and she replies that, like Hero, she is 'very ill'. In our production, I looked Zoë straight in the eyes and said, sincerely, with no ironic twist:

> *'Serve God, love me and mend.'*

It's good advice. And it was at that moment, every night, that I knew they would be happy together. There's not the shadow of a doubt about that.

4

My life during the months after I left university was, to be frank, a bit of a mess. I moved to London, a city that I found hard to navigate and even harder to love. It feels strange to write that now. London has become my home town and is a place for which I feel a great and steady affection. One of my favourite journeys is the car ride from Heathrow airport to the centre of the city after a long trip abroad. Looking through the window, I am reminded every time of just how beautiful London is. And there is no question that it is still one of the most exciting and stimulating places on earth. Even after a stay in New York or after a world tour, I feel my heart lift when I return. But I wasn't happy when I first moved there. Perhaps it's a city that yields up its riches slowly; it takes time to work its charm.

The truth is that I was used to smaller environments than London. My upbringing was very sheltered. I think my siblings would agree that they were sheltered too. In fact, one brother recently said that, even when we left our respective universities – let alone when we arrived – we were all very naive. I'm not sure that's quite the right word. Perhaps 'foolish' would be more accurate. Either way, moving to a city that was noisy, dirty and fiercely energised was bound to be something of a challenge for all of us.

This is odd, perhaps. After all, from a very early age, we siblings had become used to travelling all over the world. As a young boy, I thought nothing of boarding a plane at Heathrow – with a small badge clipped to my jumper which informed everyone that I was 'An Unaccompanied Minor' – and flying by myself to Singapore. I don't remember any visible chaperone, though there must have been one somewhere. For a short period, I did that journey three times a year. In those days, we stopped off at six or seven places on the way. I remember the freezing cold of Zurich and the savage heat of Karachi – where once I asked a barman in the terminal for an orange juice and was given undiluted orange squash. I didn't have the courage to tell him that it wasn't really quenching my thirst. On one occasion, the flight was diverted from Beirut and went on to land somewhere else. I presume this had something to do with the terrible civil war that was raging in Lebanon. So, in some ways, we were quite sophisticated young people; in others, we were idiots.

Despite the fact that I loved reading English and that I believe without reserve in the value of my studies, it can't be denied that an English degree doesn't provide a graduate with any clear indications about a future career – except for academia, of course. Despite toying unsuccessfully with that option for a while, I knew that it would never work out. I still have a faded ambition to give up acting and go into research of some kind. My academic friends will say that, even now, I get overexcited in their company as I try to match their expertise. It's probably too late to change course now; but the dream won't quite die.

Many of my fellow graduates went into merchant banking or some other type of high finance. It was the early years of Thatcher, after all, so this was predictable. But I knew that I would be hopeless in that world and, anyway, I felt uncomfortable about it. There was a couple of heady minutes when I thought I'd like to be a diplomat; but my interest was skin-deep. I had heard that there might be tough exams to pass and high hurdles to clear before there was any chance of becoming our man in

Paris or Washington – and even that was apparently not assured. So that ambition, too, faded away.

I finally decided to apply for a place at the Guildhall School of Music and Drama in London. I was going to be a professional singer. My choice of pieces for the audition was ambitious, perhaps even foolhardy. Alongside some Handel, I sang an aria from Mozart's *The Magic Flute* – in German – which I knew was beyond me. I have no idea why I chose a piece that everyone told me was fiendishly difficult. My breath control was so weak that, by the time I got to the last bars, the physical effort had turned my face a dark crimson. The college, nevertheless, offered to take me on. In those halcyon days, it was relatively easy to get a grant for postgraduate work – inconceivable now, of course. I wouldn't otherwise have been able to afford it: it meant I could go and train properly for what, I had no doubt, would be a dazzling career in opera.

I was following a path that many choral scholars had trod before me. Some, including a few of my fellow undergraduates, have become great stars. But, if I'm honest, my heart wasn't in it. I didn't really believe that my voice was good enough; and one of the many things a singer needs is confidence in their instrument. Furthermore, and I hesitate to say it, I wasn't prepared to put in the hard work that was going to be being asked of me. I also knew that I probably wouldn't end up on the stages of La Scala or Covent Garden or the Met; and, although I'm half-joking when I say that, I knew that I would resent it.

I was sent to a very famous teacher called Rudolf Piernay. Other students told me that he had been responsible for some big singers – Bryn Terfel among them, apparently – and was known for 'breaking a voice down before building it up again'. I was not entirely sure what this process entailed, but I think I knew what it was aiming at. The great choral tradition – in England and elsewhere – tends to use voices that are light and accurate. A high standard of musicianship is expected – including sight-reading, of course. I presume the ideal choral voice is therefore one that can deal with a wide range of repertoire and blend effortlessly with other singers. It's a case of the individual being absorbed into the collective. As a result, the great choirs, at least in England, have a smooth, rich and homogenous sound. It appears effortless, even when the music is tough to sing. I know there are exceptions, but, as a rule, I think this an accurate description. A teacher such as Mr Piernay would see one of his tasks as taking choral singers – the majority of his pupils, I would guess – and turn them into soloists, who are very different animals. After all, a Verdian or Wagnerian, even a Mozartian, would find a choral technique of limited use.

Mr Piernay was not very impressed with me. A major issue was the old problem of whether I was really a tenor and not some kind of light baritone. One of my minor weaknesses was a blanket incompetence when it came to languages. That could be dealt with, but would require intensive study of German, Italian and French. More fundamentally, I knew nothing about how my voice was produced. I had never been taught about things such as breath control or placement or proper legato. I had picked things up along the way, but that was about it. The break in my voice as I tried to get into my higher register – a common difficulty for tenors, I believe – would have to be properly dealt with. In short, there was a lot of work to be done.

Of course, in addition to this, there was one big, unmentionable issue – the elephant in the room. As its name suggested, the school trained both musicians and actors. A single building housed both groups. There was a large entrance hall – a corridor, in effect – and at one end of this, the singers used to congregate whenever they had a break. At the other end, were the actors. Looking at them every day, I felt that I was in the wrong group. Mr Piernay felt it too. After only a couple of weeks, we parted company. He was very kind about it – and probably, let's be honest, relieved. He later came to see me in a couple of plays, which was good of him; and, years after, I heard him perform a Rachmaninov song at the memorial service for a friend. His voice was dark and rich and it filled the church. The performance served as a reminder of what my voice might have been.

I rang my parents to tell them of my decision to drop the singing. It's odd that I felt no trepidation about this call. You would think that, given that they had been, for years now, sending me money to pay the rent and to keep me in food and drink, I would worry that they might be irritated – frustrated at my lack of focus as much as the waste of money. It's an indication of their generosity of spirit that it never occurred to me to be worried. And I was right. When I told Dad that I was going to be an actor, he said cheerfully, 'Thank God for that. We all knew that's what you'd end up doing.'

I still wonder whether a small part of him was not disappointed. Singing is very important to Dad. He was rightly proud when his youngest son grew up to have a wonderful voice and pursued a career in opera and choral music. I think he would have relished my doing the same. On a more personal level, music was something he and I did together. It was unlikely that I would ever join him on the golf course or the hockey pitch; my twin brothers did that. But Dad and I could both sing. Before I went to university, I spent six months at home with my parents, living in the house near Swindon where they had finally settled after their travels around the world. During the day, I worked as a porter in a local hospital, but in the evenings, often two or three times a week, Dad would take us both to join a choir somewhere in the wilds of Wiltshire. We were tenors for hire, as it were. After each concert, we would drive home, through the dark, twisting country roads, listening to music on the car's sound system. Often it was Dietrich Fischer-Dieskau – 'the perfect voice', Dad would always say. Sometimes, it was Fritz Wunderlich and we would, on cue, bemoan the singer's early and violent death. We put on Gundula Janowitz, Christa

Ludwig and Janet Baker. All were singers whom Dad had grown up with. As a final treat, we would stop off for a pint as we neared our village.

After leaving the music course at the Guildhall, I never sang seriously again. Over the years, I've appeared in a couple of musicals and enjoyed the experience, but, other than that, there was no more singing. I confess that I haven't missed it. In tandem, my listening changed too – less choral repertoire and more orchestral and instrumental music. The sound system in my father's car played its part in this change. When I was a teenager, the family lived in Germany. At the beginning of the school holidays, I would fly from England to a small military airport near Düsseldorf. Mum and Dad would pick me up. On one occasion, as we were driving home, Dad put on a tape, saying, 'You really must hear this.' There was a huge blast of sound as the first bars of Mahler's Eighth Symphony – the famous 'Symphony of a Thousand' – flooded the car. It took my breath away; and planted the seeds of a keen interest in Mahler and the long, Germanic symphonic tradition. As I sat in the car, I knew that I had to find out what such an enormous array of forces – full orchestra, organ, eight soloists, double choir and more – looked like on the page. I had some pocket money and, as soon as I could, I went into town to buy the score. It was the size of a paperback and had a rich maroon cover and tiny print. It was also criminally expensive. I loved it – the first orchestral score that I had bought for my own pleasure. It has since disappeared, which is an unsolved mystery. I have no idea where it is now; perhaps it's being studied somewhere by another teenager.

So I left singing behind me, auditioned for the college drama course, was accepted and crossed the floor to join the actors. A friend from university, Cathy, had won a scholarship to study drama at the Guildhall and was there to hold my hand when I arrived to start my new life. She explained to me the arcane complexities of voicework and movement workshops and mask technique. It was a strict regime and any sloppiness, especially when it came to things such as timekeeping, was frowned upon.

One of the principals of drama at the Guildhall – and thereby an enforcer of the rules – was called Tony Church. He was a genial and wise figure who wore open-toed sandals, I remember, even in winter. He was also a founding actor of the Royal Shakespeare Company and had performed so often with them that he was known affectionately as 'the established Church'. I would later act alongside him, playing his son in a Ben Jonson comedy during my first season at Stratford; but for now he was simply the boss.

He was aware, early on, that I was finding things difficult. Perhaps it was because I had already spent three years in higher education. Perhaps it was because, like every young actor I have ever met, I was impatient to start a career as soon as possible. Perhaps it was because I was unhappy in London; but the fact is that I was, whatever the reason, unsettled. I enjoyed the training and learned many valuable things, but I always felt that the grass was greener somewhere else.

At the end of the first year, Cathy and I decided to put on our own production of a play. This was frowned upon by the authorities, who discouraged any public performance until our training was complete; but, in this case, unexpectedly, they turned a blind eye. We scraped together a tiny budget for this small act of rebellion and asked a friend, Jenny Killick, to lead the project. I had met Jenny at university – although she wasn't a fellow student – when she directed me as Sir Epicure Mammon in *The Alchemist* by Jonson. She was older than Cathy and I were – or, at least, seemed to be – and she was already a professional director; so we were delighted when she agreed to help us out at the Guildhall. We were equally delighted and more than a little bemused when she proposed to direct us in a play by Carl Sternheim – *Die Hose*. Sternheim was a writer from the early twentieth century; I had never heard of him. The play was described by Jenny as one of the finest examples of German expressionist comedy. This sounded, to our ignorant ears, like a contradiction in terms; but we nevertheless agreed with her choice and, in our spare time and in near-secret, we started work.

The production was as cheap as chips. The set was no more than a large cloth – lent by a London theatre, I think – that was hung at the back of the stage and spread down over the full area of the floor. Since the story took place in the living room of a small city apartment, we borrowed a table and some chairs. The total budget for costumes and props was fifty pounds. That was it.

The play tells the story of a petit bourgeois couple. They are not happy. The husband is aggressive and small minded, his wife sensitive and frustrated. One day, at some public event attended by a large crowd, the wife's knickers (*Die Hose* in German) fall down and are seen fleetingly beneath her long skirts. Her husband is furious at the humiliation; but two male bystanders are intrigued and aroused by this brief, illicit glimpse of a woman's underwear. One of these men is a failed poet, the other a right-wing political activist of the sort that, a few years later, would support the National Socialists. They both rent rooms in the building where the couple live and attempt to seduce the wife.

It sounds rather grim and heavy handed; but it was actually very funny. And it proved to be an unexpected success, largely due to Jenny's stylish direction and the minimalist design. We were given a space in the college for a couple of performances – a welcome and unexpected gesture of support – and were then invited to the National Student Drama Festival, where, that year, among others, Meera Syal gave a wonderful performance in a one-woman show as a waitress wearing roller skates and a hat in the shape of a large prawn. *Die Hose* ended up months later at the Traverse Theatre in Edinburgh. Our tiny project just grew and grew.

For me, it felt like the beginning of a professional career.

Among other things that boosted my confidence, an agent expressed an interest in me after seeing the show. I think I remember that correctly. I do know that I went to see Tony Church and we agreed that I could leave the college if I wanted to – with no hard feelings on either side. However, he felt obliged to point out that I would miss the course on Chekhov that was just coming up and perhaps I should wait until I had completed that. I decided to go. Tony wished me the best of luck and waved me off. My student days were over.

Like any other young actor, I did odd jobs here and there and accepted everything that I was offered. I had an agent backing me up, so I was lucky. Stephen Fry, remembering me from university, asked me to play in a show that he had written and which had already won an award at the Edinburgh festival. One of my most memorable engagements was playing an Ugly Sister, called Belladonna, in a pantomime of *Cinderella*, that a small company took to residential care homes and geriatric wards around London. I wore a mini-skirt and silver high-heeled shoes and was given a short black wig, cut in a bob. We all travelled together in an old van and visited elderly people in establishments that ranged from the relatively luxurious to the utterly bleak. At the end of each performance, we led our audience in a rendition of 'Roll Out the Barrel'. At that moment, enthusiasm outweighed any musical accuracy, but the quality of the final result was hardly the point. Apparently, incontinence rates among the residents improved immediately after each of our visits, which is intriguing. The company knew that what they were doing was unquestionably worthwhile and we had fun together, but it was hard work and often depressing. As has been said many times, old age is not for the faint-hearted.

One name is missing from this account of an unsteady year – William Shakespeare. I hardly thought of him during this period, though I suppose he was always there in the back of my mind. I wouldn't have been able to articulate it precisely, but my ambition was to appear in his plays – although in what capacity I didn't know. Back then, I think actors were more rigidly categorised than they are now. One of the benefits of the changes that have followed on from the demands of identity politics is that great parts are now available to a wider range of actors. This has affected performers everywhere, whatever their size, shape, skin colour, class, gender. I was told, when I started out, that I was a comic performer and no more. I thought of myself in that way too. It was no surprise that my first agent wanted to change my surname from Beale to Beagle, because he said it sounded jollier. At the time, I resisted his suggestion, possibly because, subconsciously, I thought things might change and that I would, one day, be asked to do big, serious parts. It seemed unlikely, but then I was invited to audition for a play at the Royal Court Theatre in London, directed by the legendary director Bill Gaskill, in 1985. It was an adaptation of a Jacobean tragedy. This led, a few months later, to my first professional Shakespeare – *The Winter's Tale* – with the Royal Shakespeare Company. Everything began to change. I felt happy and secure and stimulated. I was even asked, eventually, to play serious roles. And I stayed with the Royal Shakespeare Company for the next eight years.

A Magical World

The Young Shepherd

The sheep-shearing festival in *The Winter's Tale* seems to go on for ever. In fact, it's reputed to be the longest scene in Shakespeare. The host of the party is a Bohemian shepherd. He has two children. The elder is a young man, who is a shepherd like his father; the younger is a beautiful young woman who, since their mother is dead, is the official 'mistress o'th'feast'.

This plot summary sounds like the beginning of a fairy tale; and that's appropriate, because the play is a magical fantasy of death and rebirth, of terrible cruelty, of remorse and forgiveness. I played the young man, who is often referred to as a clown, in my Shakespearean debut for the RSC. He speaks entirely in prose. I hadn't anticipated this. I assumed that, as soon as I joined the company, I would be speaking yards of great poetry. But, as it happened, a couple of years would pass before I was trusted with any of Shakespeare's verse – when I was asked to play the King of Navarre in *Love's Labour's Lost*.

Even early on in my career, I was wary of the clowns in Shakespeare. I realised that I looked the part – I had come to terms with the fact that I was never going to be a romantic lead – but I knew that clowns were notoriously difficult to do well. For a start, the language that they use is often obscure and, on top of that, they require a range of skills – singing, dancing, comic patter, for instance – that I was not sure that I possessed. When, years after *The Winter's Tale*, I was offered the Fool in *King Lear*, I turned it down. I knew that the Fool is a truly great role. He's wise, sad and complicated, but in addition he seemed to me to employ certain performance skills, almost those of a music-hall artist, that I didn't have.

There is another clown figure in *The Winter's Tale*. He is called Autolycus. He gatecrashes the party, ostensibly to sell trinkets – ribbons and suchlike – to the guests. He sings songs on request; and he is also a petty thief. He is a very different type of comic character from the Young Shepherd, who is innocent, good-natured and, to be frank, not very bright. Autolycus conforms more closely to our idea of a clown as a figure who displays a variety of different performance skills. He obviously made quite a splash when he first appeared on the English stage. An early audience member, Simon Forman, wrote about him. Forman was a regular and enthusiastic playgoer and he talks about what he saw in his 'Book of Plays'. His description of the Bohemian scene in *The Winter's Tale* is focused on Autolycus; and he draws a useful moral from his afternoon at the theatre: 'Beware of trusting feigned beggars or fawning fellows.'

It seems that Autolycus was played by the leading comic actor in Shakespeare's company of the time – Robert Armin. We know quite a lot about Armin and about the other company clowns, because, I suppose, like comedians throughout history, they were big stars at the time and people such as Simon Forman talked and wrote about them. As it happens, Armin was also a writer himself. As far as I can tell, he was a spiky character, quick to take offence and protective of his contribution to the London theatre. He could sing, which was useful, and often performed his own music. Shakespeare wrote to highlight his skills. Characters such as Feste in *Twelfth Night*, the Fool in *King Lear* and Autolycus all sing and they all employ a comic register that is sharp, cynical and world weary. They are very different from Shakespeare's earlier clowns, who were written for a different man – Will Kemp.

Kemp's story is fascinating. He clearly had a rougher edge, a more muscular style, than Armin. When, in *Hamlet*, the prince talks about the irritating habit of clowns' improvising during performances, he seems to have been alluding to Kemp. The latter decided to leave Shakespeare's company around the end of the sixteenth century. For some reason, as a publicity stunt and, presumably, to make a bit of money, he then danced to Norwich. God knows why a marathon jig through East Anglia was thought to be a good idea. I wonder if this could be the worst career move in theatrical history. Shakespeare was just about to write the greatest plays in the English language; Kemp could have been part of that, I presume. But, instead, capering across the English countryside, he missed out.

The point of all this is that the actor playing Autolycus needs a particular set of attributes. I was cast in *The Winter's Tale* again, years after my 1986 debut at the RSC – this time as the king, Leontes – and Autolycus was played by Ethan Hawke, the American film and stage actor. He had the performance skills that I'm talking about. He is an entertainer as well as an actor; and, like Robert Armin, he happens to be a writer too – and a rather brilliant one. In the earlier production at Stratford, Autolycus was played by an actor called Joe Melia. He was older than me and was a man of exciting contradictions. He was balding and had tufts of feathery hair sticking out of the side of his head. He was very fit and employed a lithe physicality on stage. It was said that, in his long career, he had never missed a performance through ill health. I'm certain this was true. He pursued an ambitious intellectual life. The books he read and the music he listened to were at the more demanding end of the range. Earlier in his life, he had presented a very highbrow arts programme on the television. I imagine that he would have been comfortable striding through the febrile streets of turn-of-the-century Paris or Vienna.

But, on stage, his instincts were vaudevillian. So he was perfect casting for Autolycus. He transformed the sheep-shearing festival into an evening at a classic variety show. As the Young Shepherd, all but one of my scenes were with Joe. In the early days of rehearsal, we spent the minimum amount of time looking at the script and concentrated rather on physical comedy routines – just like circus clowns, I suppose. Since Autolycus is a skilled pickpocket, these routines involved an elaborate choreography with a large number of props; and, while this was happening, we had to keep speaking Shakespeare's words. It was like that age-old challenge of rubbing your stomach and patting your head at the same time.

Of the four plays I did that year, Joe was in three of them. One evening, while I was enjoying a post-performance beer in the local pub, an American visitor, who had seen all the shows that season, came up to me and asked if I always acted with 'that bald guy'. I didn't, of course, and told him so; but it wouldn't have been such a bad thing (and I would have learned a great deal more about comic technique) if that had been the case.

Before Shakespeare's time, the word 'clown' was used to describe a rustic character; and it seems that the playwright employs it in this sense in *The Winter's Tale*. The later connotations of a professional fool do not seem to apply here. Clowns were sometimes boorish figures, but the Young Shepherd, although unsophisticated, is a delight. He is much loved by his younger sister and his father. He relishes the company of the sexy young women he encounters at the party. He is puzzled but not distressed by the small misfortunes that come his way – like, for instance, the theft of all his pocket money by Autolycus. For the clown, life is good. His reactions to events around him are slow and easy – or, at least, mine were. Terry Hands, our director, showed me a little trick that he had learned from some clown school somewhere and which I found very useful. Everything that the clown sees or hears enters his eyes or ears, travels all the way down his body to the bottom of his feet and then travels all the way back up to his head again before he is able to respond. Following Terry's tip, my clown took his time; and, as a result, he was calmer and probably happier than those around him.

The scene in which we first meet him, some sixteen years before the sheep-shearing festival, is one of the most magical in Shakespeare. For the previous hour, we have been at the court in Sicilia – a world that is torn apart by false accusations of adultery, fierce jealousy and shocking cruelty. The play then moves to Bohemia, where the two shepherds, father and son, discover an abandoned newborn baby – the tiny daughter of the Sicilian king. It's a turning point. The story is transformed from a world of death and hatred to a new world of life and love. To his son, who has just witnessed, among other things, a violent shipwreck, the Old Shepherd, who has found the child, says:

> *'Now bless thyself; thou met'st with things dying, I with things newborn.'*

As we waited in the wings, preparing ourselves to go on for this scene, Bernard Horsfall, who was playing my father, used to whisper Edward Lear's poem, 'The Owl and the Pussycat', in my ear. He happened to know it off by heart. It sounds ridiculous. But it wasn't. For a moment, he was a father telling a bedtime story to his young boy, just as he had done every night for years and years. We're fine, he was saying, all is well.

Leontes

The clown has many adventures. He and his father find gold along with the baby and so become rich men. They adopt the child, who turns out to be a princess. She falls in love with a prince. The two shepherds have to flee their home and they come eventually to Sicilia, where they are recognised by the king as gentlemen – the father and brother of a future queen. It's quite a journey; but the clown doesn't change. He retains his good humour and generosity of spirit throughout. It was not a complicated acting challenge.

Leontes, the King of Sicilia in *The Winter's Tale*, is a very different matter. I played him in 2009, many years after I had played the clown. This time I was directed again by Sam Mendes and the play featured as part of a double bill with *The Cherry Orchard* by Chekhov. Leontes behaves appallingly and, in consequence, suffers terribly, as he causes others to suffer. As the story unfolds, he, unlike the Young Shepherd, changes in many fundamental ways. It's a demanding and complex role.

One other obvious difference between the two parts is that the king speaks in verse and the clown in prose. This is to be expected. Shakespeare tends to ask his characters of a lower social status (who are often also comic characters) to speak in prose, and his upper-class characters to speak in verse. He sometimes mixes this up a bit, but as a general guide it applies throughout his plays. There are rules that have to be followed in the composition and the speaking of poetry and this makes matters complicated – but often, as I sometimes tell acting students, more complicated than they need to be. And, in fact, some of the prose, which enjoys fewer formal constraints, is, like verse, very difficult to perform effectively. For instance, in the first scene in which the Young Shepherd appears, he is given a long sequence about seeing both a shipwreck and a man being killed by a bear, which is, from a technical point of view, very demanding indeed.

So Leontes, since he is a king, speaks in verse. *The Winter's Tale* is one of the playwright's later plays and, like others from the same period, the writing can become very elaborate, even tortured. Before I started in the rehearsal room, I marked up my script – a habit that I adopted early on in my time with the RSC. It's laborious and, let's be frank, boring work; but it has to be done, I think. For any part that is written in verse, I take a pencil and go through every line, putting a dash above stressed syllables and dots above unstressed ones. The next stage for me, long before formal rehearsals begin, is to learn the script with as little emotional inflection as possible; at this stage, there is no value in making firm decisions about motive or an inner life. That will come later. I would guess that every job has its tedious moments and, for me and for many actors, line-learning is the chore that just has to be endured. Marking stress patterns is equally dull. The important point is that, unless care is taken at this stage of the process, trouble will lie ahead.

I am not a puritan about verse speaking. I'm not what some people jokingly call a verse fundamentalist. However, Shakespeare chose to write in verse; and we have to respect that. It's not too great a burden to find out how the poetry works. After all, the essential rules are few and quite simple. I know some actors who think that dissecting Shakespeare's poetry in this rather technical way is unnecessary, but I have to disagree. It's not just a question of acknowledging the form in which a particular artwork is created, important though that is. There is also a practical value. If an actor observes the verse forms, then they will enjoy both security and, paradoxically, freedom. If you know and acknowledge the underlying rhythms, you can begin to play with them without losing your grip. There is a heartbeat in any line of poetry, which keeps it alive; but the actor can dance along with it. As many have noted, speaking Shakespeare convincingly is like performing jazz.

However, the reason that I don't consider myself a verse fundamentalist is that there are moments in Shakespeare's plays – albeit rare – when I think that clarity trumps a strict observance of the rules. I don't believe, as is often suggested, that Shakespeare is always helpful. Some people will tell you that how he writes will invariably endorse what he wants to communicate. I suspect that this is just something people say about a writer who is clearly a genius and should, therefore, achieve the effect that he is aiming for every time. But he sometimes slips up or is simply perverse and, if our job as actors is to be easily comprehensible at first hearing, then sacrificing a strictly correct speaking of the verse might be necessary. I once did a workshop on *Measure for Measure* run by a couple of very famous Shakespeareans. We were given a horribly complicated speech to work on, with the advice from our teachers that we should remember that the fractured verse reflects the fractured psychological state of the speaker. I remember thinking at the time that if the audience has no idea what the actor is talking about, then, even if the rules of verse-speaking are being followed, no amount of generalised angst is going to compensate.

If you tread carefully and respectfully, though, Shakespeare will sometimes surprise you. For instance, as an example of the benefit of playing by the rules, here is a moment from a scene in *The Winter's Tale*. The king has accused his beloved wife of adultery and called her to a formal hearing so that she can respond to the charge. To those attending the trial, he describes her in the following way:

> *'The daughter of a king, our wife and one*
> *Of us too much belov'd.'*

The first line has the expected five strong beats. In fact, it's a perfect example of an iambic pentameter, the form most favoured by Shakespeare. However, it stops in the middle of a thought. Normally, my instinct would be to run through the first line straight into the second – 'one of us . . .' I would ignore the line ending and so break one of the few cardinal rules. But, in this case, I allowed myself the tiniest pause before launching into the second line. In this case, I followed the rules – one of which stipulates a slight pause at line endings. It works here because it's as if Leontes is searching for the right words to describe a woman that he loves but believes has betrayed him; and he needs the pause before he can continue. On this occasion, there was an unexpected benefit in being obedient.

I guess that the lesson I take from this is that one should do everything one can to follow the rules; but if you realise that you're speaking nonsense and that nobody understands you, then try something else.

As with *Othello* and *Hamlet*, we took *The Winter's Tale* around the world – literally, in the latter case. We visited Singapore and Auckland, and then crossed the Pacific to play Madrid and a small town called Recklinghausen in Germany. One of my favourite boasts is that, during this tour, I visited Chile for lunch. It was halfway through the long plane journey between New Zealand and Spain. Since we had stopped off for six hours in Santiago, we got off the plane, found a restaurant in town, ate and returned immediately to the airport. It was a little rushed. We barely noticed what the food was like.

Clifton College Archives

CLIFTON COLLEGE: (*Othello, King Lear, Rosencrantz and Guildenstern Are Dead*)

A toe in the water: I played Desdemona soon after I arrived at my senior school (opposite Andrew Mach Wilson as Emilia) and went on to do other plays, including ones by Tom Stoppard and Shakespeare. Here, joining Desdemona, are King Lear and Guildenstern (with Darren Gerrish as Rosencrantz).

Photograph by Neil Libbert/Barbican Centre, London

CASSIUS: (*Julius Caesar*, Barbican Theatre, 2005)
A picture of political tension: arguing fiercely after the murder of Caesar with Mark Antony (Ralph Fiennes) and, listening behind us, Brutus (Anton Lesser).

IAGO: (*Othello*, National Theatre, 1997)
Talking to the audience: but it is debatable whether Iago ever tells the whole truth.

MALVOLIO: (*Twelfth Night*, Donmar Warehouse, 2002)
Dressed up in the famous yellow stockings with cross-gartering: a sad and ultimately futile attempt to look sexy.

© Marc Brenner

RICHARD II: (*Richard II*, Almeida Theatre, 2019)

His story is one of impossible arrogance punished by terrible humiliation. Only at the end, just before his death, does he achieve some fragile sense of genuine self-worth. In our show, he was soaked through and covered with blood and dirt.

Donald Cooper/Photostage

RICHARD III: (*Richard III*, RSC, 1992)

Plotting with one of his few friends, the wily and untrustworthy Duke of Buckingham (Stephen Boxer). Richard will later order his assassination.

MACBETH: (*Macbeth*, Almeida Theatre, 2004)

A rare moment of laughter with his wife, Lady Macbeth (Emma Fielding): theirs is a close and loving relationship that cannot possibly survive after they acce to the crown of Scotland.

BENEDICK: (*Much Ado About Nothing*, National Theatre, 2007)

Unalloyed joy: emerging from a pool in which he has been hiding, now aware that his love for Beatrice is reciprocated.

THE YOUNG SHEPHERD: (*The Winter's Tale*, RSC, 1986)

Early days: my first ›fessional Shakespeare. A happy scene in which her (Bernard Horsfall) and son celebrate their v relationship with the ing of Sicilia, alongside the small-time thief Autolycus (Joe Melia).

The Winter's Tale, 1986: Joe Cocks Studio Collection © Shakespeare Birthplace Trust

© Tristram Kenton

LEONTES: (*The Winter's Tale*, BAM, New York, 2009)

The agony of a man being presented with a tiny child whom he believes is the result of his wife's adulterous affair. Paulina (Sinéad Cusack) insists that he is wrong and is determined that he will pay for his irrational cruelty.

HAMLET: (*Hamlet*, National Theatre, 2000)

One of the greatest explorations of grief ever written: I played him just after my mother's death and the result was a very sweet prince who knew that he would never be capable of the violence that is asked of him.

The highlight of our travels was a short trip to Greece. In truth, it was too short – just a week. We were invited to put the play on in the ancient theatre at Epidaurus. This is a site in the Peloponnese, an amphitheatre that seats up to twelve thousand people at any one time. Many will tell you that the acoustics are so good in these Classical buildings that an actor can whisper from the stage and be heard clearly in the last, back row of seats. This is not true; or, rather, it's true in a very limited sense. If an actor stands in one particular spot and faces front it might work; and if he or she is wearing a mask, as actors did in ancient Greece, with a megaphone built in front of the mouth, then audibility might not be problem. Otherwise, acting at Epidaurus is very, very hard work. I'm maybe being facetious, but there is a real problem in that these large amphitheatres were built for a particular type of play and a particular type of acting. They are not suitable for modern naturalism – even heightened Shakespearean naturalism. After each performance – we did the play twice in Epidaurus, to thousands and thousands of people – I felt as if I had gone through several rounds of a boxing match against a world champion; and had been soundly beaten both times.

Despite this minor difficulty, Greece was relentlessly seductive. I have been lucky to have seen wonderful things in my travels around the world, both natural and man-made. My first sight of some buildings has literally made me gasp. Turning a corner in snow-covered Kyoto and coming across the Golden Pavilion shimmering above an ice-cold lake was one of those moments; as was the chance to stand alone, bathed in the blue light of the Sainte-Chapelle in Paris – a medieval and very convincing depiction of paradise. I had to catch my breath when I was shown through a small door in a palace outside Stockholm and saw in front of me a perfectly preserved eighteenth-century theatre, complete with the original stage machinery. And there was the Grand Canyon, of course. Seeing the amphitheatre in Epidaurus for the first time was, for various different reasons, in the same league.

I remember every detail of that moment. We walked into the building at the height of a blisteringly hot day. The tiers of seats shone white and bright. The impact was almost physical. We knew beforehand that the theatre would be impressive. But the effect was not ethereal – as in Kyoto or Paris – but somehow earthbound, human, even aggressive. After all, a very large number of people could gather here. One could imagine the noise. And the smell. The seats had been worn down by the bottoms of thousands of excited Greeks, perhaps comparing performances of Oedipus and Jocasta with those they'd seen in Athens, or arguing about who should win first prize in the drama festival. I could clearly see them in my mind's eye. Debate among the audience members must have been relentless and tempers must have flared. The applause would have been thunderous and the adulation overwhelming. Vivid pictures ran hurtling through my mind and, above all, I couldn't stop thinking that this is where it had all started. Everything that I was doing in my professional life – and elsewhere – owed its existence to this.

After those first few visits, we did not see the theatre again in the full glare of the day. It was too hot to work in the midday heat, so we would start rehearsing or performing as the sun began to set; and we would often continue into the middle of the night. Our free days would be spent relaxing – reading, swimming, eating – or taking in the sights. We visited Mycenae, where thousands of years before, Agamemnon had ruled; and we looked across the plain to Argos and the kingdom of Menelaus and Helen, his unhappy wife. The countryside pulsated with a bright, unforgiving combination of white, blue and green. At night, we played under a velvet sky and a canopy of countless stars. The hill on which the theatre was built fell away behind us.

Towards the end of *The Winter's Tale,* there is a scene in which we see Leontes talking to his confidante, Paulina. It is many years now since his wife, Hermione, died. The king is being urged by his courtiers to marry again. He resists. He refuses to consider a second wife; and, talking about his dead queen, he refers to her eyes:

> *'Stars, stars,*
> *And all eyes else dead coals . . .'*

In Greece, I had no choice but to look up and melt helplessly into the night sky.

A strange thing happened while I was on stage in Epidaurus. I swear that what I'm about to tell you is true. In fact, I have witnesses. When Leontes puts his innocent wife on trial for adultery, as part of this grim event and as an attempt to legitimise the proceedings, he sends two of his men to Apollo's oracle in Delphos to obtain the god's verdict on the queen's possible crime. They return to declare that Hermione is innocent. Leontes cannot accept this. To the assembled company, he says:

> *'There is no truth at all i'th'oracle . . .'*

On both nights in Greece, at precisely this moment, a tight ball of wind bowled down the bank of seats, crossed the stage and hit me hard in the chest. I repeat, on both nights. I hate to be whimsical, but surely Apollo himself was reminding me, in his homeland, that he was listening, that he was not happy and, most importantly, that he was not dead yet.

The Winter's Tale presents the actor playing Leontes with something of a puzzle – an irritant, I suppose one might call it. This problem is present at the very start of the play. Before the story begins, Leontes, the King of Sicilia, invites his oldest friend, Polixenes, the King of Bohemia, to come and visit. Polixenes accepts the invitation and stays with Leontes and his wife, Hermione, for nine months. By the end of this period,

Hermione is heavily pregnant, which, I suppose, might raise questions in a suspicious mind; and, although the paternity of the future child never seems to be in doubt, Leontes, as we will later learn, unquestionably has a suspicious mind. When we first see him, he seems cheerful enough. Hermione is trying to persuade Polixenes to stay longer, and her husband, too, is eager for his friend to extend his visit. The scene plays out, the queen and Polixenes move aside, then Leontes, to the audience's great surprise, launches into a brutal soliloquy during which we discover that he is tortured by sexual jealousy.

The difficulty lies in the fact that this is so unexpected. There have been no earlier clues to the king's state of mind. Frankly, there hasn't been time. Has Leontes been jealous for a while now or is this a new development? I guess that either option is workable; but the difference between the two is of importance for an actor constructing a convincing inner life. So a decision has to be made, if only for the actor's peace of mind. I have a friend who insists that the sensation of jealousy hits the king at precisely the moment he talks about it. He may very well be right. His advice would be not to overcomplicate, to 'play the moment'. This is certainly the most Shakespearean choice; and, in naturalistic terms, jealously can sometimes appear out of the blue. What is really interesting, though, is that, in this play, Shakespeare is actually not interested in how or why jealousy develops. He was capable of such an exploration, of course. He had written detailed studies of jealousy before; but *The Winter's Tale* is not a re-run of *Othello* or *The Merry Wives of Windsor*. As in a fairy tale, Leontes is, to begin with, simply 'the jealous husband'. We have to accept this label without question because the playwright wants to pursue other lines of enquiry.

However Leontes's jealousy begins, it is presented as a disease. 'I have *tremor cordis* on me,' he says, 'My heart dances.' His story is, in part, the search for a cure for this disease. It was a surprise for me to discover, late on in rehearsal, that, once the initial distress has passed, Leontes tries to follow a logical course. In our production, he appeared calm and in control. His behaviour seemed sane. For instance, if his wife is an adulteress and her behaviour treasonous, then, in Leontes's mind, it is right and proper that she should be arrested and put on trial. A real tyrant would simply kill her without all that fuss. Leontes sees himself as a rational man. This affected both the mode of playing him and the moral landscape of the play. Leontes was surrounded by men and women who were accustomed to dealing with a reasonable man; and so they were not afraid to speak their minds. He was and had always been a good king. In our production, he was often seen at his desk, working, calmly doing what responsible kings do. He prides himself on not acting like a tyrant. For those who love him, the pursuit of an irrational aim using rational means is particularly distressing. His old friend, Paulina, insists that she will not call her king a tyrant, although she acknowledges that he is behaving suspiciously like one. To this, Leontes replies to those around him:

> *'Were I a tyrant,*
> *Where were her life? She durst not call me so*
> *If she did know me one.'*

Needless to say, Leontes is completely comfortable with his own behaviour. He believes that he is doing everything correctly. In his eyes, it is quite right that he imprisons his wife – 'the cause', as he calls her. His friend runs away, so he can do nothing about him. But his flight is obviously an admission of guilt and so Leontes remains convinced that he's on the right path. Indeed, the whole plan is perhaps easier when both Hermione and Polixenes are out of sight and unable to challenge him. It's jealousy at one remove, as it were.

It is well known that, at the time he wrote *The Winter's Tale*, Shakespeare was exploring a new theatrical genre. Critics call the plays of this period 'romances' or 'tragicomedies'. The full-bloodied tragedies, the long history cycles and the light-hearted comedies were long gone. In this new world of fable, it's appropriate that Leontes begins almost as an archetype – 'the jealous husband'. Similarly, Paulina could be seen as 'the shrew'. She is married to a man called Antigonus, 'the hen-pecked husband'. Hermione is 'the virtuous wife'. They all end up being more complex characters than this, but the bold colours of fairy tale have their effect on the tone of these first scenes of the drama. They have an energy that is absurd, even comic. Antigonus goes so far as to worry that the king's behaviour will raise us all 'to laughter'. At our performances, the audiences had no such concern. They laughed openly and I know that the cast enjoyed managing the almost imperceptible slide from comedy to the bleakest tragedy. There is something ridiculous about Leontes's behaviour and the expectation of both those watching and the characters in the story is that, once this has been pointed out, the king will come to his senses.

This is what finally happens, but at an enormous cost. Leontes's threats of death and destruction change from excitable posturing to something very dangerous indeed. Despite the expectations of those who love him, he cannot be persuaded to change his mind; and the risk he runs becomes clear to him only when, as a direct result of his actions, his little boy, Mamillius, dies.

The king's reaction to the death of his son is extreme. The fever breaks, as it were. The actor has to execute a complete volte-face – as extreme a shift as the first onset of jealousy. Leontes immediately recognises that he is wrong and is, equally speedily, overcome by remorse. During my early attempts at this scene, it felt that there was no way to act it convincingly. The scene doesn't follow the rules of naturalism. Perhaps it could be argued that, on seeing his wife earlier for the first time after her spell in prison, Leontes experiences the initial stirring of doubt. He could believe, at this point, that he is right and, simultaneously, fear that he is wrong. But there is no direct evidence for such a softening of the king's judgement. As at the beginning of the play, the details of how and why the remorse develops are not important. The playwright wants to move quickly on to something else – in this case, at this moment, the price that Leontes will have to pay for his behaviour and, then, the possibility of recovery.

Soon after his son's death, the king hears that Hermione has also died. He is told this by Paulina. In the first production of *The Winter's Tale* that I was involved in, with the RSC, Paulina was played by an actress called Gillian Barge. Since I was playing the clown, I was not involved in any of the early Sicilian scenes; but, every night, I used to stand in the wings of the theatre and watch Gillian deliver the terrible news to Jeremy Irons's Leontes. What is mesmerising about this moment in the play is that Paulina not only announces the death of the queen, but also anticipates the desperate remorse that Leontes will suffer and the punishment that he must and will endure. Gillian battered Jeremy with her voice alone. It was a vocal display that was mythic in its power and intensity. Every word was an assault:

> *'The queen, the queen,*
> *The sweetest, dearest creature's dead, and vengeance for't*
> *Not dropped down yet.'*

I will never forget it. The words were like hammer blows. The rhythmic regularity was used as a weapon. Gillian understood (as did Sinéad Cusack, who played Paulina in my second production of the play) that, at this moment, she was representing something bigger than this particular woman in this particular story. She was no longer the shrew or the nag of the fairy tale, but the personification of unforgiving rage and of cosmic justice.

At the end of the story, Hermione will return. Perdita, the little girl who is born to the king and queen just before the trial, is exiled from the court and is later presumed dead; but she will also return. This is part of the unlikely magic of the play. But

Mamillius, the son adored by both parents, will not. This is the great tragedy of the story. It cannot be ignored. It is the dark shadow from which we may not turn away. Many productions over the years have registered this and focused a great deal of attention on Mamillius. So did we – in our own way. Sam, in the 2009 production, set much of the first half of the play in the boy's nursery. We saw Leontes putting his son to bed, just as we saw the child playing with his mother. But, after he dies, he is not mentioned again. Perhaps the loss is too painful to talk about. This is familiar ground, something about which I know a little; after all, I watched my mother unable to speak about the death of her daughter. So the silence rings true for me.

Sam asked the same actress, Morven Christie, to play the two children, Mamillius and Perdita. She had a very beautiful nose and her nose played an important part in our production. In the first half of the play, as I put my son to bed, I stroked it gently, as if to calm the boy before I turned out the lights. It was clearly a bedtime ritual. When, sixteen years later, Leontes meets Perdita, who at this point is thought to be the daughter of a Bohemian shepherd, not a Sicilian princess, the king is fascinated and disturbed by her nose. Much to her surprise, he can't help going to touch it. For him, terrible memories came flooding back; just as, at the same time, the first flicker of hope that his daughter might have survived is ignited. A few moments later, of course, to great joy, her true identity is revealed.

The Winter's Tale is probably most famous for its final scene. Paulina invites the king and his newfound daughter to see a statue that she has commissioned. It represents Hermione. Shakespeare provides the name of the artist – Giulio Romano, a 'rare Italian master'. He was a real person, intriguingly, but he is not mentioned again. It's the kind of detail that we know the playwright often throws into his plays, but it's an odd, if charming, piece of useless information. Perhaps he thought it provided texture. Perhaps, more importantly, he thought it would throw us off the scent; because it is no statue that we finally see, but the living, breathing Hermione. The king, the queen and their daughter are reunited.

This is a scene that never fails. However dodgy the production, it always works. I find it almost unbearably moving. At first, Paulina refuses to allow her guests to come near the 'statue', But she finally relents and, after insisting that they 'awake [their] faith' and asking for music, she invites Leontes to touch the skin of his long-dead wife. As he does so, he exclaims:

'O, she's warm!'

I've always thought that this is a good candidate for the best line that Shakespeare ever wrote. It is monosyllabic, of course – like the love scene between Beatrice and Benedick – but it packs a punch. It distils the legacy of sixteen years of pain, the possibility of redemption, the chance to rewrite the past, the promise of rekindled love into three little words. Hermione begins to move. She turns and speaks to her daughter. She says nothing to her husband. Some people see this as an indication that she is not ready to forgive him. I'm not sure about that. I don't think this moment – the final moment of the story, after all – can work unless the promise it offers and the hope it embodies are simple and unconditional. If the moment is muddied, except, perhaps, with memories of Mamillius, then the result is too many irrelevant questions; and the final moments of the story are not as moving as they should be.

But I acknowledge that this famous scene, wonderful though it is, is also troubling; or, at least, I find it so. I hate to be grimly literal, but it doesn't make sense. It could never happen. I know, we've been here before with this play. Paulina spends some time explaining how she has hidden Hermione for over a decade and has concocted this plan involving the statue – presumably a plan that is to be activated only in the unlikely event that Perdita will reappear at court. And, as has been noted, in an attempt to make the whole trick more realistic, she has the name of the sculptor at her fingertips. Surely nobody in the audience is convinced by this long explanation; and, anyway, working out how the plan was executed misses the point. As elsewhere in the play, Shakespeare is forging ahead to the next stage of his story.

He's tapping into something that all of us feel, I think. We all dream, don't we, that our past mistakes – even our past sins – could be wiped away, forgiven and forgotten? That's what Christians, among others, believe, isn't it? That's the basis of their faith. But imagine if this could happen here and now. Imagine if we didn't have to wait until after our death. How wonderful it would be to have the chance to start again, to do better. This is why I feel that the sense of redemption at the end of the play should be as complete and inclusive as possible. Otherwise, what are we left with? A strange, rather elaborate fairytale without a fairytale ending. I realise that the final reunion of mother and daughter might, for some, be satisfying enough; but to leave out Leontes, the person most in need of forgiveness, is harsh. Shakespeare would return to the subject of forgiveness in his next plays – particularly in *The Tempest*. Perhaps, as he aged, he himself was looking for some sort of absolution. Perhaps he wanted to forget the errors of his past life. He certainly understood that many of us wish, hopelessly, for the same thing. This is surely why this last scene in *The Winter's Tale*, while it might not make sense, still works.

Oddly, one of my very first memories is of an amphitheatre – not in Greece, but in North Africa. My family must have made a day-trip out of Tripoli to visit it, presumably as a treat for one of my many great-aunts, Olive, my grandfather's sister, who was visiting us at the time. I was, perhaps, five or six years old. Auntie Olive was one of the stars of my family – the headmistress of a school in Newport, elegant, informed and kindly. In Libya, she must have looked like a descendant of those solitary nineteenth-century lady travellers who left England to explore the 'real' Middle East. During our day at the amphitheatre, after I was sent to sit in the topmost row of stone seats, Auntie Olive stood in the centre of the stage and whispered my name. Ironically, given my later experience at Epidaurus, I could hear her clearly – proof, so Auntie Olive confidently said, of the perfect acoustics. The theatre blazed bright and hot in the sun. I don't recall any other visitors. We had the whole site to ourselves.

One of my brothers, a year younger than me, remembers the same trip. A highlight for him was our stopping at a roadside stall on the journey back home to buy fizzy drinks. This was a rare luxury; and, clearly, as memorable for him as the pile of Roman ruins that we had left behind us.

5

I saw very little theatre during my first few years in London. This might have been partly to do with the expense, of course, although I'm sure that I could have found cheap tickets through some scheme or other. Other people did that, so I have no convincing excuse for not trying harder. The real reason I went to so few shows was that I had not acquired the habit; and there was so much else to do. I was ignorant of who or what was considered worth seeing. I could have done with some coaching. Apart from the theatre I had learned about at university, I knew nothing. I didn't even know the names of the most popular and successful performers. I have often been asked which role models I followed when I was younger, but, at the start of my career, I don't think I had any. I simply hadn't seen enough. Role models tended to appear later in my life; and they were often my contemporaries rather than older actors; and anyway, these contemporaries were often objects of envy as much as performers that I felt capable of imitating.

I made my first visit to the National Theatre in my early twenties and watched a production of medieval mystery plays. Everyone was talking about it and praising it to the skies. I still have a clear image of the roof of the theatre being hung with hundreds of tools and utensils – I spotted a couple of colanders – which, when they were lit, glittered like Christmas-tree decorations. Around this time I saw *Angels in America*, a landmark experience for any gay man, again at the National. In fact, I went twice. It seemed too important a piece of writing to see just once. And I saw *Evita*.

One of the theatres I got to know early on was the Royal Court. I had read a little of its proud history. I had been told by my friends about how important an institution it was. So I was well briefed but a little tentative when I walked through the stage door of the theatre for the first time to audition for their upcoming play. The director, Bill Gaskill, whom I was about to meet, was one of the most influential British theatre practitioners of the last half-century. I didn't know this; which was probably a good thing. The piece he was seeing me for was a fascinating hybrid – *Women Beware Women* by Thomas Middleton and Howard Barker. The first half was a condensed version of the Jacobean play; the second was a riff on the original – luxuriant, wild, intense work by one of our most idiosyncratic and powerful contemporary writers.

The part that I was up for had no name. The character was known simply as 'The Ward'. In the original Middleton, he is a brutish, angry young man, of a type that the Jacobeans would have called 'a roaring boy'. He is also rich and displays all the worst insensitivities of his class. There is no evidence of any complex internal life. However, in the second part of the evening, Howard Barker gave him a soul. He was no less brutish and no less self-regarding, but now we could see frustration and insecurity, even pain. At the audition, I told Mr Gaskill that he should give me the part because, I said, the Ward and I were in many ways identical; or, at least, I had lived through his insecurities. I sincerely believed this, although I realise that it sounds like a tactic. I had certainly never said anything like this in past auditions and I have never tried it since. I don't think I was aware how self-serving it sounded. But, perhaps taken aback by my shamelessness, Bill gave me the job.

In passing, the Ward's first lines were all about playing a game called Tip-Cat or Cat-and-Trap. It's similar to badminton. He rushes on stage having just finished a bout with an opponent who has thrashed him. Much of what I had to say at this point is incomprehensible. I can still remember, off the top of my head, one particular line which I had to get through:

'I tickled him
when I came once to my tippings.'

Apparently, this is to do with winning a point or two at some stage of the game. There were many other lines that were equally befuddling. I mention it only because there are times with these old plays – especially when clowns are involved – when you just have to speak clearly and with assurance and then move on. Unless the audience has studied the play and knows it well, they are unlikely to understand what you're talking about. All the actor can hope for is to give them a general idea of the subject matter and reassure them that they're in safe hands, even if they can't follow the details. Joe Melia, the older actor whom I got to know in Stratford and who specialised in Shakespearean comedy, once told me that the trick is to 'adopt a confident vernacular'. I was playing the clown in *The Winter's Tale* at the time he told me this and I took his advice. Since one of speeches I had to deliver as this particular clown is a mystery unless you know something about the seventeenth-century wool trade, I was grateful. Joe seemed to be saying that so long as you appeared to know what you were talking about, you'd be fine. I apologise if this causes offence to purists, but sometimes you have to admit that, when it comes to immediate comprehensibility, you're fighting a losing battle and must accept defeat. You either plough through the offending passage; or, of course, cut it.

The Ward is from a wealthy family and has a manservant called Sordido – a pleasing revenge-tragedy type of name. In our

1985 production, he was played by Gary Oldman. I would like to able to say that, reflecting their unequal social status, my part was bigger and more important than his. But, unfortunately, that would be untrue. Sordido was a much more impressive character than the Ward. In fact, he stood right at the centre of the story and was a principal motor of the plot. Gary was, when I met him, on the cusp of huge success. Around the time of his appearance at the Royal Court, his film *Sid and Nancy* came out to great acclaim; it was, as we all know, to make him a star. Bill Gaskill adored him, with good reason. I felt lucky to be following, unnoticed for the most part, in Gary's slipstream; because Bill could be tough, really tough, when he wanted to be. I saw him flare with impatience – especially when he felt that his cast was being too docile or passive. There was one occasion when he asked an older actor to walk diagonally across the full distance of the stage – a long journey from bottom right to top left. It seemed rather an arbitrary move and difficult to execute. The actor approached Bill for help. Why was he making this move? he asked. Could the director give him a reason, a motivation? 'Motivation?' Bill grunted, 'That's your job, not mine.'

However, Bill's rule was, by and large, benevolent; and the results he achieved were always impressive. His methods worked. There was a fashion in those days, and during the previous decades, for directors to act like dictators. That's how we all assumed they had to be; and, in truth, it made a sort of sense. After all, the buck stopped with them. Directors saw themselves, at that time, as having a responsibility to teach (and control), not to collaborate. This definition of the job has faded away now; or, at least, directors are better at disguising their authoritarian tendencies. The rehearsal room is, on the whole, a kinder place.

I was lucky in that Bill seemed to like me, and I grew to like and admire him. When he was thinking, he held his head at an angle, with his chin thrust forward and often with his eyes half shut. One day, while discussing my character, he said that

I should remember that the Ward enjoyed, whatever his vulnerabilities might be, an unbreakable social self-confidence, even arrogance. He recommended that I find some physical representation of this. So I imitated him – a private joke, which I think I got away with. On another occasion, we were sitting together in the stalls of the theatre, watching a rehearsal on the stage. For a split second, one of the actors turned their back to the auditorium and Bill, whispering in my ear, told me that the only actor he had ever seen that could act with their back to the audience was Peggy Ashcroft. I've never forgotten it; and, even during the short run at the Royal Court, I would occasionally speak with my back to the audience – just to see if I could match the great Ashcroft. I don't suppose Bill noticed; or, if he did, he probably thought I was being an idiot.

Women Beware Women was my first experience of the glamour of theatre – a shabby glamour, to be sure, but glamour nonetheless. For a start, the cast list included, alongside Gary, some very big names. Famous people came to see the show, which was a new experience for me. One night, Anthony Hopkins visited us backstage and I hung around in the stairwell to catch a sight of him as he climbed past me to visit a friend. The men shared a single dressing room, which, in the best theatre tradition, was pretty grubby. Above us were all the women. Yet, despite the uninspiring surroundings and our low wages, the men would share a bottle of champagne after every performance. And, as might be expected, the cast all had good stories. For instance, a few years before, one of my colleagues had appeared in a production at the National Theatre called *The Romans in Britain*, a show that has become a part of theatre history. In the play, there was a brutal scene in which male Britons were raped by Roman soldiers. Mary Whitehouse, a fearless fighter against the rising tide of smut that threatened to overwhelm our traditional way of life, objected to this. A much-publicised court case followed. My fellow cast member, who played one of the soldiers, had to testify. He told a complicated story about his having to prove that his thumb, which he had used in the rape scene, was not a penis. Listening to him, and the others, made me feel as if I was at the centre of things.

Towards the end of the run of *Women Beware Women*, the Royal Shakespeare Company asked me to come and meet them. Presumably, one of their people had seen the show at the Court. In fact, I had auditioned for the RSC once before, but it had been a disaster. In front of an imposing bank of senior directors, I had, on that occasion, given a speech from *The Alchemist* by Ben Jonson. The character was Sir Epicure Mammon, which I had played at university. After I had run through the speech once, Adrian Noble, a man I got to know well later in my career, gave me some fresh ideas and asked me to do it again. I started well enough but then lost my train of thought. Adrian picked this up and gently advised me to begin again. Unaccountably, instead of following his instructions, I decided that now was the moment to discuss in more detail the notes he had just given me. I felt that some of them probably wouldn't work. The directors didn't seem that interested in exploring my ideas and the audition was ended abruptly. As I walked out, I chatted to the assistant director who was helping to shepherd actors in and out of the room. During our short conversation, I asked whether he thought my audition had gone well. He said quietly that perhaps, next time, if there was a next time, I should consider trying to talk a little less.

However, here they were, a year later, asking me back. It appeared that they had forgiven me. They offered me four roles and one understudy. All the parts were small, but all of them were interesting. The offer included a Shakespeare play, a professional first for me. The package was certainly enough to keep me going through a year's work. In truth, I was thrilled. A few months earlier, my mother had given me a book by Antony Sher – *The Year of the King* – which was about his experience of playing Richard III for the RSC. He talked not only about his detailed preparations for the role but also about the excitement of going up to Stratford, of meeting new people, of embarking on a new stage in his life, of facing new challenges. There were even pictures in the book of the people he met and worked with – cartoons which Tony himself had drawn. Later, I would get to know some of those people. I lapped up every word of the book, of course, and then, a few months later, found myself doing much the same thing as the great Tony Sher – albeit on a lesser scale.

We rehearsed the first two plays for the RSC in London. I was still performing in the evening at the Royal Court, so it was a busy time. It was my first taste of a work schedule that I would follow for years to come – starting in the morning and finishing late at night. On one of those mornings, as I was working on a scene in *The Winter's Tale*, a urgent message came through to the rehearsal room from the Royal Court. Apparently, Gary Oldman was unwell – nothing serious, the theatre said, but he was unable to perform that night. No understudies had been employed by the Court and so another actor had to be found somewhere for the show that evening. We didn't have much time. A further message was from Bill Gaskill himself, who asked if I could come into the theatre to discuss our options and then rehearse with the replacement. Terry Hands, the director of the Shakespeare play, agreed to let me go – it was an emergency, after all – and so I jumped into a cab outside the Waterloo church where the RSC was based at the time, and sped across town to Sloane Square. I never took cabs in those days. They were far too expensive. This cab was being paid for. As I rushed to save the day, I felt like the most important actor in London.

The American star, Martin Sheen, was working at the Royal Court at the time – he was preparing for the first English production of *The Normal Heart*, one of the most influential early explorations of the horrors of the AIDS epidemic. He had heard about our problem and offered his services. I thought this was a splendid idea, but Bill told me not to be ridiculous. He had a much better solution to our problem. He knew a student whom he had recently directed in a college production of *Women Beware Women*. This student already knew the part and would clearly be a safer bet than another actor, however brilliant, reading from an unfamiliar script. I reluctantly agreed and it was the student-actor who appeared on stage that night. His name was Clive Owen.

As well as being in charge of *The Winter's Tale*, Terry Hands was the artistic director of the company. In other words, he was, especially from my perspective, a remote and very imposing figure. He was slim and always wore black, except in the last days of rehearsal for each play, when, in the darkened auditorium of the theatre, he would don a short red kimono. I think he wore this for good luck, as a superstition, which shows some appealing vulnerability. Otherwise, he was impressively self-contained and quietly assured. He could be sharp-tongued and quick-witted, too. Once, when an actor, whose name I don't know, was mangling some Shakespeare verse line in rehearsal, he whispered to him, pointedly but benignly enough, 'There are a thousand ways to say a Shakespeare line, and that's not one of them'.

Terry was one of the unsung heroes of British theatre over the last half-century. He was never as famous as some of his colleagues, but his influence behind the scenes was all-pervasive. He was devoted to the RSC – as he was to Theatr Clwyd, which he went on to run after he left Stratford. His great skills were in nurturing individual talents and in recognising when those talents would work well together. At one point during my time at the RSC, the junior team of directors that he helped to assemble included Nick Hytner, Sam Mendes, Deborah Warner, Katie Mitchell and Danny Boyle. The actors who worked for them were often of equal stature. How Terry managed to keep all these big personalities happy, I'll never know. But he did – or, rather, it looked as if he did. The company was criticised by many at the time for creating work that didn't match the achievements of previous decades. But, actually, we can now see how Terry – and Trevor Nunn, who co-directed the RSC with him – kept standards as high as ever. He died only a short while ago, in 2020. I was in New York at the time, sitting in my tiny dressing room on Broadway, and I got a tearful phone call from Sam Mendes, who pointed out that Terry had been responsible for our first meeting. I did not know this at the time. I was far too young a player to be told things like that; but Terry obviously saw that Sam and I would get on. He was right – thirty-five years later and we're still going strong – and I am so grateful to him for that and for much else. I assume Sam is too.

Terry went on to cast me in a couple more shows over the years – *Love's Labour's Lost* with Ralph Fiennes and as Konstantin in *The Seagull*, both in the very early 1990s. This latter play changed the course of my career. Oddly, it was the first time Terry had directed Chekhov and it was the last play he directed for the RSC. It was a fitting farewell, a production of aching beauty and delicacy. This was all the more surprising in that Terry was known for some huge, hard-edged shows, including a series of history plays with the heroic Alan Howard. These involved a great deal of metal and leather – employing a powerful, macho aesthetic. *The Seagull* couldn't have been more different; and, on a personal level, it represented an important change of direction for me. Terry was one of the first people who trusted me with a character that was complex, weighty and serious.

He once gave me a wonderful and rather elaborate note. It was during our work on the Chekhov play. He took me aside and asked whether Konstantin acted to please his mother or his father. It was a puzzling question. We never meet his father; whereas his mother is a constant, domineering presence. 'His mother, I suppose,' I answered. 'And how does he do that?' Terry asked. 'By being sensitive, kind, submissive, lovable,' I replied. 'And how would he want to appear to his father?' 'Strong, capable, mature.' 'For the next few days, I need you to play Konstantin as if he wants to please his father rather than his mother,' Terry said. It was a brilliant idea and it helped to turn the performance on its head; and, paradoxically, the harder Konstantin tried to impress, the more vulnerable he appeared to be.

While I was rehearsing the Young Shepherd in *The Winter's Tale*, Terry told me that there was a tradition that actors who played this particular part went on to perform Hamlet later in their careers. It was a curious thing to say. I couldn't see why that would be the case. But it did stick in my mind.

A Sweet Prince

Hamlet

Hamlet took his time. By the time I played him in 2000, I was turning forty; so I was unquestionably a middle-aged prince. Colleagues had for years been talking to me about taking on the role, but nobody seemed quite ready to trust me with it. Far in the back of my mind was Terry Hands's seductive comment when I first worked for him on *The Winter's Tale*; and he was also responsible for casting me as Konstantin in *The Seagull* – a part that has traditionally been linked to Hamlet. So the idea was in the air. I also played Oswald in *Ghosts*, another derivative figure who, like Hamlet, has a problematic relationship with his mother. There was even, at one point when I was in my twenties, a short article in a daily broadsheet – 'Beale heads for Elsinore', it said. The correspondent had received assurances from some trusted source that I was about to play the prince – even, perhaps, visit Elsinore, the castle in Denmark where the historical Hamlet had supposedly lived and died. This prospect of playing the prince was news to me. I was flattered, of course, and pleasantly surprised that it should be seen as a story of national interest; but nobody took the hint and nothing came of it. Playing Hamlet remained the shadow of an ambition, something that I couldn't realistically expect to achieve.

As it happens, I did visit Elsinore years later and I performed *Hamlet* there. The crew from the National Theatre built a temporary auditorium in the central courtyard of the castle and we played every night in the cold, damp air. As we looked out from the stage we would spot members of the audience desperately trying to keep warm, wrapping themselves in blankets, wearing gloves and scarves and woolly hats. Sometimes, all one could see in the dark were rows of bright eyes. In the latter half of the play, Hamlet has some time off stage. During this short break, I would walk through the scaffolding underneath the bank of seats and visit a temporary loo at the back of the castle for a quick pee. As I returned, I would take my time to look at the moon and the circling birds, and imagine that I really was a prince and that this haunted, forbidding place really was my home.

This trip to Denmark was part of a world tour that lasted, on and off, for a whole year. As with *Othello*, we saw many marvellous and unexpected things. I revisited Arizona and was reminded of how ravishing the state is – not the cities, necessarily, but the high deserts and the border country and, of course, the Grand Canyon, where I once sat with my legs dangling over the edge, watching the rocks turn slowly red as the sun set. We played *Hamlet* in both Phoenix and, way down south, in Tucson. The latter feels, even in the twenty-first century, like a frontier town. While we were there, the heat was so fierce that a local crew member insisted that I wore sunglasses when I was outside – not something I normally do – because otherwise the light would burn my eyes. In this heat, we visited a magnificent and improbable Franciscan monastery on the southern border. All I could think of was the contrast between the sheer obstinacy of the original European settlers and the misery suffered by the indigenous workmen.

The most memorable week of the tour – and the most important – was our short visit to Belgrade. The war had only recently ended and the infrastructure of the city was very badly damaged. On the coach trip from the airport, our Serbian hosts were eager to point out every building along the route that had been destroyed by recent NATO attacks. Slobodan Milošević had just gone into exile; his wife and the rest of his family were, many people believed, still in the country. Or they might have been in Russia. Nobody knew for certain. We could glimpse bombed buildings round every corner; the city had, only recently, been at the centre of a war zone. The theatre was a grand edifice in the middle of town, but it housed very little equipment. There was evidence of shortages everywhere. I sometimes felt that it was inappropriate for us to be there, performing a play that made no direct or indirect reference to the experiences that the local inhabitants had been through. Might it look as if we were ignoring the war? Was an apolitical visit really possible in such circumstances? At a press conference early on in our time there, I was concerned that the journalists who were firing questions at us might become hostile. I needn't have worried. The city appeared to welcome us with open arms. They accepted our performances in the spirit in which they were offered – as a peace offering. The theatre was packed – audience members sitting in the aisles, some with their chins pushed against the lip of the stage, each box crammed with twenty people or more.

The company spent its free days during that week indulging in some light sightseeing. We ate well, too, but, as might be expected, we didn't spend much time shopping in Belgrade. To be frank, there was very little to buy – except, strangely, leather goods. One day I decided that I needed a new pair of shoes and I knew exactly where I could find them. As I walked through the city, I noticed posters for our play stuck up everywhere. They all featured a large picture of my face. When I arrived at the shoe shop, the owner recognised me immediately and, in sign language, made it clear that she knew I was performing Hamlet. Our conversation was limited because I knew no Serbo-Croat and she knew no English – except 'To be or not to be, that is the question', which she intoned over and over again. I replied in kind, repeating the same words each time; and thought how extraordinary it was that one could probably go anywhere in the world, even to places where no other English is spoken, and find somebody there who knows that line.

This fleeting encounter inspired me to learn a little Serbo-Croat. On our last night, after the show had finished, our hosts threw a party. It was an emotional affair for all of us. We knew that it had been an extraordinary week. I was asked to make a speech, which is something I do not, in normal circumstances, find easy. But, this time, I had something that I needed to say. I wanted to tell our new friends that we would return one day. We could not predict when that would be, of course, but, as Hamlet says, 'if it be not now, yet it will come. The readiness is all.' I asked one of our new colleagues to translate Shakespeare's words into Serbo-Croat. I'm certain that my delivery that night was imperfect, perhaps incomprehensible, but the effort was appreciated, I think. I have not returned to Belgrade – at least not yet. I have not kept my promise.

There was a gap of about a year between my being cast as Hamlet and the first performance. Sam Mendes had agreed to direct the show. Trevor Nunn, who was running the National Theatre at the time, had his doubts about the project; although, much later, he wrote me a kind letter to say how pleased he was that it finally went ahead under his stewardship. A great deal happened during that year, including Sam directing his first film, *American Beauty*. This was the most extraordinary achievement and I still can't quite get my head round it. How he managed, at his first attempt, to produce such an assured piece of work, I'll never know. Perhaps it was the result of his characteristic bloody-mindedness and a genuine modesty. He has always been eager to learn from people who know more than him; and that, of course, is an indication of his self-confidence. Soon after the film was released in 1999, it became clear that it was going to be a strong contender for all the big awards. As always in these cases, this means that the workload for everyone involved – especially the director – increases exponentially. Sam decided that he would have to forgo directing *Hamlet*. I was disappointed, of course; but I couldn't, in all honesty, object. Nor did I want to. This was a big moment for Sam and it would have been churlish of me to stand in his way. And, as it turned out, he won an Oscar. So it was worth it.

The director John Caird took over the show. He's a very different man from Sam; and our relationship was predictably different too. The characters I had explored with Sam were most of them on the nastier end of the spectrum – Richard III, Thersites, Iago; and the plays in which they appeared were some of the darkest Shakespeare wrote. I knew John less well than Sam, and in the only play we had done together – *Every Man in His Humour* by Ben Jonson, back in 1986 – I had played a rather innocent, clever young man travelling through the jungle of Elizabethan London. So I have two Hamlets in my head – the one I might have played with Sam and the one I developed with John. I suspect the former would have had a harder edge than the latter, who was unquestionably a 'sweet prince', a 'noble heart'. But I will never know.

Just before I started rehearsals, my mother died. The few months before this awful event were a terrible time for her, for me and for her family. She suffered a great deal of pain. Looking back, I didn't handle it well. I don't think I appreciated that she was dying. The doctors in the family knew, but I ignored – or failed to see – the evidence and pushed the thought of her death aside. I didn't do the things one is supposed to do – like saying that I loved her – and I regret this bitterly. I was angry, I suppose. I still am – with myself and with the God I was taught to believe in. What was He/She/They playing at? For whose benefit did my mother have to go through all this? Hers? The family's? The world's? The last time I saw her, I was sitting by her bed with my father and my brother Andy. Dad was worried that Mum was dehydrated and he asked her quietly to stick out her tongue. Presumably, he thought that he would find out, through this, if she needed water. She heard him, understood and, with immense effort, did what he asked. She pushed out the tiniest tip of her tongue. I left the room a few minutes later – I presumably had a show to do – and she died soon after.

A few months later, I was on stage as Hamlet. Early in the play, the prince talks about his dead father:

> '. . . *Remember thee?*
> *Ay, thou poor ghost, whiles memory holds a seat*
> *In this distracted globe. Remember thee? . . .*'

Here is the paradox of grief. Clinging on to the memory of a person means that recovery is not possible. Forgetting, on the other hand, is a betrayal. Hamlet works hard to resolve this; as do all who are mourning. Every night, before this passage, I stuck out the tip of my tongue in memory of my mother.

Mum knew that I was about to play Hamlet. She insisted that she would remain alive long enough to see the show; but the performance dates had been changed and the opening night was now later than originally planned. I didn't tell her this; and she didn't make it.

It's a grim and tedious truth that the death of someone you love puts things into perspective. Certainly, work didn't seem particularly important; or, rather, it had a different value. My Hamlet was a tribute to my mother. At no point, when I played him, did I feel nervous – not even for the first showing of our production nor for the press night in front of the critics. This was unusual; but, frankly, I didn't care what other people thought of my interpretation. There was a table in the wings where stage management used to lay out our props. Before the first performance, I asked the team whether they would mind my putting a picture of Mum on this table – just for that one night. They kindly allowed me to do this, and she was there whenever I came off stage.

There are moments in any actor's career when their work mirrors events in their own life. My time playing in *Hamlet* is a good example of this. How many people enjoy the luxury – if that is the right word – of studying this magnificent exploration of grief at precisely the moment when it has the greatest personal significance? The whole experience felt like an honour, because, in my mind, the performance was in memory of a single, much-loved person. It was also a reminder that grief is something that the majority of us will go through at some point in our lives. A few days before my mother's funeral, I was walking in the churchyard where she was due to be buried, and met the gravedigger who was preparing her grave. I asked him, as Hamlet does, 'Whose grave's this?' For a split second, I and the prince were thinking and feeling the same thing. It was a reminder that *Hamlet* is a play that is almost unique in its universality.

One of the things that worried me before I started to work on the play was the nature of Hamlet's 'madness'. I will speak later of the decisions I took about this and give my reasons for those decisions. But, for the moment, it boils down to this: Hamlet, at one point, tells his friends Rosencrantz and Guildenstern that he is 'but mad north-north-west'. In other words, he is only a little off-kilter. To me, that sounds like a pretty accurate definition of grief.

The rehearsal period lasted eight weeks. Unusually, the first two of these were spent cutting the text. We needed to find a version of this very bulky play that was of a manageable length. The entire cast sat around a table with pencils and paper and assorted versions of *Hamlet*. Every line was analysed. We didn't get up on to our feet until the third week. Some of the actors must have found this frustrating, but it served two independently useful functions. Firstly, it ensured that every cast member was happy with the version of the play – and their part – that we ended up with. Secondly, we all got to know the text inside out; and by that I mean the whole thing. We could, each one of us, give reasons for every choice that was made and every argument that was pursued. That fortnight's work was something that couldn't be done later in the rehearsal process. Once actors are moving around in the room, other concerns have to be dealt with and detailed textual work – which sometimes seems fussy and boring – is easily ignored.

I had never approached a Shakespeare play in quite this way before, or, rather, with quite this minute and shared attention to the details of the text. It sparked an interest in me that I have never lost – a fascination with the history of editing Shakespeare. Indeed, I find it so compelling that I once developed an idea for a television series about the subject. Oddly, nobody seems to have picked it up. I can't think why. The way Shakespeare's text has been handed down to us is, I swear, genuinely interesting. Despite my work at school and university, I had always assumed that any play text by Shakespeare that I saw in print was somehow set in stone. The words I read were precisely the words that the playwright wanted me to read. Nothing could be further from the truth. All these plays are unstable entities.

In the case of *Hamlet*, there are three versions of the text that need to be considered; and they are all very different. These three versions are described by academics as authoritative, because two appeared in print during the writer's lifetime and one shortly after his death. In other words, Shakespeare would have known about them; although whether they all had his blessing is another matter. In the Jacobean period, playwrights seemed to have enjoyed very little control over their work once they had handed it over to the acting companies. *Hamlet* was printed in two different physical formats. The first appearances of the work were as a quarto – individual editions of the play, which are the size of a modern paperback. Two different quartos exist and are known as the first quarto and the second quarto. In 1623, after his death, some of his friends published Shakespeare's collected works in another bigger, grander format – not this time in quarto, but in folio. This large book, known as the First Folio, contained nearly forty plays. *Hamlet* was included.

The interest for an actor lies, of course, in the differences between these versions – some substantial and some minute. Choices have to be made, often between equally worthy alternatives. Sometimes this involves single words, sometimes whole speeches or even whole scenes. Academics consider all the three *Hamlets* that we have inherited to have some value. This was not always the case. The first quarto, which apart from anything else is relatively short, used to be dismissed as 'the bad quarto'. Now, it is read as a valid performance edition. The second quarto – the 'good quarto', as it was once known – is the longest version of *Hamlet* that we have. The First Folio version of the play, despite its being printed later, is longer than the first quarto but shorter than the second.

Quite apart from determining Shakespeare's original intentions – an almost impossible task – any actor, director or editor has to consider changes that might have occurred in the transmission of the text from the original manuscript to the early printed versions. So many people were involved in this process – scribes, printers, publishers, patrons, censors – that differing ideas (and many mistakes) were bound to have crept in. Indeed, when it comes to mistakes, it's likely that some of these are now accepted as genuine Shakespearean writing. The result of all this is that, in deciding upon a single text suitable for performance, we have to pick and mix. We have to play around with a number of authoritative versions and later editorial decisions. It's all a bit of a muddle.

Sometimes this boils down to a single word. One of the most debated examples in *Hamlet* is found in the first line of the prince's first soliloquy. The edition I have in front of me prints this line as follows:

'O that this too too sullied flesh would melt . . .'

Instead of the adjective 'sullied', the First Folio has 'solid'. Both quartos use the word 'sallied'. The actor must choose between the three options. 'Sullied' is the conjectural choice of later editors, who were writing long after Shakespeare's death. They argue that 'sallied', which feels, if we're honest, a little obscure, is the result of a misprint. I chose 'solid', not only because it's in the Folio, but because it seemed the simplest option. It's not hard to imagine that solid flesh might melt, is it? As I made my decision, I read that one editor thought that 'solid', attractive though it might be, is too easy an idea. We must be wary, he implied, of ironing out the intricacies of Shakespeare's writing. Oh well, I thought, I'll go for greater clarity rather than greater complexity.

And there were bigger debates to be had – not about single words, but about larger stretches of writing. The last of Hamlet's soliloquies appears in the second quarto, but is cut out of the Folio, a later, but authoritative, version of the play. This is intriguing, because it's a magnificent speech and deserves to be heard. Over thirty lines, Hamlet goes through the old concerns he has about his inability to act; but he then turns his attention to a war that is likely to break out in Europe. He refers to a character called Fortinbras, a rival Norwegian prince who is preparing to invade Danish territory. As might be expected, it is an intensely committed meditation on death and on the value of a single human life. It is also the final time we hear Hamlet speaking before he leaves for England. He will return a different man. So this speech is our last sight of the old Hamlet. Why is it cut out of the Folio version of the play? Did the theatre company or Shakespeare himself make this decision? And what should an actor playing Hamlet do? Should he speak the speech or leave it out?

As it happens, our *Hamlet* did not include the prince Fortinbras. Before we met for the first day of rehearsal, John Caird decided that we could do without him. This was the one decision he made that was not a result of discussion with the company. The central story of the play is set within a context of political upheaval – the threat of a Norwegian invasion – but John felt that this was less important than the essential family drama and that, since we had to make some big cuts for prosaic, practical reasons, then Fortinbras and his army were no longer necessary. This did not bother me, although it worried some people. A short time into the run, during a public interview that I was asked to do at the National Theatre, I was berated by a very elegant, elderly woman – she reminded me of Edith Sitwell – who was clearly incensed that the political subplot had disappeared and demanded that I give our reasons for this butchery. I explained that we had needed to cut the text because we were required to play *Hamlet* over a single evening, but I apologised for the fact that, other than that, I could give her no more interesting answer. Since we had to reduce the length of the show, we felt that the simplest option was to confine the story within a purely domestic environment. I did point out, though, that Hamlet himself doesn't seem particularly exercised either by the threat of war or his own political future. He says at one point that his unhappiness might be due to his lack of 'advancement', but this does not seem especially convincing. My Hamlet was not an instinctive political animal. I feel that, on the whole, he would rather be back at university in Germany and as far as possible from the centre of power and the theatre of war.

So the non-appearance of Fortinbras meant that we had to get rid of Hamlet's last soliloquy. It would, of course, have made no sense in our production. But I wonder too whether the playwright, years after the second quarto was published, looked at the play again and came to the conclusion that this particular speech was redundant. After all, a great deal of what he says at this point has been said before; and, at this late stage in the story, perhaps it's a good idea to keep things moving and not hang around for yet another meditative digression. Maybe this apparently insignificant difference between the later versions of *Hamlet* throws a light on the way Shakespeare developed his plays.

Because we know so little about Shakespeare, any clue, however faint, about his working life is worth pursuing. Like many of the writers that I have known, he was clearly prepared to collaborate. We will never know whether he enjoyed this process or, rather, found it difficult, but he collaborated nonetheless. I suspect that he adapted his plays throughout his life. He must have had to respond to changes in personnel and fluid performance conditions. He was also willing to offer his services as a co-writer. He appears to have been an adaptable and generous craftsman as well as an individual genius.

A further thought about editing *Hamlet*: I've always felt that the most famous soliloquy in the play – 'To be or not to be' – is in the wrong place. I know other Hamlets have felt the same. For instance, when Benedict Cumberbatch played Hamlet, he and his director moved it to the very start of the play. This might have been, in part, to get this very famous speech out of the way, but it made sense. It's a great piece of writing, of course, but it doesn't move the story or the psychology of the central character forward in any significant way. It stands alone – a universally applicable meditation on death. The possibility of Hamlet's suicide, considered in the speech, is mentioned very early in the play – in a different context. So 'To be or not to be' could appear at any point in the story. In fact, it might be better placed where the last soliloquy – the one we cut – now stands, just before Hamlet's departure for England. It would then serve as a summary or climax of all that has preceded it. I thought of this only after we had finished the run. Otherwise, we might have tried it out.

The story begins and ends with the military threat of Fortinbras and his army. So the structure as well as the narrative of our play were different without his presence. We could have plunged straight into the Hamlet family drama and finished with a lot of dead bodies on the stage and no further comment, but John found a more elegant and meaningful framing device. It was a lesson in making a virtue of necessity. So much work in putting on a Shakespeare play – indeed, any work from the established European canon – is matching the text to the requirements of the present moment and to local demands. We knew that the show could not be more than three hours long. If it were too long, then the many different venues we were due to visit would not be happy. To make up for the large chunk of the Fortinbras story that we had excised, John decided to use one of the characters in a slightly different way from normal. That character was Horatio. Horatio is one of the prince's friends from university and a man who is modest, respectful and honourable. He is trustworthy, too; and John exploited these qualities. At the National, the audience saw him, alone, as the lights came up; and they saw him, the only person left alive, as the lights went down. Horatio is the man to whom, just before his death, Hamlet entrusts his story. 'If thou didst ever hold me in thy heart', the prince says to him:

> *'Absent thee from felicity awhile,*
> *And in this harsh world draw thy breath in pain*
> *To tell my story.'*

Horatio, the audience can safely assume, tells his friend's story. In 'this harsh world', it will be painful, but the commission is accepted. And that's where we left the play, as Horatio walked out into another world, into our world perhaps, haunted by his own ghosts. And, of course, he succeeds in his task. The story of

Hamlet has been told, and will continue to be told, many, many times.

Our set was dominated by a huge crucifix. Every so often, snatches of smooth Renaissance polyphony could be heard – as if there was a chapel nearby. (By chance. my youngest brother, Matt, was one of the singers who contributed to our soundtrack. I could hear his voice in the mix, which pleased me. It would have pleased Mum, too, I think.) It was clear to every audience member that this was a devout, even repressive, Christian world. Claudius, the new Danish king, was dressed in clothes that made him look rather like an orthodox Byzantine emperor. He was both king and high priest. I liked this visual reference to an environment so far removed from our own. I don't think that I know another play by Shakespeare that is so steeped in Christian theology. Not everyone would agree. One critic insisted that we were misguided because, as he saw it, *Hamlet* is clearly set in a fiercely secular world. I'm not sure this is right. At the most basic level, the central debate about the value of revenge is couched in theological terms and reflects similar contemporary concerns in the world of which Shakespeare was a part. At one point in the play, Hamlet sees Claudius, whom he now believes to have murdered the old king, at prayer. He could kill him then and there, but he hesitates. The reason he gives for his inaction is that killing a man while he is praying will ensure that the victim goes straight to heaven. When Hamlet first talks about suicide, he points out that such an action is prohibited by church law. The ghost of Hamlet's father visits his son from purgatory, a location recognised by Catholics but not by the Protestant churches. Hamlet is concerned that his father died without being officially absolved of his sins. The list goes on and on. Many productions have emphasised the authoritarian nature of the Danish court. This is fair enough. After all, Hamlet himself describes Denmark as 'a prison' – though he might, in this instance, merely be alluding to his state of mind rather than making a wider, political point. He worries that, as in every totalitarian state, spies are everywhere. We acknowledged all this, but added God. In our production, He was everywhere – Denmark as a theocracy, I suppose.

It is also no accident that the prince is a student at a university in Wittenberg – the birthplace of the Reformation. Presumably he is studying the early modern curriculum, which would include scholastic theological debate. I would guess that like his friend Horatio, his outlook is essentially conservative, although he seems willing to question received opinion. Or rather, his meeting with the ghost of his father jolts him out of complacency and forces him to recognise that he must abandon previously held convictions and start again. To Horatio, who is enjoying a similar education to his, Hamlet says:

> *'There are more things in heaven and earth, Horatio,*
> *Than are dreamt of in your philosophy . . .'*

This is said in the immediate excitement of having just talked to the ghost, but I always felt that, at this point, Hamlet is as frightened as he is stimulated. He knows that his life – his physical, emotional and intellectual life – has to change; and he is scared.

Hamlet might be clever, but he has his intellectual weak spots. We have to assume that he knows nothing about sex – or, at least, sex with women. He is a misogynist; and this misogyny looks grotesque to a modern eye. He can be excused, perhaps, since this attitude was, at the time, a lazy convention – and it's a sign of his conservatism, perhaps – but his understanding of how sexual desire works must have seemed puerile, even to an Elizabethan audience. He is particularly vicious with his mother. In the course of a long argument, he tells her that she is far too old to be having a sexual relationship with anybody, let alone her new husband. That's insensitive enough, but he then goes on to give her some advice:

> *'Refrain tonight,*
> *And that shall lend a kind of easiness*
> *To the next abstinence; the next more easy . . .'*

I really can't see how this could work. It's as if Hamlet, the intellectual powerhouse, the sophisticated man we thought we knew, has disappeared and been replaced by an angry little boy.

I found the idea of Hamlet as a little boy very useful. I don't mean that he is ever childish or cute, but rather that he is, in many ways, an innocent, the product of a protected environment; and his story, at least as he would see it, is a long series of betrayals. These betrayals surprise, even appal, him and, predictably, he lashes out – as many boys would. He had assumed that the world is a better place than it proves to be. He is betrayed by his mother, of course; by his uncle; by his two college friends, Rosencrantz and Guildenstern. Ophelia, the young woman whom he loves, lies to him. So does her father, Polonius. Even the ghost of his father, in asking him to kill his uncle, puts him under an intolerable pressure. The father doesn't set out clearly the ramifications of his instructions. In essence, he demands that Hamlet risks his own life – an appalling request – and, since the risk is never directly alluded to, this is, in effect, another type of lie. Only Horatio remains on his side, but then I'm not sure Hamlet knows Horatio very well. Their relationship is too formal to be intimate. This is why Hamlet turns to the audience. They are the only people whom he can trust; and he maintains this relationship until the hours just before his death.

In a play that is so concerned with religious belief, then death and its meaning for every individual human being take on an overwhelming significance. How Hamlet dies is important.

When, in the final act, Hamlet stops talking to the audience, he effectively severs his last real tie to other human beings. Even with Horatio, the person with whom he continues to have some meaningful conversation, he is, to say the least, remote. Hamlet ends his story and experiences his own death absolutely alone. How this happens, and what this means in psychological terms, is one of the mysteries of the play; and it is one of the reasons why the role of the prince represents such a unique challenge to the actor.

The final beats of the story run as follows: Hamlet is exiled to England by an exasperated Claudius. He is accompanied by his old friends Rosencrantz and Guildenstern, whom he no longer trusts. During the course of their travels, his friends are murdered. Hamlet is, in part, responsible for this. With the help of some pirates, he makes his way back to Denmark, where he manages to kill Claudius and, effectively, his own mother. He also fights a duel with his old friend Laertes, in which both men die.

Put so baldly, this sounds ludicrous – like the plot of a second-rate opera; Tom Stoppard was so tickled by the idea of the pirates – or, rather, the comic version of piracy – that he famously wrote a play, *Rosencrantz and Guildenstern Are Dead,* in which they feature. It makes for a very funny and exhilarating scene. But, unlike Stoppard, comedy is not what Shakespeare is after. So it is probably a good thing that, in Shakespeare's story, the pirates' contribution is played out offstage. As for what we actually see enacted in *Hamlet,* a summary of the action could sound grim as well as absurd. A large number of people die. A reader might get the impression that Hamlet has transformed himself, as his father would have wished, into an avenging angel. But this is not how it comes across on the stage. It's almost as if the prince loses any interest in revenge and, although this feels callous, I felt, when I played him, that the long list of the dead is somehow irrelevant – at least from his perspective. The fact is that, from the moment Hamlet returns home, he is making his own, private preparations to die. Nothing else is important. And for the actor, it requires a stripping away of any sense of display or contrivance or self-consciousness. After all, at this point, facing the necessity of dying alone, Hamlet is speaking for all of us. It is particularly in this spiritual exploration that we can locate the power and durability of the role.

In one of the most famous passages in the play, Hamlet talks to Horatio about his preparations for death. He states his belief that any death – even the most apparently insignificant – reflects a greater, if hidden, purpose; and, taking that on board, he seems resigned to his own inevitable end. He finishes the speech with two short words: 'Let be.' For me, this moment encapsulated everything that I loved about the prince and about the play. It could feel passive or fatalistic. It could seem despairing. But here is love and a universal sympathy and a rejection of easy judgement. It's the perfect epitaph. I'd quite like 'Let be' written on my gravestone.

I wanted to die standing up. I mean that literally. My Hamlet didn't need or want the physical support of Horatio or, indeed, anyone else. So, after his last words, 'The rest is silence,' he stepped away from his friend, sank to the floor and died, alone and silent, curled up like a foetus.

I would like to write something detailed and perceptive about Hamlet's 'madness'. But, in fact, there's not much for me to say. My Hamlet was not mad – it's as simple as that. He was not frightened of losing his mind. He didn't even pretend to be mad – except for one short moment with Polonius, the senior counsellor at the Danish court. I have acknowledged that I was unsure of how to act a 'mad' Hamlet and therefore avoided the subject, but, in truth, I could find very little evidence for the prince's insanity. When Shakespeare wants to indicate that someone has lost their mind, he tends to use a different linguistic register. Ophelia is a good example of this. There is no such shift in the way Hamlet speaks. The playwright simply does not seem to be that interested in his central character losing his mind. In the earliest source material, from the twelfth century, the Danish prince feigns madness as a self-protective tactic. He does not want to appear to threaten the legitimacy of the new king. Apparent insanity also disguises any future ambitions. But in Shakespeare's play, the situation is different. Apart from anything else, Hamlet barely mentions any desire to be king himself. Talk of madness feels to me like the faintest trace of an older story.

It is Polonius who is the first person to describe Hamlet as mad. He claims that the prince's disturbed state of mind is the result of a love for his own daughter, Ophelia. The problem with Polonius is that, however wise a statesman he may be, his understanding of human nature is pretty weak. In Hamlet's case, he gets the cause, the diagnosis and the treatment wildly wrong. Once Hamlet hears of Polonius's analysis, he, of course, plays up to it; but only in front of Polonius. That's all the insanity we see. It takes time and effort pretending to be mad. Frankly, he has other, more important, things to think about.

Madness is part of the history of Hamlet in performance, of course. So any actor playing him must confront the problem. Many solutions have been explored, from wearing provocative clothes to setting the whole play in a lunatic asylum. As an addendum to the question of Hamlet's shifting state of mind, a recent tradition has been established that concerns Hamlet's relationship with his mother, Gertrude. Early in the twentieth century, a great Freudian analyst, Ernest Jones, proposed the idea that Hamlet reveals some version of an Oedipal fantasy with Gertrude – particularly in their long scene together late in the play. It is a convincing argument. Laurence Olivier was understandably fascinated by it and, when he played Hamlet, physically attacked Gertrude. In fact, his behaviour amounted to sexual assault. Over time, this reading of the scene has remained unchallenged.

I know that it's an exciting idea, but I could see no evidence for it. Through the long period of rehearsal for this scene, I kept thinking that Hamlet has no desire to have sex with his mother, even subconsciously; he just wants her to stop having sex with his uncle. I know unacknowledged or infantile desires are the bedrock of Freudian thinking, but I was not interested in this particular hidden world coming to light. Maybe I'm too middle class and repressed to follow Olivier's example, but I felt that this big scene could be about the love of mother and son, and not principally about anger and aggression. At one point, the ghost of Hamlet's father appears. Hamlet can see him; Gertrude cannot. In our production, the father put his hand on his son's shoulder, just as his mother went to touch him too. For one brief moment, the family unit was re-established – at least in Hamlet's mind. The prince delighted in this, even as he realised that his longing for things to be as they were can never be satisfied.

At that moment, my Hamlet gave up. (A few moments later, he would acquiesce without protest to Claudius's sending him into exile.) Simultaneously, it became clear to Gertrude, in Sara Kestelman's heartbroken performance, that her first loyalty was to her son and not to her new husband. This rediscovered sense of priorities is not put into words, but it was a shift that Hamlet saw and understood. Perhaps this is the affirmation that he was looking for. He could see some evidence of a family unit being re-established, even if not in its pure, original form. By the end of the scene, Hamlet and Gertrude began to enjoy each other's company again. Anger evaporated and some sort of love was reaffirmed.

Hamlet is such a hospitable creation that he can absorb widely divergent readings. Unlike more potentially heroic or fiercer interpretations, the prince I discovered never had a chance. One of my favourite moments in our production came just before the interval. Hamlet and the rest of the court have watched a performance of a play. Hamlet commissioned this from a visiting theatrical troupe; and it presents a series of events that bear an uncanny resemblance to those that Hamlet suspects led up to his father's murder. Claudius sits watching for a short while and then, unable to take any more, storms out. For Hamlet, this behaviour is a clear sign of his uncle's guilt. He asks for music to be played. It appears, from the words on the page, that he is elated, triumphant. This was not the case in our production. Now he has proof, my Hamlet has no means of escape; and he knows he cannot do what has been asked of him. Turning to the musicians, he said:

> *'Come, some music; come, the recorders.*
> *For if the king like not the comedy,*
> *Why then, belike he likes it not, perdie.*
> *Come, some music.'*

The repeated word – 'Come' – became a soft appeal or, rather, a search for reassurance. There was no celebration. After his request for music, Hamlet then sat down, immobilised, and the recorders played. The lights went down and, after a fifteen-minute interval, came up again. Hamlet hadn't moved. He was sitting in the same place, listening to the music.

6

When I signed up for the RSC, I was living in a small flat in London with an old school friend. My elder siblings were by now all based in town. At this point, they were training or working as junior doctors; so inevitably they had almost no free time. Despite this, one brother – Tim, I think – took me up to Stratford in a hired van. I couldn't drive and, bless him, he took pity on me. The van was packed with clothes, bed linen, CDs – and books. I had found out, on a previous trip, that Stratford had no big, commercial bookstore, which was surprising, given that her most famous son was a writer. There were plenty of small antiquarian, specialist and second-hand bookshops, but nothing more wide ranging. These small and often pricey outlets weren't of much use to me. Knowing that I would be stuck in Warwickshire for a long year, I dropped into the university bookstore off Tottenham Court Road in London before I left town and stocked up on twelve months' supply of reading material.

What caught my eye first was a history of the Normans in Sicily and a three-volume account of the Byzantine Empire – both subjects about which I knew nothing. They looked fascinating and were written in a easily digestible style aimed at non-specialists like me. Who knew that the Byzantine Empire had lasted a thousand years? I felt it was essential that I should find out more. I then added some studies of medieval Europe to the pile. It was a very eccentric collection; and, to be honest, in the event, some of the books proved to be very hard work. However, over the year, since I had few other options, I read them all. I became quite an expert, though I have forgotten everything since. It surprised visitors to my digs in Stratford that I had no fiction on my bookshelves, but I hadn't read fiction for a long time. Immediately after my last exam at university, I stormed off to the nearest bookshop, determined to buy something that I actually wanted to read – something for pleasure and not for my studies. Unaccountably, I settled on a novel by Henry James called *Roderick Hudson*. I never opened it; and it remains unopened. I didn't read fiction for the next twenty years. It was only at the turn of the millennium that I decided that I couldn't grow old without having experienced some of the great novels that I had missed at university – *Great Expectations* and *Jane Eyre*, for instance. I think I was trying to make up for the fact that I didn't take my degree seriously enough. It had begun to seem ludicrous that I hadn't at least tried to read *Ulysses*, although I recognised that I would probably never attempt *Finnegans Wake*. Ticking off the big writers became something of a compulsion.

On that millennial New Year's Day, I started with one of the toughest challenges I could think of – Marcel Proust. A part of me was dreading it; and, as expected, he proved to be, in many ways, infuriating. But he was also surprisingly funny, always sharp and sly, and many passages were ravishing. Once I had pushed through the pain barrier, it was easy to see how addictive his writing could be.

All the hard work on nineteenth- and twentieth-century fiction – because, if one's honest, it's very often hard work – led me unexpectedly to contemporary writing. I spent a few years immersed in stories from South Asia, for instance. I don't think we ever considered this type of work at school. All the writers we studied then were long dead – and either British or American. And at university, I could have finished my degree, if I had wanted to, knowing nothing of literature after 1850. Now, for a period, I couldn't get enough of Salman Rushdie, Arundhati Roy, Vikram Seth, Monica Ali.

Once you had arrived and settled in, Stratford was, quite literally, a very difficult town to leave – unless you had a car, of course. I didn't drive. In those days, very few trains used the tiny station, which squatted at the end of a correspondingly tiny, grass-covered branch line. After a show, late at night, with thousands of audience members milling around, a single coach was available outside the theatre to take customers to Coventry station. That was the only option. I learned very quickly that it was easier to spend my free Sundays in Warwickshire than try to escape to London.

This didn't worry me. I feel comfortable in small market towns. I always have done. If there's a decent pub and an easy walk to the supermarket, then I'm quite happy. In any case, the workload was so heavy – as it was for all the youngest actors in the company – that there was precious little time to explore anything beyond the theatre. Once the performance schedule got underway, I had one evening off during the whole year. I still remember the date – 5 December. I don't know why I was free; but I do know that Imelda Staunton, Penny Downie and I went off to see *Top Gun*. It was splendid – good-looking pilots playing around with their planes. Otherwise, there was only the work – and the new friendships I made. The whole experience felt rather like an extended summer school – only, marvellously, we were being paid.

One of my fellow actors was called Susie Fairfax. She has remained a close friend – from the first day I met her during that season with the RSC, when she warned me that she had taken a Valium and, consequently, might behave oddly. I took her warning seriously and was understandably wary of engaging her in conversation; but it transpired that she had taken the sedative after a morning of extensive root-canal treatment and it was not the result of a long-established addiction. I think she enjoyed my confusion. I talk to her almost every day. It is impossible to explain how important a figure she is in my life. She's witty, perceptive and limitlessly kind. She's also one of only two people that I know who is willing to test me over and over on my lines – a task that most sensible people find intolerable.

I've been told that Stratford is England's second most popular tourist destination – all because of Shakespeare. He's everywhere. There are the sights to be seen – Shakespeare's birthplace, his grave, his wife's house – and a couple of important academic institutions; and there are also the regular shows by the RSC. Oddly, though, in my first years there, I had no sense of being in any way closer to the playwright. I didn't picture him walking the streets or sitting in his big house, which, after all, was just down the road from the theatre. I went only once to see where he was buried. Perhaps it was because I performed so little of Shakespeare's work during that time that he wasn't yet a clearly defined part of my world. It was different twenty-five years later, in 2016, when I was playing Prospero in *The Tempest* in Stratford. As I spoke his extraordinary words night after night, I had an acute sense that Shakespeare himself had literally been here before me. After all, I thought, he had probably written *The Tempest* – his last solo-authored work – only a few yards away from the stage on which I was standing.

My first digs weren't actually in the town itself. My fellow actor Nathaniel Parker invited me to join him in a small cottage just outside Stratford. Nat was effortlessly and consistently stylish. He knew about lighting wood fires, recognising types of fruit trees, cooking on an Aga and other essential attributes of country life. At least, that's how it looked to my rather suburban eyes. He himself would probably be surprised that I describe him in this way. Sadly, a cottage outside town, lovely though it was, proved to be an impractical choice, since the only way I could get home at night and back into work in the morning was in a very expensive taxi. Despite enjoying my short rural experience, Nat and I agreed that I should go somewhere else and I went to live in a modern semi-detached house in town. My fellow lodger was called Gary Love.

Gary was a delight. Sharing a house with him was very easy – although he tells me that we argued a great deal. Apparently, I used to eat his cornflakes and steal his socks. Once, in rehearsal, our most recent and seemingly endless spat was so noisy that the director, Trevor Nunn, had to tell us to shut up or go home. I loved Gary. After his time at the RSC, he went on to enjoy huge success as an actor and director in television. He was extremely good looking, always beautifully dressed and drove a rather chic vintage Beetle convertible. Jeremy Irons, who was also a member of the company, owned a similar model, which only confirms how chic the car was. Gary had a London accent and was once stopped by the Stratford police as he was driving – perfectly innocently – around town. In answer to their questions, he told them that he was an actor with the Royal Shakespeare Company. Because of the way he spoke, they didn't believe him – which was a touch old-fashioned of them, I thought at the time. Happily, Gary finally convinced them that he was telling the truth – perhaps he tossed off a short passage of Ben Jonson or something – and they let him go.

We were both cast in *The Winter's Tale*, and we both had understudy duties. Gary covered my part, the Young Shepherd, and I was understudying Joe Melia, who was playing the principal clown, Autolycus. These two characters have all their scenes together. On occasion, when we felt guilty about our lack of commitment and our imperceptible work ethic, we would attempt to run through our scenes at home. It was a total waste of time. It was impossible to take this exercise seriously. The truth is that we were both terrified at the idea of going on for our principals, and didn't want to spend any more time than absolutely necessary thinking about it. Because, let's face it, understudying is a ghastly job. That popular and thrilling narrative of a young actor replacing another actor at the last moment and thereby becoming a star does happen, but it's very rare. It certainly wouldn't have been like that if I had ever gone on as Autolycus. A few performers must enjoy being an understudy, I suppose. Perhaps some younger actors see it as a valuable part of the learning process. There was a friend of mine in our company who was desperate to take over from the big star he was understudying. I thought he was mad. I was pretty certain that Joe Melia would never miss a show; but, on the days when we had a performance of *The Winter's Tale*, I would wake in the morning, dry-mouthed with anxiety. There was one day at work when Joe fell and twisted his ankle. I'm ashamed to admit that my sympathy was minimal. So was Gary's. All we could think about was getting him back on his feet as quickly as possible, fit enough to play his part. Joe didn't let us down.

There were three theatres in Stratford. The largest, the Royal Shakespeare Theatre (originally known as the Shakespeare Memorial Theatre), was a beautiful Art Deco building from the early years of the twentieth century, designed, unusually for the time, by a woman, Elisabeth Scott. The auditorium was a touch four-square and felt like a barn, but was beautiful nonetheless. It was a demanding space to play. We all knew how difficult it was, though that didn't make it any easier. Before I first appeared there, one older actor warned me that trying to be heard by the back row of seats was rather like shouting from Dover to Calais.

The smallest performing venue was the Other Place – a shed dropped into the middle of a large car park. It has since been rebuilt and is now rather smart, but at that time the facilities, for both actors and audience, were pretty basic. When it rained, we would tiptoe on unsteady planks of wood over large, muddy puddles to get to the entrance of the building. It was usually worth the effort; because the Other Place was responsible for some of the most important work the company ever produced.

The big excitement during my first year in Stratford was a new theatre, of middling size, that had just been built. It was called the Swan, after our house playwright (Ben Jonson called Shakespeare 'the Swan of Avon'), but also as a nod to one of the venues on the South Bank of the Thames that Shakespeare himself would have known. It was a gorgeous building. The substantial stage was thrust into a horseshoe of seats, which were made from warm, golden wood. The interior glowed under the lights. The auditorium was constructed within a nineteenth-century brick shell. The original space had been used as a large rehearsal room. Some of the older members of the company talked in hushed – and, sometimes, weary – tones about the harsh experience of creating one of the most famous Shakespeare productions of the twentieth century – Peter Brook's *A Midsummer Night's Dream* – there in that very room. Built above the theatre was a new rehearsal space. I spent many hours there over three seasons. It was unquestionably a lovely room, although the views of the Warwickshire countryside stretching out far into the distance, and the very comfortable window seats, didn't always help our concentration. The majority of the shows I worked on over the next few years were performed in the Swan, so I got to know it well. I was playing there when the theatre was officially opened by Queen Elizabeth II in November 1986. I was introduced to her before the show. I was in costume, looking very shabby, and I was clutching one of my props, a large broom. She looked politely curious; I looked blank. I felt self-conscious. No words were exchanged, which was, frankly, a relief. I would only have seized up with embarrassment.

The play that had been chosen to show Her Majesty was

a swashbuckling adventure story called *The Fair Maid of the West*. It featured a young woman called Bess, acted by Imelda Staunton, who enjoyed an exhilarating time fighting pirates and outwitting the evil King of Morocco. She ended up capturing the heart of a dashing soldier of fortune, played by Sean Bean. The evening's entertainment actually consisted of two plays cobbled together by the director, Trevor Nunn. Songs by Shaun Davey had been added. These showed off Imelda's spectacular singing voice. The playwright was one of Shakespeare's contemporaries, Thomas Heywood, whose major claim to fame is that, over his lifetime, he had 'had a hand' in over two hundred plays. Perhaps he should have tried to do a little less. He wrote some good stuff in his time, but I'm not sure that *The Fair Maid* shows him at his best. However, Trevor Nunn, that great alchemist, transformed the two plays into something celebratory and furiously energetic. It was a riot and a triumph.

On the page, it looked as if I had almost nothing to do. This worried me; but one of the creative team, sensing my disappointment, took me aside after the first read-through and assured me that Trevor would turn my tiny role into something special. He was right. Trevor's big idea was to start the evening with a troupe of players who arrive at an inn where they plan to put on a performance of *Henry V*. As they start their show, they are shouted down by their audience, who demand something less serious and more action-packed. The troupe come up with *The Fair Maid of the West*, which the audience judges to be acceptable. My part, a shy man called Fawcett, is the stage manager of the troupe. He is perfectly content organising costumes and props, entrances and exits, sitting at the edge of the stage following the script, quietly prompting when necessary. Unfortunately, it becomes clear early on that there are not enough actors available to fill all the roles in the new play. Needless to say, and much to Fawcett's discomfort, he is forced to join his actors on the stage. He becomes a player; and, furthermore, it was no longer an insignificant role.

There is a moment in the play when one of the characters delivers an impassioned encomium to the queen – originally Queen Elizabeth I, of course. Fawcett was so caught up in this song of praise that, as it finished, he muttered very quietly, but with deep feeling, 'God save the Queen.' The audience laughed. When our queen came to visit, I asked Trevor whether I should cut this – just for this one performance. I thought it might be offensive, especially if people laughed. He told me to keep it in. Instead of a laugh, the response that night, from a large well-fed audience of the great and the good, was a soft murmur of 'hear, hear'. I found it very funny, even if they didn't; and it was probably closer to the response of the original Elizabethan audience than the laugh had been.

That year, I did one other play in the Swan – *Every Man in His Humour* by Ben Jonson, directed by John Caird. This was another happy experience, although, in rehearsal, we thought we were heading for a disaster. There were many panicked, whispered meetings in pubs and dressing rooms and corridors. We should have trusted John more because, among many other talents, he really knows about casting. For this show, he gathered together a hugely accomplished group of actors: Pete Postlethwaite, Henry Goodman, David Haig, David Troughton, Philip Franks, Nathaniel Parker, Joely Richardson. Tony Church, my principal at the Guildhall, was there too, playing my father. Frankly, give a group like that free rein with any Elizabethan text and you'll find that it's in very safe hands.

There is no doubt that Ben Jonson's writing is elaborate and demanding. A ferocious technique is required for all the principal parts in *EveryMan*. I was playing a supporting role; and so spent my time watching the others. If you want to know how a master deals with Jonson's words, and if there is a recording available, then listen to the late Pete Postlethwaite in *Every Man*. Watch him, if you can, dance his way through a bewilderingly elaborate description of his heroism in some fictitious military campaign – he was playing an old braggart soldier in our play – and marvel at both his clarity and his exuberance. Every night, I had the privilege of watching him, open-mouthed in admiration. I don't suppose one can teach the skills that he had in such abundance, but I thought then that it was worth trying to learn.

My last play that year was at the Other Place – a scabrous and very funny story about William Hogarth. It was called *The Art of Success* and was written by Nick Dear. It dealt, among much else, with the establishment of the first law of copyright, which sounds a very dry subject, but there was nothing dry about Nick's script or, indeed, Michael Kitchen's central performance. The latter employed a hesitant, knowing delivery that somehow conveyed both puzzlement and world-weariness. There is one line – the funniest in the play – which, forty years later, is locked in my memory and which I can still deliver in the same way as Michael did. Joe Melia was there on the stage too – our third time together. I met another actor then, David Killick, who became a lifelong friend. I mention him not only because he's a wonderful man, but also because it was, at that time, always fascinating for me to discover how and where my colleagues, especially the older performers, had started their careers. David had spent his early years in the Royal Navy. Joe, while presenting an arts programme on television, continued to perform and had also worked for Joan Littlewood on the original production of *Oh! What a Lovely War*. For a while, as a young man, he had studied in the Soviet Union. Another actor in the company, Dilys Laye, began her career singing alongside Julie Andrews in musical comedies. Yet another had spent time as a straight man to the comedian John Inman. I would later meet an ex-lawyer, a retired schoolmaster, a doctor, a footballer, even an acrobat. We were all working in a group that specialised in Shakespeare, but to call all of us Shakespeare specialists would be wrong. I think many people believe that the performers up at Stratford in those years somehow represented a homogenous group, men and women with identical backgrounds and training. They didn't.

On the first day that I walked into the big theatre in Stratford, the Royal Shakespeare Theatre, it was to put *The Winter's Tale* on to the stage. I naturally brought all the stuff I needed for my dressing room – make-up, tissues, shower gel, a big towel, paracetamol. I was given a key by the stage-door keeper and she waved me on my way. I was told that my dressing room could be found across the back of the stage and up two flights of stairs. On the way, I caught a glimpse of a row of four dressing rooms, where the leading actors were housed. It was not until my last season with the RSC that I was allocated one of these. They weren't grand; in fact, they were rather small and needed a lick of paint. But they each had a pair of French windows that opened on to a small balcony. From there, one could look out over the River Avon, with the Clopton Bridge to one's left and, far away to the right, the spire of Holy Trinity church, where Shakespeare and his family once worshipped and are now buried. Beneath the balcony, swans glided past. Each room had a single bed. On a summer afternoon, with the windows open and the net curtains billowing in the breeze, one could take quick nap before the evening show while listening to the muffled sound of people outside, tourists mostly, messing about in boats.

I climbed another final flight of stairs and arrived at my dressing room on the second floor. I was to share it with Nat Parker and we were looked after by a man, our dresser, who played a very important part in my daily life with the RSC. He was called Black Mac; he must have once had black hair, though there was precious little evidence of that when I met him. A stocky man from the northeast, his day job was in the stores of a military depot just outside town. He had no teeth. His story was that he had lost them in a bet. That seemed unlikely, I thought. A couple of decades before I worked with him, a friend of his who was employed as a dresser – for the large number of supernumeraries that the company hired at the time – asked Mac to come and lend a hand. One evening, despite some scepticism and a professed contempt for actors, he answered his friend's call for help. Although he would never have said as much, Mac clearly loved the experience and he kept on working in the theatre for the rest of his life.

He ran the dressing room with military precision. As he forcefully pointed out on the day that I arrived, he was in charge – and nobody else. There was no use in resisting. Mac's language was colourful, to say the least, and would not be acceptable now. He had a habit of referring to his actors with a nickname of his invention. Mine was 'The Body' – referring to my bulk, I think, more than my beauty. When the show was finally up and running, he would provide a cup of hot, sweet tea during the interval. I hadn't asked for it and didn't need it, but I dutifully drank it for the whole year. At the end of each performance, Mac would run me a bath. We had no shower, but rather a strange, square hipbath in which one would sit on a small shelf in order to wash. Mac would add bubbles. The water was always scalding hot. I didn't dare run the cold tap, in case Mac would hear and interpret it as an implied criticism. So I would lower myself into the water, sit on the shelf for as long as I could bear it and then get out, my skin as pink and tender as a lobster.

After that first season, I didn't return to the main theatre – nor to be looked after by Black Mac – for a couple of years. Then it was to perform my first Shakespearean verse roles, in *Love's Labour's Lost* and *King Lear*. In the intervening period, I was at the Swan in Restoration comedy. I saw Mac around, of course – he was hard to miss – but now he had other young actors in his care. As a memento of our first year together, he made me a rather beautiful bird table. I didn't have anywhere to put it, but I gave it to my parents, whom Mac had once entertained in our dressing room, and, for years, it stood proudly in their garden. It has since disappeared – destroyed, I presume, by the wind and the rain.

Two Good Men

The King of Navarre

The King of Navarre, in *Love's Labour's Lost,* has a first name – Ferdinand; but it's almost never used. He's usually known simply as the King. He's a rather sweet man, a little pompous, but well-meaning. He has three friends with whom he concocts an elaborate plan for their mutual self-improvement. The King proposes that they should live together for three years. They will devote their lives to study, limit their sleep to three hours a night, fast for one day in the week and, most impressively, avoid the company of women. As the audience listens to the four of them make their vows, they must know that the whole thing is absurd and that the boys are bound to fail.

And so it proves. After all, as king, Ferdinand still has a job to do, so he can't just hide himself away. An embassy has been sent from the neighbouring kingdom of France, with whom the King is required to negotiate. This embassy is headed by the French king's daughter; and accompanying her are three ladies-in-waiting. They are all irresistibly beautiful, witty and clever. The four young men haven't a hope in hell of keeping their vows.

There's not a lot to say about the King as a character. He doesn't undergo much change. He doesn't really suffer, even as he falls in love with the Princess. Actually, he seems pretty content most of the time – rather like the Young Shepherd in *The Winter's Tale*. The king would be simple to play, were it not for one thing – the writing, both verse and prose, is very elaborate, difficult to understand and to perform. *Love's Labour's Lost* is one of the most refined plays in Shakespeare's canon. Even the clowns make jokes in Latin. It would be fascinating to know how the original audience felt about it. Did the aristocrats see it as a mirror of their own lives? Did they worry that they were being gently mocked? Did they, on the other hand, enjoy the mockery? Surely they can't have spent their time playing word games as relentlessly as the fictional King of Navarre and his friends. But who knows? Perhaps life with Sir Philip Sidney and his sister, for instance, or Francis Bacon and his friends, really was like the world of *Love's Labour's Lost*. Did the rest of the audience – those who weren't aristocrats – enjoy it in the same way that we enjoy popular period drama? Did they think it was an essentially accurate, if romanticised, depiction of courtly life? Maybe they did. It has to be said that, despite a whiff of satire, everyone in the story is rather lovely to look at and a pleasure to listen to.

It seems that the play has always divided opinion. I've just read, in a recent edition, that William Hazlitt, the nineteenth-century critic, could happily have lived without it. Dr Johnson, in contrast, saw 'scattered through the whole many sparks of genius'. A long list of actors have fallen in love with it – including the late Richard Griffiths, who, like me, once played the King. He adored the piece; and I guess that if the production is particularly skilful, like the one he was involved with, then it can deliver a charming, even moving, evening in the theatre.

I am damning with faint praise. I'll admit that *Love's Labour's Lost* is not one of my favourite Shakespeare plays, but it has its glories. There's lots to admire. In fact, Shakespeare's achievements, even as a young man, are astonishing. He was, at this time, still a relatively immature writer in many ways, but he was already something of a technical wizard. Frankly, it's fun to watch the young master showing off. In *The Comedy of Errors*, an early play, he followed his source material pretty closely, but changed the story and doubled the number of identical twins. He knew he was capable of manipulating quadruple the amount of confusion. Similarly, here in *Love's Labour's Lost,* there's a breathless scene in which the writer has the four young men eavesdrop on each other. They have all fallen in love and therefore have all broken their vows of celibacy – if not in deed, then at least in thought. One of the boys, Berowne, has written a sonnet to his beloved and is telling the audience all about it when the King enters. Berowne hides as the King reads a poem that he too has composed – this one in honour of the Princess. Then, as a third young man, Longaville, comes on to read yet another poem, the King himself hides. Inevitably and deliciously, the last remaining friend, Dumaine, enters to read his poem. Longaville hides. As the men emerge one by one from their respective hiding places, feigned outrage and accusations of hypocrisy ensue. But it's all very good-natured and, again, it's quadruple the amount of fun than one has the right to expect.

However, it is at the end of the play that we see glimpses of the unique voice that future readers would recognise as Shakespearean. Contrary to expectations, the story does not end happily. One would predict that the four couples would marry. Surely, that's what always happens in comedies like this. But here, just as the story is cantering to the expected happy ending, it is stopped in its tracks. In a supremely theatrical twist, a man arrives from the French court with a message for the Princess. He is called Marcade. Their conversation goes like this:

Marcade: I am sorry, madam, for the news I bring
Is heavy in my tongue. The King, your father –
Princess: Dead, for my life!
Marcade: Even so; my tale is told.

It's a bleak and unexpected moment. The string of simple words, particularly after the elaborate rhetoric that has gone before, is like the soft beat of a muffled drum. The Princess's interruption is a masterstroke. It's as if she has been expecting this terrible news. Everyone freezes. The four women know that they must leave immediately. All the weddings are postponed for the foreseeable future. Perhaps, we may think, they will never happen. Perhaps we have been watching nothing more than giddy, holiday flirtations. The young people have had their fun and now it's time to face reality – and death. The change that Marcade effects with his couple of lines is seismic. That's why it could be argued that it's the best small part Shakespeare ever wrote. The actor who played Marcade in our production, Griffith Jones, had a head of white hair and a long white beard. He was dressed all in black – not a colour we had seen up to this point – and he looked like God in a child's illustrated Bible. He spoke like God, too, with a voice that was rich and deep. I am not the only one who feels that Marcade comes from a different world. I was told of a student production years ago at Oxford University that was presented in a beautiful college garden with a large lake. Somehow, they contrived that Marcade made his entrance walking across the water.

Who knows what will happen to the youngsters after the play ends? One director, Ian Judge, set his production in the early years of the twentieth century. As the lights went down at the story's end, we heard the sound of distant guns. It was clear that the boys were off to fight in the trenches of Flanders. They would, in all likelihood, never return.

After the news of the old King's death, there is just time for a short, melancholy song. And then one of the characters turns to the audience and says:

> *'The words of Mercury are harsh after the songs of Apollo.*
> *You that way, we this way.'*

There is, after all the displays of verbal athleticism, nothing left to say. Perhaps what happened during the previous two hours didn't really amount to much. The characters leave the stage in silence. It's difficult to think of a sadder, more mournful farewell.

Love's Labour's Lost was the second play I did that was directed by Terry Hands. The set was ravishing – a circular, bright green lawn surrounded by a large number of trees. There was a dab of primary colour painted on each leaf. The effect was that of an Impressionist painting or, more accurately perhaps, given the technique that was employed, a work by Georges Seurat. It felt appropriately French. Indeed, providing further Gallic flavour, the design of the costumes was indebted to nineteenth-century Paris. In the first scene, in which the King and his three friends take their vows to study together, the boys sat on a beautiful quilted cloth, enjoying a picnic. It was a direct reference to *Le Dejeuner sur l'herbe* by Édouard Manet – but without the naked woman. Although perhaps Terry was dropping a hint that she was indeed present, if only in the minds of the young men. At that time, I was too inexperienced an actor to query the choices that were made for my costume. The frock coat and trousers that I wore for most of the play were cut from a light powder-blue corduroy. I never stopped feeling that this was unwise; and I didn't dare hint that I thought it might be unflattering. So, despite the fact that it felt needlessly fluffy, I just had to shrug my shoulders and inhabit it with as much grace as I could muster.

The King, although he enjoys regal status, is not really a leading role. He is there to support others, especially the most loquacious of his companions, Berowne. This latter figure was played, in our 1990 production, by Ralph Fiennes, the new star in the theatrical firmament. He projected a tightly controlled energy and was already employing that awesome accuracy for which he later became famous. We three boys – his fictional colleagues – would sit down every night at the start of the show and happily watch him fly.

The other big star of the evening was playing a character that has little to do with the principal plotline. This is Don Armado, a Spanish knight, who, for some unexplained reason, is living in a small house on the King's estate. He is desperately in love with a young woman, who sadly seems indifferent to his advances. He also has a rival for her hand and this rival, who is a simple country clown, appears to enjoy more success than the Spanish knight. Don Armado is sad, dignified, ridiculous and, in many ways, magnificent. His use of the English language is, to put it mildly, idiosyncratic; but it has its own peculiar, mangled beauty. I presume that, in late Elizabethan England, it was acceptable to think of Spanish men as both absurd and dangerous and, therefore, they were fair game for playwrights. I also know that, as Elizabeth came to the end of her reign and James prepared to ascend the throne, readers began to show a more sympathetic interest in Spanish writers. The literature pouring out of Spain became rather fashionable in England. This was the period when Cervantes's *Don Quixote* first appeared in English; and, although *Love's Labour's Lost* predates that seminal event, there is something quixotic about Don Armado.

The actor who played him in our production was called John Wood. In the same period of his life, he also took on King Lear and Prospero. So he was a very busy man. I'd never met an actor quite like him. He was ferociously clever – I was told he read law at Oxford – and any script that was given to him underwent severe forensic examination. I watched him many times in performance, in different plays, and I knew that there was not a word or a thought or an emotion that was not both worked through, often reappraised and fully invested. His vocal dexterity was legendary. It was no surprise to learn that he had become famous for his work in Tom Stoppard's plays. I don't know whether he had a beautiful voice – whatever that might be – but he understood and used the full range of its expressive potential.

A few months after his death in 2011, I was invited to read at his memorial service. This was a somewhat daunting prospect, since the passage that had been chosen came from Stoppard's *Travesties*, a play in which John had triumphed many years previously. After I had read my piece, I returned to my seat. They then played a recording of John's voice. He was performing one of Prospero's most beautiful speeches. This type of tribute – the chance to hear an old recording – has recently become something of a fashion at actors' memorial services. It wouldn't have been possible a century ago, of course. What came through the sound system this time was an elaborate and virtuosic display of vocal technique. It was thrilling. Here was an actor absolutely aware of his voice as an instrument – or, rather, as an orchestra. And the display wasn't meaningless. The voice perfectly matched the sense of the verse. It also, incidentally, sounded like something from a period long ago, a lost age, although it could only have been twenty years since John had recorded the speech. I whispered to Nick Hytner, who was sitting beside me, that nobody would accept John's style of acting now. People would think it was unnecessarily baroque. 'Oh no,' Nick replied. 'They would accept it, but only if the actor himself really believed in it.'

It was a reminder that actors fool themselves if they consider their particular performance style as somehow truer than what has gone before. Naturalism is always a shifting and receding target, after all. There is no acting that is absolutely realistic – especially with a writer as complex as Shakespeare. Furthermore, there are many roads to truth and many different destinations. Garrick was as truthful as Burton, Sarah Siddons as Judi Dench.

John Wood could also deliver surprises – a result of his desire to reinvent, I guess. There was a marvellous moment in his King Lear, which I should have found the courage to steal when I came to play the part myself. At a point late in the story, Lear loses his mind and, wandering through the Kentish countryside, comes across an old friend and his son. He stays to talk; and, while talking, he sees a mouse – he may be hallucinating – and offers it an imaginary piece of toasted cheese. John's mouse was huge, the size of an elephant. The piece of cheese that was offered was similarly large. Lear was simultaneously terrified and fascinated by the giant rodent; and the scene was, consequently, both funny and disturbing.

While watching John's work, it occurred to me that, at least with a writer as complex as Shakespeare, it is imperative that an actor locate and clarify the sequence of thoughts before attempting any exploration of the emotional landscape. This is more difficult than it sounds; and, conversely, it is all too easy to fall back on generalisations – Hamlet is essentially indecisive, for instance, or Prospero is noble. Many of the characters in Shakespeare – the majority, perhaps – are supremely articulate and if the complexity of their thoughts is presented clearly, then the details of their emotional life will follow. In other words, the expression of thought is an emotional activity. The results may very well be surprising. There are moments when Hamlet is decisive and Prospero ignoble.

The last time I saw John on stage was in Nick Hytner's production of *Henry IV* at the National Theatre in London. He had always been thin and wiry, but now he seemed skeletal. He had some difficulty breathing. The part he played was of an old man, Justice Shallow, who spends his time looking compulsively back over his life. Like all great actors, John had an instinct for mapping out a vast hinterland behind the words that he spoke. In this instance, though little was said, a history of youthful excitement – misremembered, perhaps, and glamourised – followed by a later disappointment and resignation was clearly evident. But there was something ruthless and unsentimental about John's interpretation, a determination in the character not to show any weakness or to compromise his dignity. John must have been aware that such efforts only made his Justice Shallow more ridiculous – and sadder. Like all his performances, it was a winning combination of rigour, complexity and delicacy.

Edgar

A couple of years after meeting John Wood, I worked with another actor whom many, including me, consider to have been great – Robert Stephens. Where John was sharp and tightly coiled, Robert was fleshy and expansive. John worried about everything – but especially his work. He seemed to have genuine doubts about his prodigious talent; Robert had a secure self-confidence. As I write this, I realise that the opposite may be simultaneously true. John could be imperious; and Robert struggled with his demons. Robert wasn't proud or self-important. I would regularly spot him, after the Saturday evening show, queuing patiently with everyone else for the one coach out of Stratford. As he waited, he clutched a couple of plastic bags. The last stage performance he gave, before his death in 1995, was as King Lear. I was cast as Edgar. Robert had drunk heavily throughout his life and was frequently ill during the long run, but he never uttered a word of complaint. When I played Lear, I complained all the time – of tiredness, of a series of aches and pains – so I consider Robert's self-control and restraint almost superhuman. On stage and in rehearsal, he could access big emotions and made some brave choices – an indication of his imaginative power. Some worked, some didn't; but when he was on top form, he was electrifying.

Robert tried an unusual reading in one rehearsal, which was dropped almost immediately. At the time, I thought it was wonderful. Late in the play, Lear, keening over the corpse of his daughter, fails to recognise an old friend, who steps forward to offer his king some support. The excuse Lear gives for his weakness is simple: 'I am old now,' he says. In normal circumstances, the word 'old' is stressed – it's the natural focus of the thought. Robert decided one day to stress heavily the word 'now', and accompanied this with a violent, downward jab of a finger – as if to locate precisely the time and place. It's a tiny change; but suddenly it was clear that, up until this point, his Lear had never really, in his heart, believed that he was old. Whatever he might have said on various occasions, he had never considered that he was frail or incapacitated. Only now, holding his dead child, anticipating his own death perhaps, does he recognise that he is properly old.

I wish, as with John Wood's giant mouse and the enormous piece of cheese, I had used Robert's discarded idea when I came to play Lear myself. But I didn't. I don't know why.

Before I started on the show with Robert, in 1993, I was talking one day with Imelda Staunton. She knew I was going up to Stratford to begin working on Edgar and she asked who was playing King Lear. 'I'm not sure,' I replied, 'I think he's called Robert Stephens.' She was appalled, and explained how big a star Robert had been in the past. I knew nothing of this. Imelda told me that he had been married to Maggie Smith; and that the two of them were the power couple of British theatre in the sixties and seventies. As a young woman, Imelda went to see Robert in the first production of *The Royal Hunt of the Sun* by Peter Shaffer. Robert played the god-king Atahualpa – 'one of the most beautiful things I have ever seen on stage', Imelda said.

The part of Edgar is a large one. In the first quarto edition of the play, he is given his own paragraph on the title page. This mentions King Lear, of course, and then we read that the story includes 'the unfortunate life of Edgar, son and heir to the Earl of Gloucester and his sullen and assumed humour of Tom of Bedlam'. It's an unusual, though not unique, place to find such a long and elaborate description of a subsidiary character. The printers must have known that Edgar would be of great interest to the first audiences and readers. I was flattered to be asked to play him, because I anticipated that he would be interesting and knew that he would be a challenge. I had heard that many actors have found him difficult and some unsatisfying. I read a passage by a Shakespeare academic recently that describes him as boring. Edgar has a half-brother – Edmund – who is sexy and dynamic and very unpleasant; he always appears to be more fun to play than Edgar. I hoped my experience would be different.

I'm not sure that I succeeded in changing the old narrative. I knew what I wanted to do with Edgar but, in retrospect, I fell short. The performance wasn't a disaster, but it was less complete than I had hoped. As the short mention on the cover of the quarto might imply, Edgar's story is complicated. It starts like this: Edgar is the only legitimate son of the Earl of Gloucester. Edmund, his illegitimate half-brother, persuades their father that Edgar is planning to kill him. A death warrant is issued and Edgar is forced to flee. He disguises himself as a mad beggar – Poor Tom.

We're only halfway through, but already questions need to be answered. Before his transformation into Poor Tom, Edgar is seen very little. He barely speaks. Apart from some harmless and fleeting banter with Edmund, there is almost nothing else for an actor to latch onto. What kind of man is he? We can't say. Here is one of those gaps in Shakespeare's writing that I have already talked about; but, in this instance, the gap doesn't feel to me like a missed opportunity, as with Malvolio, or a mystery resonant with possibilities, as with Hamlet. It seems that Shakespeare wants Edgar, at the start of his story, to be a blank page, as it were. It's a deliberate choice. I decided to carry a book in my very first scene, which I felt implied that Edgar is a quiet and thoughtful young man – in contrast to his wilder half-brother. It wasn't necessary. For all we know, he's never read a book in his life. Perhaps it's better that we don't know anything about

Edgar's thoughts and feelings. If things are left as simple as possible, then there are no psychological complications to negotiate as Edgar transforms himself into the beggar; and it also allows for his other transformations.

Because Edgar changes his identity more than once. He plays many different consecutive roles. During his short period as Poor Tom, the mad beggar, he meets his father, who has been thrown out of his home and, appallingly, blinded by the king's son-in-law. Despite his profound shock, Edgar doesn't reveal his true identity to Gloucester. He sticks to his adopted persona of Poor Tom, but, since his father wants to go to the coast near Dover, he offers his help as a guide. Later, Gloucester will confess that, at this point, standing in despair at the cliff's edge, he believed the mysterious man beside him to be a demon. It gets more complicated. Tom changes slowly and imperceptibly from Poor Tom into a more neutral figure – a Kent countryman, perhaps. He uses a new, thick, rural accent as he challenges and then kills a man who is threatening his father. The two men arrive in Dover just as the final battle for control of the kingdom begins. Edgar disappears for a short period and reappears as an unnamed knight. He challenges his brother to a duel and kills him. Only then, in the last moments of the play, as he takes off his final disguise, do we see the real or – more accurately, I suppose – the basic Edgar.

It's a dizzying journey. It is possible that Edgar's function, or functions, are more significant than his character. In other words, is what he does more important than who he is? He plays a series of parts; and it seems that the unconscious aim of this series is essentially redemptive. Paul Rhys, in his wonderful performance for Richard Eyre at the National in 1997, understood this. Indeed, there was something Christ-like about his Edgar. Paul can effortlessly access that quality. So can Tom Brooke, who played Edgar when I finally played King Lear in 2014. I'm not sure that I could. But I desperately wanted to.

How does one locate and exercise this nebulous, spiritual quality? Clearly, I had a few hurdles to clear. Adrian Noble, the director of our 1993 production, employed a movement director in the rehearsal room. We had to work together to find a physical vocabulary for the various disguises that Edgar adopts through the play – Poor Tom in particular. It is implied that Poor Tom, being a beggar, is naked, exposed to the elements; and the elements are, for a good part of the play, ferocious. I wore a small loincloth and my body was covered in a light clay. As he develops his first disguise, Edgar talks of self-harm with 'pins, wooden pricks, nails'. So my skin had a number of small, bleeding puncture marks. This strange, savage image had to be matched with an appropriate choreography. The movement director thought that I should aim to look like a figure in an El Greco painting – appropriately spiritual and anguished, I suppose. I replied that, as far as I could remember, El Greco figures were all thin, bilious and seven-feet tall; and that this might be a bit of a push for me. Perhaps, I said, Brueghel would be an easier option – something more earthy, in other words. I was reassured that all would be well; and we went for El Greco. I spent much of my time stretching my arms up to the skies, trying to look taller and thinner. It was odd, but then, by definition, so is Poor Tom.

When in disguise, Edgar matches the way he speaks to the way he looks. In presenting a man who has ostensibly lost his mind, he proves to be supremely skilful in his employment of a radically new voice. The transformation is extreme. There is no possible naturalistic explanation for this; nor need we look for one. Edgar is simply fulfilling his function in Shakespeare's story. The playwright wanted to focus on 'unaccommodated man'; and so chose to present a character who has nothing – no food, no clothes, no home. Poor Tom is also, in the eyes of Lear (who meets him as a great storm is raging around them), a 'noble philosopher'; and, therefore, the writer ensures that his speech must change too. He must speak elliptically. Lear could then easily read his gnomic pronouncements as expressions of wisdom. I know no other character in Shakespeare whose thought processes are as unfathomable as Poor Tom's. The Fool, who, in the early stages of the play, never leaves the king's side and who also specialises in oblique commentary, sees Poor Tom as a threat. Or rather, he did in our production. Our Fool became very truculent and rather needy as he saw his role as Lear's confidant – and a sage – superseded.

During my time with Edgar, I was introduced to a psychiatrist called Murray Cox. In his professional life, Murray dealt with very disturbed and dangerous people – many of them criminals, in fact. He was an enthusiastic reader of Shakespeare and was particularly fascinated by Poor Tom. He used *King Lear* as a therapeutic tool. He wrote a book about his techniques – a signed copy of which he once gave me. His method of treatment had started when Murray had shown one of Poor Tom's speeches to a recalcitrant and incommunicative patient and the latter had responded positively to a particular line:

> *'Nero is an angler in the lake of darkness.'*

Nobody knows what this line means; but we can all follow the components of the image and, even if we can't define it further, the thought, as a whole, has a dark, magnetic power. I was not surprised to hear of the patient's response. To be honest, all of Poor Tom's language is evocative of something – indefinable though it may be. It's expressive of mental and physical pain, certainly, but also of defiance, even aggression. In addition, Poor Tom seems to be on a search for some meaning in a life that is otherwise ignored and insignificant. This quality – a sort of pained puzzlement – is something that Tom Brooke captured perfectly in his performance of Edgar at the National. Edgar as Poor Tom, perhaps even in his other disguises, wants answers; which is why stretching upwards towards a godless (or, maybe, God-filled) sky seemed, after my initial doubts, appropriate.

Later in the play, Edgar will appear as an instrument of retribution – the mysterious knight who kills his evil brother. So, perhaps, in his story, we can see a shift from a hidden anger through an anger that is half-acknowledged to an anger that is fully focused. This was a journey that I felt I had the equipment to chart. I might find Christ-like qualities difficult to play, but I can do anger. Edgar must, of course, be enraged by his initial banishment; but it is the sight of his blinded father that I used to fuel his onward journey and to inspire his final appearance as a warrior. It's always been a puzzle for the actor playing Edgar that he keeps his real identity hidden from his wounded father. Actually, it puzzles everybody. R. A. Foakes, a distinguished editor of the play, sees no credible reason for his behaviour 'except in terms of the needs of the plot'. Edgar, it seems, tries to bury his fury. Perhaps this suppression of his real feelings is necessary if he is to continue to play his part in the story. However, it occurred to me that he might find his father's mutilation so appalling that his response, despite his best efforts, is violent. If his father has lost his eyes, then those responsible should lose theirs. When he murdered Oswald, the time-serving courtier who threatens to kill Gloucester, my Edgar took the staff he was carrying and used it to batter Oswald's head, attacking his eyes again and again. At the end of the duel with Edmund, as his brother lies defeated on the ground, Edgar went to gouge out his eyes – old-fashioned retributive justice, I suppose.

However, I'm not sure that an Edgar who finds it difficult to control his anger necessarily helps the final moments of the story. The last voice we hear in the play is Edgar's. Sometimes the final speech is entrusted to Albany, Lear's son-in-law. The early editions leave us these two options. But, either way, the man who takes over the kingdom after Lear's death is recognised as both virtuous and honourable. This is important. It seems that, after the horrors we have witnessed, peace will be restored. However, many people read the end of *King Lear* differently. They don't trust this sense of restored order. The end of many Shakespeare plays presents a similar difficulty. I've already talked about the possibility that Hermione might not forgive Leontes at the end of *The Winter's Tale*. In *Richard III*, are we to take Richmond's promise of stability at the end of the play at face value? Knowing what we know about the historical Richmond, can we trust that, as King Henry VII, he will rule wisely and well? Is Katherina's speech of submission at the end of *The Taming of the Shrew* genuine or ironic? What about the triumph of Christian values at the end of *The Merchant of Venice*? All of these examples have made people anxious; and, of course, this is by no means an exhaustive list.

The truthful – and tentative – answer to all these questions is that it depends. It depends on the nature of the production and the instinct of the actor. Sometimes I find a particular problem insurmountable. I personally feel that the end of *The Merchant of Venice* is repulsive and I'm not sure that any presentation of it can render it acceptable. Despite his sympathetic portrait of Shylock and his repudiation of antisemitic violence, Shakespeare does not challenge the Christian triumph in any meaningful way. An ironic reading of Katherina's last speech in *The Taming of the Shrew* seems forced to me; but a public submission of a wife before her husband is clearly problematic for a modern audience. So there is not always a solution, easy or otherwise. The most convincing reading of this passage that I ever saw – from the actress Alexandra Gilbreath, in Stratford in 2003 – was absolutely genuine; but it was a free and conscious declaration of love rather than an enforced submission. She ostensibly did what Shakespeare and her new husband asked of her, played it without comment or distortion, but acknowledged that some internal qualification is needed if the scene is to be acceptable to a contemporary ear.

(Incidentally, some years after the appearance of *The Taming of the Shrew*, John Fletcher, one of Shakespeare's younger colleagues, wrote a play called *The Tamer Tamed*. It served as a riposte to the central assumptions of the earlier Shakespeare work. The male protagonist is Petruchio, who is also a leading figure from *The Taming of the Shrew*. At the beginning of Fletcher's play, we find out that Katherina has died and Petruchio has remarried. His new wife does not respond to the abusive treatment that appeared to work on Katherina and she exacts an aggressive, if comic, revenge. Clearly, if Shakespeare's play did not seem to celebrate the benefits of a submissive, docile wife, then this satirical response would not have been written.)

In contrast, it's sometimes better to leave the final moments of a Shakespeare play alone, free of interpretative complications, even if there is a temptation for the actor to go for a more sophisticated, nuanced reading. I think that Edgar's last speech, Richmond's pledge on winning the crown from Richard III and Hermione's attitude to her repentant husband are best played without irony. I'm pretty confident that this is what Shakespeare intended and that he was aiming for resolution and not instability, however valid the idea of instability might be. This is a challenge, I know. In some ways, a 'straight' reading is more difficult to play than other options, because it requires an absolute self-belief on the part of the actor. Cynicism is easy; it feels safe. It's often more interesting to perform. It's not easy – and, of course, some would say that it's deluded – to trust completely that Hermione can forgive or that Richmond and Edgar will usher in a better world. But I believe that, in these and many other instances, the promise of a better world is what the playwright was aiming for.

At the same time that I was playing Edgar, I was involved in a production of *Troilus and Cressida*. This show was memorable for many things – but particularly for a spectacular cast list. I look back now and marvel that the RSC managed to assemble such a weight of talent in a single production. One of this dazzling group was an actor called Norman Rodway. It so happened that he and I shared a hour-long break during each performance. It was during these breaks, over a long two years, that Norman, who was older than I was, taught me about cryptic crosswords. Within a few years, I was an addict.

At home, when I was a teenager, my father and brothers used to tackle the crossword in one of the daily broadsheets, albeit in a rather desultory fashion. I never joined them in this exercise, claiming that I didn't have 'the right kind of brain'. I've heard this excuse many times since, from all kinds of people, and, needless to say, it's nonsense; or rather, in order to complete a bog-standard, regular cryptic crossword – not one of the more fiendish puzzles one sometimes comes across – no special skills are needed, just the patience and the desire to learn a host of verbal tricks. Unaccountably, and much to my own surprise, I was persuaded by Norman to put in the work. Every evening that we were playing *Troilus and Cressida*, I would walk to the theatre, clutching my copy of the *Guardian*, and, sitting at my place in the communal dressing room, under Norman's beady supervision, I would try to solve the daily puzzle. Months went by before I managed a clue on my own. I can still recall Norman's look of bemusement when, for the hundredth time, I failed to grasp something that was blindingly obvious to him and that he felt didn't need further explanation. However, despite the slow progress, he (and I) persisted. Time passed. The company moved from Stratford to Newcastle and then on to London. I was still plugging away, every day, with little to show for my efforts. Finally, a year after I had begun this adventure, sitting on a London tube train and without Norman by my side, I managed to complete a crossword all by myself – a significant and memorable triumph.

I can't explain why I love an activity at which I've never been anything more than mediocre. One of my brothers, Andy, is so quick in finding solutions that I always struggle to keep up with him – he clearly has 'the right kind of brain' – and, in his company, I'm regularly reminded of my limitations. I suspect that I keep trying, despite repeated frustrations, because I think crosswords are beautiful – and witty. As many solvers will tell you, some of the clues make you laugh out loud. And, in addition, the history of crosswords is fascinating. During my long apprenticeship, I learned how they had started in the USA, how a distinct British style developed, how the rules were determined and by whom, who the most famous setters were and why they were so good. As it happened, Norman was friendly with the greatest setter of recent times. The latter, like all his crossword colleagues, used an alias – Araucaria. His real name was John Graham. He lived a very long life – well into his nineties – and kept working to the end. In fact, he told his host of fans about the cancer that would kill him (and the treatment he was undergoing) in a crossword published in the *Guardian* in January 2013. It was a gesture that was simultaneously resigned, blackly humorous and self-mocking; and it was considered important enough to be mentioned on that day's evening news. I was lucky enough to bump into Araucaria a couple of times, once at a birthday party and once at Broadcasting House in London, when we were both guests on a BBC radio documentary about crosswords. At the time of this latter event, Norman was seriously ill and in hospital. I managed to send a message to let him know that I was meeting one of our heroes. Norman was ultimately responsible for this piece of luck, after all, and, of course, I wanted to show off. I heard later that, on hearing my message, he muttered that I was 'a lucky bastard' – and undeserving. Not long after, and only a few hours before the broadcast, Norman died. He never heard the programme or my singing his praises.

Crosswords were also one of the reasons why I got to know Stephen Sondheim, a man whom many would agree was a bona fide genius. I can't remember exactly how we were first introduced – it must have been through Sam Mendes – but, during one of my visits to New York, I was invited to join Stephen for dinner in his apartment. I had never worked for Stephen and, frankly, it was unlikely that I would ever do so. (In fact, the only time I ever sang any of his music was for a birthday celebration at the Albert Hall in London; and I guess that I was involved with that event because I was a friend rather than because of my experience of performing Stephen's work.) So our dinner date had no professional subtext and was, consequently, an easy, if extraordinary, evening.

After we had eaten, we played through some of the music that Stephen was writing at the time. This was what a friend of mine would have called 'a New York moment' – one of those occasions when one can't quite believe what is happening or how one got there. This sense of unanticipated delight was compounded by the fact that Stephen's piano overlooked the rear of an apartment where Katharine Hepburn used to live – something that my host gleefully pointed out to me. We talked about Stephen's music, of course, but also about his interest in puzzles. He told me that as a young man he had loved theatrical thrillers – indeed, years before, he had co-written one – and that he regretted that the genre had died out. He also told me of his interest in the British cryptic crossword – a very different beast from the equally difficult American crossword. In fact, for a short period, he had submitted cryptic crosswords that he himself had composed for a New York magazine, but they hadn't caught on and the series had died out. I left him at the end of the evening, after too many Martinis, to return to my rather drab midtown digs, walking on air.

We were never close friends, but we would meet when he was in London and take in a couple of plays together. I loved his company and I liked the fact that we never needed to discuss our work, except in the most general terms. I must admit, too, that it was thrilling to be asked to escort such a giant on his visits to the theatre. And he gave me, some time after our first dinner, a packet containing a collection of his own cryptic crosswords. I confess that I have not tried to solve any of them. They are, no doubt, fiendish.

7

In those days, after a year in Stratford, the company would move to Newcastle. This visit was a regular annual event. During our short stay in the city, we presented our entire repertoire – about twelve plays – in three different theatres. This sounds like a substantial workload – and it certainly was a heavy schedule for the crew and the technical teams – but for the actors, since there were very few rehearsals during the day, it felt like a holiday. Our time in Newcastle was party-time; and Newcastle, as everyone knows, is a great place to party.

Unlike many of my colleagues, I can't say that I went clubbing – a local speciality. It was a missed opportunity, perhaps, because there were a lot of different clubs to choose from. A couple of friends and I spent one night at the biggest gay club in the city, but it wasn't particularly enjoyable. I didn't have the courage to dance and felt like a lump. I drank too much and I didn't go again. There were, however, plenty of fine restaurants, great pubs and, of course, trips outside the city into some of the most spectacular countryside that England has to offer. We stumbled along the river in Durham, stretching our necks to glimpse, above us, through the trees, the oppressive bulk of the cathedral; we strode across the sand to Holy Island, pretending that we were medieval pilgrims; and, most memorably, we walked miles along the vast, inhospitable coastline that shone a pale grey in the winter light.

We unquestionably had a great time. There was only one concern that exercised us – and it was a minor one, perhaps. Once our visit to the northeast was over, we were due to travel on to London and take up residence in the Barbican Centre. There we would repeat the dozen shows that were already up and running; but we would also be asked to add a few more. In other words, new roles were on offer. There was no sense of any aggressive competition for these – the actors, as I remember, remained characteristically courteous – but people were anxious. Many, especially those who had just joined the company, had, despite working long hours over a long period, done very little on the stage that had challenged them. These were the 'spear-carriers' – as they were once disparagingly called. Officially, they were known as 'play-as-cast' – actors who had signed up for two years on the understanding that they would be cast when and where the company needed them. Some were given small speaking parts and sometimes these were actually interesting, but there was never any possibility that Hamlet or Rosalind might be on the cards; and so a great deal of their time was spent at the back of the stage silently supporting the leading players.

This is the sort of situation where the worthy idea of a semi-permanent company of actors comes under strain. It's not easy being a 'spear-carrier'. It can be frustrating, especially if you feel invisible and if promotion to bigger and better roles seems unlikely. I was lucky in that, during my first season with the RSC, I was asked to play 'named' parts. They might have been small, but they had some impact; and I was accorded some status by the company. I have the kindness of the casting director of the time, Joyce Nettles, to thank for this. After my first, disastrous audition for the RSC, she asked to see me. She really wasn't required to talk to me, but she clearly felt that I was in need of some guidance. Joyce told me that if I wanted to join the RSC at some point, it would be a good move if I were to go out into the wide world and gain some experience before coming back. I could then, with confidence, apply for decent roles, the first step on a ladder that might lead somewhere fulfilling. Needless to say, I took her advice and returned to the company with, I think, a little more to offer.

If, however, an actor decided to join the company and play as cast, then the unspoken hope on their part would be that, after a year or so, better roles would come their way. This, of course, was not always the case; so signing up was as much of a risk as an investment. A young actor could easily waste a year or two – or so it would seem to them. The workings of the company system were not predictable and the nature of any outcome was due to many factors outside anyone's control – talent and luck, principally. I still wonder whether the climb up the ladder could have been made more secure; but then I also wonder whether the notion of a national acting company, romantic though it is, remains a viable model. Maybe it can only work if permanent, lifelong salaries are on offer for the theatre practitioners; but, of course, the danger then is that a group of actors might calcify. Perhaps it's more fruitful to stick to the principle of casting each show from scratch.

I don't know the answer to this; and I'm not sure that I'm the best person to find a solution. I have a sentimental attachment to the idea of a semi-permanent company, because that's how I learned my trade. But so much has changed since I joined the RSC. I suspect that things were a little easier and simpler thirty years ago. Now it's much harder. For a start, there was then less competition from other media. Difficult choices have to be made these days and careers have to be planned. It is possible now for a talented young actor to launch their career by playing leading roles for television or in the movies and, with luck, playing them brilliantly. We – or, rather, many of us – didn't have such a range of seductive options. Movies were part of another world. Now they are a realistic option in this country and a long apprenticeship in the theatre is not particularly attractive or, frankly, interesting. I shared a car journey once with an old friend of mine, who had played, to great success, all the most important women in Shakespeare. She pointed out, rather sheepishly, that forty years ago she would, for that alone, have been recognised as a star. In contrast, I had a chat with an actor some years back – a man of prodigious talent – who told me that he planned to make his name in the movies and then come back to the theatre later in his career, when he would be assured of great parts – and full houses; and that is precisely (and triumphantly) what he did.

My instinct was that I would probably spend most of my career in the theatre, which felt like home, rather than in the movies, a scary *terra incognita*. If that was to be the case, then I needed to do something about my technique, which, frankly, was a bit rough around the edges. A great deal of what I learned during those first years at the RSC was, predictably, gleaned from watching other, more experienced actors. But more formal teaching was also on offer. For instance, there was a large department devoted to vocal training. Oddly, there was no particular interest in physical movement as a discipline and, therefore, no department devoted to that. But then I suppose this reflects the central tradition of British theatre, which has always been rooted in the words that actors speak rather than in the way they move. I think I'm right in saying that John Gielgud, who possessed one of the most glorious and recognisable voices of the last century, was once described as having the most 'meaningless legs' in the business. It didn't stop him becoming a star. That about sums it up.

There were also classes in verse speaking. These were compulsory, attended by everyone from the most experienced actors to those who were just starting out, and they were led by a man called John Barton. John was a genial, patriarchal figure, a teacher, academic, writer and director, who had helped to lead the company in its glory days – the days of Judi Dench, Helen Mirren, Ian McKellen, Alan Howard, Ian Holm. John seemed to me to be as old as the hills and I found him remote and terrifying. I don't think we exchanged more than a couple of words in all the years that I knew him. In retrospect, this is a shame, since it was clear, even to me, that John wasn't there to judge us. He was there to help; and he did this, as he chewed ceaselessly on his nicotine-soaked gum, by working with us on Shakespeare's sonnets.

The sonnets provide good material for lessons in verse speaking, but there are drawbacks. All technical matters can be covered pretty comprehensively – stress, metre, syntax and so on. They are also useful because each fourteen-line poem presents a single argument and the twists and turns of this argument need to be teased out, fully understood and, if spoken aloud, clearly presented. After all, similar rhetoric is used throughout Shakespeare's plays. There is even, in many of the sonnets, a 'turn' – introduced by a word such as 'so' or 'but' – when the writer changes direction and charges onward to his conclusion. Again, this provides a fine exercise for any actor preparing for Shakespeare's dramatic writing. But problems arise when, as sometimes happened in John's classes, the actor is asked to present one of the poems as if it were a speech in a play, to speak in the present tense, as it were. The words don't respond to that sort of emotional pressure. After all, the sonnets are about intense feeling 'recollected in tranquillity', as William Wordsworth would have it. They are written at one remove from the events that they describe. Consequently, the liberties that are acceptable, indeed desirable, in a dramatic situation – pauses, changes in volume and pace, crying, laughing – feel out of place, affected and unconvincing.

One of John's party pieces was speaking from memory a

passage out of Malory's *Morte d'Arthur*. It comprised a long list of names – the names of Arthurian knights, I presume. It sounds rather uninspiring, but, in fact, on the rare occasions that he could be persuaded to perform this passage, John was always mesmerising. He never hurried through the list. Every name was given time and space. It was as if he could see the men he was talking about and knew their histories. They became real and individual. The problem of lists might seem a rather odd and insignificant thing to worry about, but Shakespeare employs them quite often – most famously in *Henry V*, when the king reads out the tally of English and French warriors who have died in battle. Two of the parts that I have played, Macbeth and Thersites in *Troilus and Cressida*, employ long lists, both, as it happens, of animals. What John taught us was not be frightened of lists, not to skate through them as if they might be boring, but, rather, to relish each component. A good list can be spellbinding and, if they're embraced wholeheartedly, an actor can conjure up new, unfamiliar worlds.

John Barton was a supreme example of someone who effortlessly combined his roles as academic and theatre practitioner. There were others like him, of course, though perhaps less eminent than John. The fact is that when it comes to Shakespeare, work in the study and work on the stage have, for centuries, existed side by side; and both disciplines were well represented in Stratford. Alongside actors, directors and designers, the town was host to a large community of scholars. Not far from the RSC headquarters were both the Shakespeare Institute, an outcrop of the University of Birmingham – with a rather lovely garden – and the Shakespeare Centre, a modern building that housed a large collection of material about the playwright and that loomed over the house where he was born. Students and scholars came to Stratford from all over the world; and actors from the company were often invited to meet them. Some of these students were still at college, some were just starting out on their academic careers; but sometimes we would be asked to talk to very senior academics.

Around 1990, during the time that we were playing *Troilus and Cressida,* the Shakespeare Institute hosted a very grand international conference of scholars. Amanda Root, who was playing Cressida, was invited to meet them and, for some reason, I went along with her – to keep her company, I suppose. Cressida is one of those parts that provokes fiery debate among professional Shakespeareans and Amanda was understandably nervous at the prospect of talking about her. She pointed out to me that she had had no academic training herself and here she was, preparing to face a barrage of questions from a bunch of very clever people with very strong opinions – particularly about Cressida. I remember thinking that nobody at the conference knew the part as well as she did. She could say every word that Cressida spoke and had traced her every thought and emotion. In my mind, she had no need to worry. As it happened, the questions were kindly and generous and Amanda was, as everyone had anticipated, both modest and incisive.

Amanda's trepidation was not unusual. For a long time – centuries, in fact – it seems that actors have been wary of Shakespearean scholars. It was always assumed, I think, that whatever we did on stage would disappoint them, that we would fail to come up to their exacting standards. In actors' eyes, academics were essentially no different from professional critics; and sometimes their views seemed equally extreme. I have met scholars who believe that *Macbeth* and *King Lear* should never be performed, because any attempt to do those plays justice will fail. And, of course, they may very well be right; but that is no reason, actors would argue, to throw in the towel and stop trying.

In truth, it was more often the case that theatre practitioners were suspicious and defensive, rather than that academics were aggressive and judgemental; and the academics that I met during my first years with the RSC were eager to bridge the divide. Luckily, they happened to be really good company as well. The University of Warwick, just up the road, sent scholars to talk to us and, as I have said, we were regular visitors to the Shakespeare Institute and the Shakespeare Centre. Academia was changing. It seemed that a new type of literary analysis was developing – the now well-established genre of Performance Criticism. The scholars that I knew wanted to acknowledge that any performance of a great text is, by definition, an act of criticism. This was, for theatre practitioners, a marvellous development. The idea that actors and directors might have something valuable to say, something that can stand alongside more conventional academic criticism, is to be celebrated. I have a memory – accurate, I think – of reading the work of a scholar from an earlier generation who, talking about a particular line of verse in a Shakespeare play, pointed out that it was metrically absurd and, anyway, made no sense. The only explanation for this aberration that the scholar could come up with was that it must have been invented by an actor – a careless and incompetent actor, it was silently implied. Those days of scholarly contempt are long gone, I hope.

I did a couple of new plays in the 1987 London season after that first trip to Newcastle. I acted alongside Janet McTeer and Lesley Sharp, two of the greatest actors of my generation, so, for that alone, it was worth the extra effort. Neither of the two productions made much of a splash, if I'm honest, but then they were rather hidden away, playing in the smaller of the Barbican theatres, which was called the Pit. This studio space was buried deep in the bowels of the building. The story was that it had been built over the graveyard of impoverished plague victims – a plague pit, in other words – though nobody I talked to was able to confirm this. This subterranean theatre was somehow symptomatic of the difficulties of working in the Barbican Centre. There was lots to admire about the place, to be sure. The public areas and the main auditorium were grand and beautiful; the location, so close to the heart of the financial district, was exhilarating; but life backstage was rather grim. A great deal of our working life was spent underground. The only windows in the series of dressing rooms opened out on to the ramp that led down to the car park; so there was not much light or air and rather too many exhaust fumes. A few floors below the dressing rooms, next to a small canteen, two rooms were set aside for rehearsals; but they were never used – presumably because with so little oxygen available, any rehearsals would have ended with the cast lying unconscious on the floor.

It was while I was at the Barbican that I was asked, once our London residency was over, to go back to Stratford and join the new season. I had spent such a happy couple of years with the RSC and so enjoyed life in a large company that I found it easy enough to accept the offer. My mission – and the director Adrian Noble really made it sound like a mission – was to study Restoration comedy and, in particular, the character of the fop. I was to act in three plays. They included a piece from early in the reign of Charles II, George Etherege's *The Man of Mode*; a comedy from later in the period, George Farquhar's *The Constant Couple*; and a play by a living writer, Edward Bond, called *Restoration*. All three included a figure who could loosely be described as a 'fop' and, to my delight and despite my worst fears, they all proved to be very different.

Plays from the Restoration period have fallen out of fashion. Over the last few years, their eclipse has been almost total and they are seen very rarely indeed. There are good, or, at least, understandable, reasons for this. For a start, comedy dates; the plays are no longer thought to be very funny. Secondly, the sexual politics that underpin them seem unacceptable, even offensive. In addition, there are hidden issues and unspoken questions about the slave trade not far below the surface. Finally, the language is elaborate and self-conscious; we, both performers and audience, find that increasingly difficult to understand and enjoy.

I suppose it's predictable that I find this sad. However, I wouldn't say that, even after a long time living with them, I'm an uncritical fan of Restoration comedies – some of them are rather irritating, in fact – but, at their best, I think they still have a great deal to say to us. A play such as *The Man of Mode*, the most complex of the three that I was involved in, resonates directly with the world we live in. It's a very dark piece, cynical and unforgiving, which explores cruelty, self-loathing, narcissism, sexual predation, stalking, social ambition – things that concern us just as much as they did our Restoration forebears. There must be a way of looking behind the arch dialogue, the fluttering of fans and the absurd periwigs to locate familiar human characteristics.

Our 1988 production of *The Man of Mode* was directed by Garry Hynes, who was, at the time, enjoying huge success leading her own theatre company, Druid, in Ireland. Garry was physically tiny and intellectually charged. She did not shy away from the darker elements of the story and her judgement of the characters' behaviour was often, quite rightly, severe; but, surprisingly, she was keen to allow the fop, who was called, unimaginatively, Sir Fopling Flutter, the benefit of the doubt. She seemed to like him. This is unusual. Fops are not likeable. They are men who are obsessively, almost pathologically, fashion conscious. Their principal concern in life is how to earn the approval and admiration of other members of high society. They are also oddly sexless and, as a result of their egomania, solitary. They are, above all, ridiculous.

Fops often look absurd – like a male version of Edwina in *Absolutely Fabulous*. But Garry wanted Sir Fopling to look gorgeous, wearing essentially the same clothes as his colleagues – just in slightly brighter colours. Where they wore black, he wore midnight blue. Their shirts were white, his were of the same design but in a pale lilac. Sir Fopling was his own living work of art; and the result was good. The reason why his companions laugh at him is not because he fails at what he does but rather because he succeeds brilliantly, and because, inevitably, this self-presentation, this work of art, is all Sir Fopling thinks about. I'm not sure that he is even aiming for social advancement; the admiration of his peers would have been quite enough to satisfy him. His behaviour – the exquisite manners, the care taken over his appearance – was not the means to an end, but an end in itself. Consequently, the laughter of those around him was crueller than it sometimes seems. It was aimed not at mere affectation or, more seriously, at an unattractive ambition, but at the very core of the fop's existence. Even if he had noticed his friends' derision, Sir Fopling wouldn't understand it and, anyway, couldn't painlessly change his behaviour. Indeed, he doesn't change, in any noticeable way, during the play; and neither, of course, should he have to. After all, his version of self-love causes no real harm. He doesn't need to be punished. As it happens, it's as if, after the story is done, he will float away mildly humiliated, but essentially unharmed, and try his luck elsewhere.

Two moments in the production stood out for me. At one point, all the characters gather together for a masked ball. Sir Fopling is, of course, invited. He arrives fashionably late – and in disguise. He is accompanied by a small number of attendants. They wear identical masks; and, in our production, these masks were all of Sir Fopling's face. Even Sir Fopling himself was disguised as Sir Fopling. It was ludicrous; but, because the gesture was without irony, the overwhelming egocentricity was somehow impressive. If, in Sir Fopling's mind, there was nobody on stage who could match his beauty, then he was doing everybody at the party a favour by bringing along five or six identical copies of himself.

After the run had ended, I asked if I could keep one of the masks, but I was refused. Years later, I was buying an interval drink at the bar in the Barbican and noticed all six or seven masks hung up as decoration on the wall behind the banked rows of bottles. I told the barman the story behind them and he kindly took one down and surreptitiously gave it to me. I still have it – in my study. I'm looking at it now, as I write.

The second moment was more melancholy. At the centre of the play is a gang of four wealthy, indolent men. Sir Fopling is one of them. Like the idle rich throughout history, they have little to do except drink, go to parties and hunt for sex. At one point in the play, after a disappointing evening, all four end up in Sir Fopling's small apartment. We worked out that this scene must be set in the middle of the night – four o'clock in the morning, say. One of the men has just indulged in a bout of unsatisfactory sex with a woman who has been obsessively following him for years. Again, we worked out that this encounter – an encounter that the woman had longed for – lasted for all of twenty minutes. The sex must have been either brutal or grimly uneventful. The men are all tired, angry and drunk. Sir Fopling is asked to sing a song. His companions expect to laugh at this, but Garry Hynes insisted that the song should be rather beautiful. After this delicate performance, Sir Fopling stands in front of a mirror in the corner of the room, staring at his reflection. When asked why he is doing this, he replies that studying his appearance is 'the best diversion of our retirements'. He then leaves to take a bath.

I found this unbearably sad. It was a short glimpse into the private life of a very lonely man. One could have guessed that Sir Fopling might be lonely, but what made the scene so sad, in Garry's production, was that he was also an innocent; and his innocence – and his firm belief that what he was doing with his life was worthwhile – gave him some dignity.

The other fops that I was asked to play were not as complex as Sir Fopling. One was a vile, abusive aristocrat and the other a boy up from the country who tries to make a splash in the big city – and fails, of course. This latter story was, at least in comparison with *The Man of Mode*, a predictable cautionary tale about the dangers of social climbing; but, again in contrast to the earlier play, it provided a light-hearted and generous evening in the theatre. The most important thing for me was that all three fops were very different. That was unexpected; and playing them led to a genuinely fascinating year of work.

The only odd thing was that, after four years with a company devoted to Shakespeare, I had performed in only one of his plays; and even that part was in prose. I had not said a line of Shakespeare's verse. For that, I would have to wait. In the next season, I would at last be trusted with some poetry: an important moment for me. Equally important was my first meeting with the director that I would go on to work with, on and off, for the next thirty-five years – Sam Mendes.

Two Servants

Thersites

When Dad became a brigadier, he and Mum went to live in Tidworth, a small garrison town in the middle of Salisbury Plain. I was enjoying my second season with the RSC, but would regularly travel down from Stratford or London to see them. I've not much to say about Tidworth. The town comprised hundreds of quarters, a mess or two, an athletics track, a golf club and a polo field. The latter was of only passing interest to my family, none of whom has ever had much interest in horses, and, predictably, I never used the athletics track (and I'm not sure my siblings did either), but the golf club became a significant part of my father's life. I once visited the clubhouse to meet him after a round, but I wasn't allowed inside because I was wearing jeans and a leather jacket. Some incomprehensible dress code seemed to be in play. I sat in the car, mildly pissed off and rather bored.

One of my favourite stories about Tidworth concerns the royal family. The old Duke of Gloucester – the brother of King George VI and a very senior figure in the British Army – was visiting the Middle East during the Second World War. In Cairo, he was introduced to a dancer. Some sources say that she was a local belly-dancer. The poor duke found himself at a loss for anything to talk about – a familiar problem for members of the royal family, I would guess – and, in desperation, fell back on the first thing that came into his head – 'Do you know Tidworth?' he barked. There is no record of how the dancer responded or whether she simply looked puzzled or blank. Perhaps she *did* know Tidworth and had a lot to say in reply. I don't know. Either way, I do hope the story is true.

Our quarters were a large, draughty house, built, I presume, in the early years of the twentieth century. It was called, reflecting the imperial confidence of the time, Jalalabad House. If my parents had been looking forward to some whiff of Mughal splendour, they must have been disappointed. All the rooms in the house were square and high-ceilinged. One attractive feature was a small vegetable garden, which I know Mum appreciated. Otherwise, it was a building that inspired little affection, as was the case with most of the quarters that my parents lived in over Dad's long military career. This is no surprise, since army housing was, for the most part, meant to be no more than functional and, in any case, no family stayed in any particular house for long. I can't remember with clarity any of the accommodation we lived in when I was young – except the house in Singapore, which was beautiful and which I revisited years later when I was on tour in the Far East. Most of the company of *The Winter's Tale*, with whom I was working at the time, decided to come with me. Our old house had been turned into a restaurant. It was closed and dark. Frankly, the trip was a bit of a damp squib and, since I had gone on at length to everyone in the cast about how lovely it was, I felt rather embarrassed.

The fact that we had to move so often put a tremendous strain on my mother. Predictably, she was responsible for getting the family out safely and for cleaning the property. Standards, as one might expect in the army, were very high indeed. Mum used to talk with dread of a man who would come to look over the house immediately prior to our departure. He would put on a pair of white gloves and, as part of a silent and protracted ritual, run his finger along the inside of the oven to check for any residue of dirt. I never saw this manoeuvre myself, but I have no doubt that it happened.

I was staying with my parents in Tidworth one weekend when, around dinnertime, the phone rang in the study. I call it a study, but in reality it was more of a storeroom than a place where anybody went to work. Mum got up to answer the phone and came back to tell me that a chap called Sam Mendes wanted to talk to me. Up to this point in my life, although we had met a couple of times, I had said barely two consecutive sentences to Sam; but I knew who he was and what an impressive reputation he enjoyed. When he was still in his early twenties, he had gone to work in Chichester as an assistant director. One of the plays that he was involved with – *London Assurance* by a nineteenth-century playwright called Dion Boucicault – lost its principal director halfway through rehearsal. Sam, though only a lowly associate, swept in to save the day, restore confidence and, finally, effortlessly, deliver a triumph. It made his name in theatrical circles and soon he was doing things like directing Judi Dench in the West End. The press began to call him a wunderkind, a label that soon became inappropriate and of which he himself grew rather weary. But they were essentially right. He was a wonder; and he was very young, clearly brilliant and, whatever private insecurities he may have felt, supremely confident.

So, of course, I took his call in the study of Jalalabad House. During our conversation, Sam offered me the clown – Thersites – in *Troilus and Cressida*. Oh dear, I thought, another clown. My heart sank; but I had to accept. Sam, at the time, was the most talked-of young director in the business; and, anyhow, he has always been an expert in the arts of persuasion. I'm not being facetious when I say this; I mean it quite seriously. His persuasive skills have meant that, throughout his career, he has been as successful a producer as he is a director. This was part of the reason why his leadership of the small London theatre, the Donmar Warehouse, which he began to revitalise in 1990, around the time we started working together on *Troilus and Cressida*, was so dazzling. He always seems to know how to choose the right project at exactly the right time – and, usually, with exactly the right team behind him.

This was certainly true of *Troilus and Cressida*. The list of actors that Sam assembled was astonishing – though I suppose, given the collaborative nature of the company's casting policy, that was not entirely the result of his brilliance. More importantly, the production itself was a revelation, an object lesson in clarity and simplicity; and neither clarity nor simplicity is what people associate with *Troilus and Cressida*. It is a very tricky, knotty play. There is a large number of major roles. They are all, despite the title of the play, of equal status. There is more than one storyline for a director to deal with. The language is complicated and the rhetoric is sometimes Byzantine. Sam refused to disguise the difficulties; but neither did he over-elaborate or show off. For a young director, his production was a masterly display of restraint.

I remember one clear example of this restraint. Since the play is set during the Trojan War, Sam felt that it would be fun if the evening started with some display of fighting prowess, of unashamed machismo. He had seen footage of an American regiment that specialised in elaborate, ceremonial displays that involved spinning large guns in the air. These guns were tossed back and forth to fellow soldiers in ever more complicated patterns. Sam gathered together all his 'warriors', showed them some footage of the American soldiers and asked his actors to develop a similar routine – with spears. They spent hours on this, meeting every morning to put in an hour's practice before the day's rehearsal. In only a few weeks, they had something very special on their hands. But, just before we opened to the public, Sam decided to scrap the whole thing. Explaining his decision to his disappointed and weary cast, he pointed out that Shakespeare had decided to start the play with a relatively quiet, conversational scene about love, not combat, and that we should trust the playwright's judgement. There was no point in adding a display of barely repressed violence – however impressive it might be – just for the hell of it.

In our production, Thersites was not a warrior. I think I'm right in saying that in the Homeric poem, on which the play is based, he is a fighting soldier, but there is precious little indication of this in Shakespeare's play. Admittedly, the story is set in the middle of a truce, so, for most of the time, there's not much evidence of actual fighting by any of the characters. Achilles is sulking in his tent and, without their greatest fighter, the Greeks seem unwilling to engage with their enemy. So I suppose Thersites could be a soldier; he's just not fighting at the moment. But, even taking all this into account, it seems that, when we first meet him, Thersites is not expecting to go into battle himself. Rather, he is working as a servant – or batman, perhaps – for one of the senior warriors, Ajax. Interestingly, despite the fact that he appears to hate his job, Thersites takes pains to emphasise that this employment is voluntary. He is a free man. He is not a slave. He has chosen to be where he is.

It was important for me that, even if he doesn't expect to fight, Thersites should have some proper, recognised function in the Greek camp. At one point, Achilles calls him 'a privileged man' – in other words, a licensed fool. There are problems with this. Firstly, even if Achilles is speaking metaphorically and not describing Thersites' actual job, the role of licensed fool feels more Shakespearean than Homeric; or, rather, Shakespeare seems to be introducing a Jacobean figure into a Classical environment. This is entirely characteristic of the writer, of course, but here, in this play, I think it disempowers Thersites if one confines him to the role of fool. In the *Iliad*, Thersites is an angry man who believes he can speak truth to power. However, he is not employed to do so. I felt that Shakespeare's figure is similar. He is not like Feste in *Twelfth Night* or the Fool in *King Lear*. Furthermore, the job of professional jester has little resonance for me or, I suspect, for a contemporary audience. I may be wrong – this may simply be a prejudice of mine – but it's how I feel. So Sam and I decided to highlight my discomfort about the idea of licensed foolery. My Thersites carried a conventional joker's stick, jolly, brightly coloured and equipped with rather irritating bells, wherever he went. It was like a badge of office or, rather, a name tag on a lanyard. Thersites never really used it; but it served as a reminder of his lowly status and of the role that some might expect him to play. In other words, the furious tirades that characterise Thersites' attitude to the world around him may not be a professional requirement, but, rather, have a deeper source.

Pushing these ideas further, I found it useful that, rather than choosing not to fight, my Thersites is unable to do so for more fundamental reasons. Perhaps, I thought, he's not of the right class – all the warriors that we meet in the play are aristocrats. Perhaps, on the other hand, he is prevented from active service by some physical incapacity. I decided on the latter rather than the former. My Thersites ended up with, among other things, a severe limp. He would be a liability in battle. But, like the Cassius in *Julius Caesar* that I played later in my career, Thersites had grown up around the men with whom he now works; he was probably the sort of child who was patronised or ignored and who, unsurprisingly, reacted with violence or fury. I tried to register this shared, but unhappy, background in my costume.

My trousers were held up by a couple of ties, the most exclusive I could think of – an Old Etonian tie and an MCC tie. David Troughton, who played the Trojan hero, Hector, in our production and who was a devoted cricket fan, pretended to be horrified at the sacrilege of using the MCC tie as a rudimentary belt; but he realised that sacrilege was the whole point. I hoped that, if anyone noticed the ties, they would understand that Thersites is part of a world that he cannot escape and of which he is both admiring and contemptuous.

We designed my costume bit by bit. Anthony Ward, Sam's designer, had built a supremely elegant set – a floor of pale wood, a central, circular pool and, leaning against the back wall, a large, decayed Classical mask. This mask hinted at the satirical nature of Shakespeare's play. It was the sort of simple set that allowed the costumes to register clearly. These were eclectic in their components and not tied down to any particular period – certainly not the periods of the Trojan War or Shakespeare's England. Rather, each costume was, in essence, a thumbnail sketch of an individual character. For instance, Agamemnon, the incompetent and indecisive leader of the Greek forces, wore a breastplate, but over this was slung an old, moth-eaten cardigan covered in food stains. His hair and beard were unkempt. Pandarus, a wealthy and unpleasant member of Trojan high society, was given a rather splendid blazer and a boater – like someone you might have seen at the Henley Regatta in the Edwardian era. In contrast, Helen, the most beautiful woman in the world, wore a figure-hugging red dress that made her look, simultaneously, sexy and untrustworthy.

In my case, Anthony started with nothing – or rather, with just a few, unfocused ideas. It was one of the first times that I had worked with a designer in this way. In effect, we made it up as we went along; and the result was a rather glorious mess. I wore a string vest under an old mac – provided by Anthony himself – a pair of pinstriped trousers and heavy, rotting boots. This was the basic look; but there was more to come. I've mentioned the ties that served as a belt. I also had a tight leather cap that made my head look tiny. We had holes cut in it so that my ears stuck out. I didn't wash it for the length of the run – nearly two years – and by the end, thrillingly, it stank. I pinned two small badges to the lapel of my coat – a CND badge and a gay-rights pink triangle. These were both ironic, since Thersites, despite loudly declaring his aversion to war, finds it addictive; and he is also contemptuous of Achilles spending so much time lounging around with his male lover, Patroclus. One final flourish was the decision that he should wear gloves.

Achilles calls Thersites a 'crusty botch of nature', and so I imagined that the latter's skin would be flaking, pustulant and sore. It was as if, over the years, he had contracted a whole host of diseases. I felt that, in order to protect his hands, Thersites would have to wear gloves. Originally, these were white – like those of a butler. After all, at the beginning of the play, he's working as a servant. But, in the final analysis, I felt that these gloves looked too clown-like. I then remembered a boy at school who, before he went to bed, had to put plastic bags over his feet to protect his flaking, painful skin. So Anthony and I replaced the white cotton gloves with surgical plastic ones. I discovered later that as I wore them, my sweat would turn the plastic from an opaque grey into a nicotine yellow. One day, by chance, I put them on the wrong way round and this distorted the shape of my hands. My little fingers were pulled away and my thumbs were drawn closer to my palms. My hands had turned into claws.

I also used a make-up technique that I first heard about while watching, years before, the television coverage of the wedding of Prince Charles and Lady Diana Spencer. As we all know, Lady Diana blushed easily. Her make-up artist for the day told us during the commentary that she was worried that the pressure of the occasion might bring the blood to the bride's face and so she had put a layer of green moisturiser under Lady

Diana's foundation. I had never heard of such a thing as green moisturiser, but now I rushed to the local chemist and bought some. I applied it to my face, but I didn't cover it with foundation. Gratifyingly, all the colour was drained from my skin and I looked very ill indeed.

So, slowly, Thersites appeared – in his full glory. Years ago, I read a study of acting that compared actors who worked 'from the inside out' to those who worked 'from the outside in'. Laurence Olivier was held up as an example of the latter type. He worked hard on his appearance in each role that he played and prided himself on the physical transformations that he achieved. In contrast, some of his fellow performers were more concerned with creating a new internal life and less with how they looked. The writer of the study implied that one method was better – truer – than the other. It was the 'inside out' technique that earned his seal of approval.

Of course, things are never as simple as this neat dichotomy might imply. There is no doubt that my version of Thersites didn't cohere until I saw him in the mirror. The same applied to Richard III and to Ariel in *The Tempest* – both shows that, coincidentally or not, I did with Sam. In all these cases, how I looked was very important. But sometimes the costume is almost irrelevant. As I've grown older, I've found that I am increasingly happy with an anonymous shirt and a pair of unremarkable trousers. I'm also very happy to get rid of any shoes, wandering around the stage in socks or barefooted. I hope that this simplicity doesn't mean that the internal life of a character is less or more complex than that of someone who is elaborately dressed. I trust – as John Gielgud once said – that different projects demand different methods.

The power of Anthony's costume for Thersites lay in the fact that it fuelled the character's fury. Thersites looked terrible. He probably smelled worse. His legs ached and his hands hurt. There was no doubt that he was chronically unwell. Life for him is hard work; and this makes him very unhappy and very angry. In addition to the physical constraints he suffers, he is doing a job he hates. When we first see him, he has agreed to offer his services to Ajax, but Ajax is a man whom Thersites regards, with reason, as irredeemably stupid. Ajax beats Thersites regularly. Early in the play, he leaves Ajax and tries his luck with Achilles – a very different beast from his former employer. Achilles is refusing to fight after a row with his commander-in-chief. Since he is, by a long way, the most impressive warrior in the Greek camp, it is felt by his colleagues that it is imperative that Achilles return to the fighting. This is the storyline that runs alongside the love affair between Troilus and Cressida. As it happens, far from being persuaded by the arguments of his fellow generals, Achilles takes up his sword again only when his lover, Patroclus, is slain by the Trojans. Then, in his fury, he kills Hector, the greatest warrior on the opposing side.

As I see it, Thersites can't help admiring Achilles. Like many cynics, he has a sentimental, even romantic, streak. Like many satirists, he is conservative. In his mind, things are going from bad to worse. In the past, things were better, surely. Thersites believes in heroes; and loathes those same heroes when they disappoint him. This is why Patroclus is one of the principal victims of his venomous attacks. Patroclus is a junior member of the Greek hierarchy, but he has an intimate, loving relationship with one of the most senior – a real hero – and Thersites sees this relationship as symptomatic of Achilles' abdication of responsibility and of his failure to fulfil his heroic potential. He tries to attack Achilles directly; but it doesn't really work. Achilles is mildly surprised, but not concerned, when Thersites sends a barb or two in his direction: 'What, with me, too, Thersites?' is the great warrior's response. As for the other generals, any criticism from Thersites is always well out of earshot. That leaves Patroclus – smaller prey – open to attack. Because Thersites, despite having the aggressive instincts of a bully, is a coward.

THERSITES: (*Troilus and Cressida*, RSC, 1990)

A genuinely funny clown – even after 400 years – and that's not something that can be said of many Shakespearean comic characters. The analysis he provides for the audience is always acerbic and consistently accurate.

EDGAR: (*King Lear*, RSC, 1993)

One of Shakespeare's most mysterious figures and a master of disguise: here he is with his blinded father (David Bradley) after an unsuccessful suicide attempt. Who is the real Edgar? That's a question that is almost impossible to answer.

KING LEAR: (*King Lear*, National Theatre, 2013)

I wonder if this is the greatest play – and the greatest role – that Shakespeare ever wrote. Here the king has just made the catastrophic decision to divide his kingdom in two. Chaos an misery inevitably follow – as the king's friend, the Earl of Kent (Stanley Townsend), predicts.

THE KING OF NAVARRE: (*Love's Labour's Lost*, RSC, 1990)

The king with his closest friend Berowne (Ralph Fiennes): the latter character is a wordsmith who can weave marvellous spells that bewitch all who hear him. All I had to do was keep quiet and listen.

Reg Wilson © RSC

ARIEL: (*The Tempest*, RSC, 1993)

Not a human being: he worked very hard our production and never left the stage. I order to give some sort of impression of t spirit world, he moved very, very slowly.

PROSPERO: (*The Tempest*, RSC, 2016)

This marked my return to the RSC after twenty-five years. The design was luxurious and elaborate, involving extraordinary technical wizardry. And a whole range of rich, deep colours.

Johan Persson/ArenaPAL

TIMON OF ATHENS: (*Timon of Athens*, National Theatre, 2012)

The moment when Timon, now destitute, discovered gold buried in the ground was difficult to pull off. It felt like something out of a fairy tale; and, furthermore, after the lucky find, Timon ignored it for the rest of the play.

Marilyn Kingwill/ArenaPAL

VOLPONE and *THE ALCHEMIST*: (Nationa
Theatre, 1995 and 2006)

My two attempts with the plays of one of Shakespear great rivals – Ben Jonson: the first with Michael Gambon and the second with Alex Jennings.

THE DEATH OF STALIN: (2017)

Armando Iannucci's wonderful film, which charts the improvisatory madness that follows the death of a dictator. Here the senior Politburo members gather around the body of their leader.

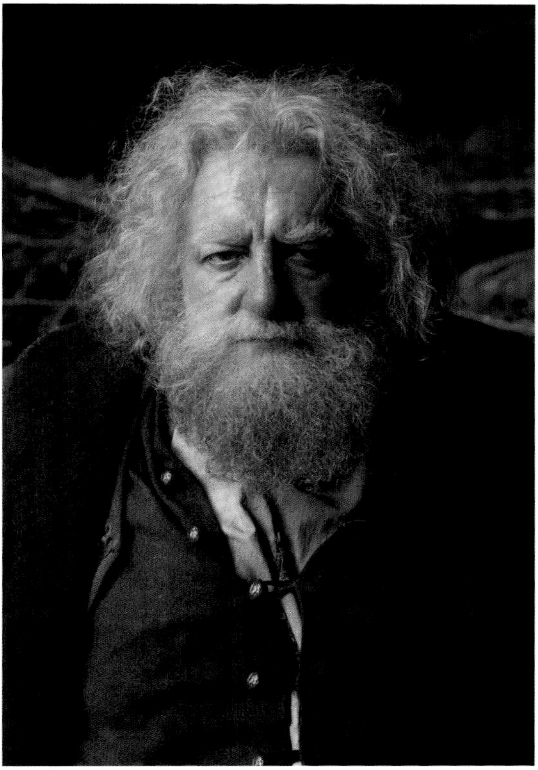

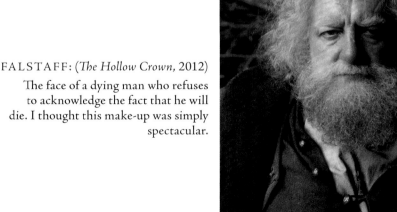

FALSTAFF: (*The Hollow Crown*, 2012)

The face of a dying man who refuses to acknowledge the fact that he will die. I thought this make-up was simply spectacular.

KING ARTHUR: (*Spamalot*, Broadway, 2007)
A new world: my first (and only?) genuine Broadway musical.

When Achilles is finally roused to action and marches out to fight Hector, his opposite number on the Trojan side, my Thersites was thrilled. At last, his hero was behaving heroically. I wanted to be there for the kill, despite there being nothing in the text to support this. Unfortunately, the death of Hector is simply grim; Achilles' tactics are underhand and despicable. At the back of the stage, Thersites screamed – a silent scream – as he watched a defenceless Hector being stabbed multiple times by the half-dozen Greek fighters whom Achilles had brought along with him. This scream started out as an expression of pain; but, over the course of the run, this pain was mixed, almost imperceptibly, with triumph. In the final analysis, Thersites, to his profound disappointment, has been proved right.

His experience of war is mirrored by his experience of love and sex – all at one remove, of course. By chance, he is a witness to the final moments of Cressida's story. After one night with Troilus, Cressida is forced to leave Troy and go over to the Greek camp. She has little choice but to forget her previous lover. Thersites watches as she decides to attach herself to another man – the Greek Diomedes. This is one of those moments in Shakespeare's work when the playwright's technical mastery is unquestionably awesome. The encounter between Cressida and her new lover is witnessed by Troilus and a Greek general, Ulysses, who are both hiding. All four are unaware that they are, in turn, being watched by Thersites – a double layer of eavesdropping, in other words. It feels like a darker re-run of the scene in *Love's Labour's Lost,* where the four young men listen to each other's love poems; but here, in *Troilus and Cressida,* the three contrasting lines of polyphony play simultaneously – Cressida careful, even tentative, with her new lover, Troilus burning with a sense of betrayal and Thersites gleeful, savage and self-righteous.

Thersites' judgement of Cressida's behaviour is unforgiving. It comes as no surprise that he is a misogynist; and it is equally predictable that, as far as I can judge, he has never loved, liked or even known any women. For him, Cressida is simply a 'whore'. I presume that a modern audience would find this offensive. After all, Cressida is in a very vulnerable position and, if she is to survive, she has few choices available to her. But, for Thersites, there is clearly no honour to be found in either love or war, whatever reasons or excuses may be put forward for either. In our production, as Cressida left the stage with Diomedes, she dropped a pale, diaphanous scarf. Thersites picked it up and held it to his nose. It smelled faintly of Cressida's scent – a smell far, far removed from a world of war. It stopped Thersites in his tracks, but only for a moment. Dismissing any compassion or sentiment, he spat out a string of words – words that could stand as his creed:

> *'Lechery, lechery, still wars and lechery; nothing else holds fashion!'*

We played *Troilus and Cressida* on the evening of 16 January 1991, when the UK declared war against Iraq – the beginning of the first, short-lived Gulf War. I rushed home after the show to switch on the television and watch, as so many of us did, the strange, green-lit pictures of the conflict as it unfolded. It was difficult to know what to think; I was watching a conflict that was in real time but as remote as some early computer game. I sat there for hours. I did the same night after night. War held fashion.

Ariel

When I was starting out as an actor, I never thought that I would one day be asked to play Ariel in *The Tempest*. I have been cast in many roles that I knew would be challenging. My critics would no doubt say that, all too often, I have been badly miscast. But Ariel is in a different league. For a start, he is not a human being. He is a spirit. Furthermore, he is a creature of air, fire and water. There is nothing remotely earthbound about him; and, as a human, I've always felt and looked quite earthbound. (Forgive me if I keep using 'he/him', rather than other pronouns, when I talk about Ariel. 'She/her', 'they/them' would be confusing and 'it' feels ugly and just plain rude.)

The Tempest, which opened in 1993, was the third show that I did with Sam Mendes. It tells the story of a man – a magician – who lives with his daughter on a small, remote island. He is called Prospero; she is called Miranda. Through his magic, Prospero is seen to control two creatures, both of whom were living on the island when he first arrived. He treats them as his slaves. One is Ariel; the other is 'a monster' called Caliban. There are other characters in the play, of course. Many of these would have suited me quite well. Indeed, when Sam first talked to me about the project, he asked whether I would be interested in playing Caliban. This seemed to both of us quite a good idea. It's a wonderful role, the portrait of a creature who is profoundly unhappy and frustrated. He is both violent and gentle, resentful and loving. He spends most of his time on stage with the comic characters, but Shakespeare still finds time to give him one of the most ravishing speeches that he ever wrote. It would, I told Sam, be a joy to play him.

The conversation that we had was on the phone and so Sam could not see my face. I'm not sure that my voice sounded enthused enough by his proposal. But, and I know this sounds arrogant, I wasn't surprised by his offer. If I were to do a production of *The Tempest* with Sam at this particular time, then everyone would expect me to play Caliban. It wouldn't exactly be surprising casting. Caliban was similar, in some ways, to many of the parts that I had been playing over the last few years. In other words, the timing wasn't quite right. I was unconsciously looking for something more demanding. However, I accepted Sam's offer. Of course I did; it would have been churlish not to.

Later, Sam told me that, after our phone call, he had had a conversation with a fellow director, who asked about his future projects. He talked about *The Tempest*. She enquired about casting. He mentioned Alec McCowen as Prospero. His colleague thought that was a great idea. He then told her that I might play Caliban. She nodded as if that was a predictable choice – which was not exactly the response he had been hoping for. A few days later, Sam rang me, withdrew his offer of Caliban and asked me to play Ariel instead.

It was an extraordinary change of direction. My stomach lurched with excitement. My first thought was that I didn't want to fly – a tradition that many Ariels followed in the old days. The image that this idea conjured up in my head was terrifying – a human Zeppelin floating above the stage. To be honest, I don't think many Ariels fly nowadays; so this wasn't a genuine worry. But Ariel, like Puck, his fellow spirit, has traditionally been a role that demands some pretty serious athleticism. Without flying or something equally light-footed, the challenge was to find a way of turning myself into a creature of air; and I had no idea how to do that.

I didn't find an answer for a long time. There were moments in rehearsal when I thought that I never would. My version of Ariel was the result of chance discoveries and lucky finds. There wasn't a clearly defined plan in my head. This was partly because, in Ariel's case, normal rules don't apply. Ariel is not a human being, so we never really know what he thinks or feels. His emotional life is, as it were, beyond the human spectrum. There are indications that he takes pride in his skill and he wants to be free again, but other than that, he is, from a human perspective, a mystery. More significantly for an actor, the possibilities are limitless. Quite apart from delineating a non-human psychology, how does one chart the relationship between a man and a spirit? It's a question, as always, of ferreting out tiny clues. There is a wonderful moment in the play when Ariel advises his master to show some compassion to his enemies. He tells Prospero that, if he saw how distressed they were, his 'affections/Would become tender.' His master looks sceptical and makes his scepticism clear; and so Ariel says, gently but firmly:

> *'Mine would, sir, were I human.'*

It's a turning point in the story; and how weird and wonderful it is. A human being is reminded by a non-human both of his moral duty and of the benefits of humane behaviour. It's as if, over his lifetime, Ariel has been watching, with curiosity but without judgement, how human beings behave – what makes them happy or unhappy, cruel or kind – and, now that he has discovered how humans work, he can offer disinterested advice. Interestingly, this little exchange is also indicative of a shift in status between master and slave. Prospero has no effective response to Ariel's super-rationality. He accepts his servant's advice and forgives his enemies.

It was predictable that, since Ariel's internal life is mysterious or unknowable, most of my efforts would be centred on the external components of the character – essentially, how he looked and how he moved. After his triumphant design for Sam's *Troilus and Cressida*, Anthony Ward provided an equally beautiful set for *The Tempest*. Again, it was very simple – an empty space with, curved gently round the back of the stage, a huge cobalt-blue cyclorama. Depending on the lighting, this could change colour. I never saw this myself, but apparently, from the auditorium, it sometimes looked dark blue or violet or pale lilac. Anthony decided to dress me in the same shade of blue, so that, at times, my body would fade away into the background, leaving only my face clearly visible.

I was given a simple two-piece linen suit. The jacket was buttoned all the way down the front and it had a Mao collar. Along with the blue suit, I was given a pair of gloves and a pair of socks and shoes of the same colour. My hair, too, was blue. This was decided early on in the rehearsal period and I didn't think about any modifications to it until we finally got on to the stage. There were many things about the original costume design that I liked very much. For instance, *The Tempest* is a play that many readers see as threaded through with the assumptions of early English colonialism. Prospero's treatment of both Ariel and Caliban can be read as a reflection – maybe even a critique – of the treatment meted out by the British to indigenous populations all over the world. My simple linen suit looked like one that might have been worn by a servant in a colonial household in the Far East. It was modest and unassuming. It suited the Ariel that we were developing – a character who was skilled, efficient and obedient.

Ariel does not have much to say in the play, but he does a lot of physical work. Sam decided that I should do even more work than was demanded in the text. Consequently, I almost never left the stage. Every character, every prop, every change of scene was controlled by Ariel and a small group of fellow spirits. I learned the words early on – which was easy enough, since there were relatively few of them – but the choreography was much more difficult to remember. This made me increasingly anxious, especially as we approached the first run-through of the play in the rehearsal room. This is always a nerve-racking moment anyway, but this time it felt different, because my concerns about Ariel were technical, not emotional or psychological. So I told myself to take everything very slowly and carefully. It worked in the sense that I and my band of helpers didn't make any obvious mistakes and we hadn't, it seemed, messed up anybody else's performance. However, as Sam pointed out after the run, it really was very boring to watch. As we talked, we realised that we had two options: either to scrap everything we had done and start again from scratch or do the same thing but much, much slower. We chose the latter.

Later, when we moved to the stage, I put on the costume that I had last seen a few weeks before. Much of it now seemed redundant. In slowing down Ariel's movements – they were now glacial – we had also simplified them. Only the most economical version of any particular move was used. Ariel's face was correspondingly impassive. There was no hint of love or hatred or any other emotion. He was simply doing his job. I felt now that his costume should be as simple; and so out went the gloves and the shoes and the blue hair. Ariel now padded around the stage in bare feet, which both grounded him and, paradoxically, transformed him into the creature of air that I had been searching for.

There was a psychological as well as a physical dividend to enjoy from all this. From the outset, Ariel wants his freedom. He makes that very clear. Prospero has promised to release him and Ariel, understandably, would like that promise to be kept – and kept as soon as possible. But Prospero delays, asking the spirit for yet more and more service. I said earlier that Ariel delights in his skills – the exuberant way he describes his work supports that reading – but that does not necessarily mean that he enjoys his servitude. At one point, Caliban says of the spirits that inhabit the island that they 'all do hate [Prospero]/As rootedly as I'. I had assumed that, when he says this, Caliban is exaggerating or lying. But what if he's telling the truth? What if, behind my Ariel's unmoving face, there is contempt, even hatred. What if he feels the same way about Prospero as Caliban does?

I decided that he did; but he plays a subtler game than Caliban. He calculates that the more submissive his behaviour and the more impeccable his work, the more likely it is that he will eventually be given his freedom. This tactic meant that the blank face Ariel presented to his master was not neutral but fuelled with repressed anger. He was also hiding a profound impatience – after all, he's been waiting for a long time to be set free. Whatever Prospero might wish to believe, there is no mutual love between him and Ariel.

This is a very harsh reading, I know; and it was made harsher by something that Sam came up with late in rehearsal. I wish I could lay claim to this idea, since it was rather brilliant; but I can't. It all came from Sam; I just got the credit – and the small amount of censure. At the end of the play, Prospero finally grants Ariel his freedom. Like the short scene that I mentioned earlier, it's one of the great, iconic moments in Shakespeare's work. Prospero calls Ariel 'my chick', a lovely term of endearment which he has not used before, sends him off to do one last job and then says a final goodbye:

> *'. . . Then to the elements*
> *Be free, and fare thou well!'*

Ariel says nothing. Sam came into the rehearsal room one day and told me that he had had a dream in which, at this point in the story, Ariel spat in Prospero's face before walking away. I'm not sure I was convinced by the story of the dream, but the idea of the spit was very exciting. We had a word with Alec McCowen, who was playing Prospero. He was wary but was willing to try it out in our next run of the play. We didn't tell the rest of the cast. When it came, the spit was, inevitably, a surprise, even a shock. Many of the cast liked it; a few made it very clear that they didn't. I noticed that, on the whole, those who were playing characters who were treated well by Prospero disapproved of the spit; those who were mistreated by him – Caliban and the other spirits, for instance – approved. We kept it in. A close friend of mine in the company pointed out that it would dominate the reviews of the production – and he thought that this was a shame.

He was right, of course. All the critics wrote about it. Many were complimentary; but others were horrified. A major broadsheet called it a 'catastrophic' choice. At one performance, I was heckled from the auditorium. A man shouted 'Rubbish!' – although it came so quickly after the spit itself that the heckler must either have read about the production or seen it before. Either way, it was obvious that he found it offensive; and had the courage to make that clear. After all, heckling is not a common occurrence at the Royal Shakespeare Theatre in Stratford-upon-Avon.

I think some people were hurt by our decision. *The Tempest* is a play that inspires a deep, unshakeable loyalty. It is the playwright's last solo-authored work and, consequently, many regard it as Shakespeare's farewell to the stage. And they would argue that a farewell from such a gentle genius must necessarily be generous, warm, loving. I understand this, although I believe the play is a fiercer beast than this analysis might imply. As it happens, a year into the run, I cut the spit. This was not, as some have written, because there had been adverse comments about it. Rather, I began to feel that such an aggressive gesture didn't sit comfortably with the Ariel that we had developed. He had become too remote and dignified a figure. He was now almost haughty. The spit felt vulgar. Ariel was still resentful and angry, but he would never stoop so low as to show it. More significantly, I also began to wonder whether Ariel could hate and love his master at the same time, whether he too feels some regret at their parting. Perhaps, I thought, this new farewell – without the spit – would be closer to what Shakespeare intended. In any case, over a long run, this blurring of clear distinctions happens more often than one might think. Elsewhere, I've called it a sort of theatrical uncertainty principle. A character can think or feel several contradictory things at the same time. Sometimes it's best to let motive, intention, a particular emotional state remain muddied or, at least, to leave options open; and then to hand it over to each individual audience member to interpret what they see and hear.

When Sam first talked to me on the phone about Ariel, he promised me a spectacular final exit. He kept his promise. At the end of the play, after Prospero's gentle dismissal, Ariel walked very slowly up to the blue cyclorama at the back of the stage. Hidden in the cyclorama was a small door – invisible up to this point. Ariel opened it and let in a flood of bright, white light. He turned to look at his former master for one last time; and then disappeared. Ariel was finally free, returned to a world that we humans will never discover or understand. Perhaps, I thought every time we played *The Tempest,* this is what the playwright himself was looking for as he said goodbye – freedom.

8

It's curious how little Shakespeare I played in my first six years with the RSC. Perhaps they were trying to tell me something. If so, I ignored them. The repertoire that I worked on was indicative of the range of writing that the company was keen to promote. The RSC was there not just to present their house playwright. They understood how deadening such a limited diet would have been. There has been, over the years, a rumbling and unresolved debate about whether the RSC should devote less time to Shakespeare, although it's clear that part of the appeal of the company – and its distinctive profile in Stratford and around the country – is dependent on a continuous supply of his plays. If someone somewhere has a sudden urge to take in a little Shakespeare, then the idea is that the RSC will always be there to provide it. For me, though, my years with the company – despite verse workshops, sonnet classes and the like – were as much about other playwrights as about the big man himself. Indeed, the Swan Theatre, the second-biggest house in Stratford, where I did most of my work, was originally dedicated not to the plays of Shakespeare, but rather to those of his contemporaries. That noble ambition was compromised over time, but the original remit remained essentially the same – Shakespeare, it was thought, is better understood when he is judged alongside his contemporaries.

At last, in my third season with the RSC, I was given a part that was written in verse. It was not, however, by Shakespeare. An actor in the company, Gerard Murphy, had been asked to direct a play. He decided on *Edward II* by Christopher Marlowe and offered me the title role. Marlowe, Shakespeare's great contemporary, had a dangerous, subversive personality the like of which no other playwright of the time possessed; and his plays reflect this. He was brilliant – effortlessly, it seems. It is often said that had he lived longer – he was murdered, still a young man, in a tavern brawl – then his writing would have outshone Shakespeare's. As it stands, it's still impressive and his abilities must have cowed his fellow writers – including the young man from Stratford. Marlowe was born in the same year as Shakespeare and enjoyed a similar background; both their fathers were small-town artisans and both boys were educated in the local school. But Marlowe went on to university; Shakespeare did not. Marlowe was both learned and outrageous; Shakespeare, I sense, was less learned and a little more careful. Shakespeare imitated Marlowe and refers to him admiringly in his own work; although, maybe, in his heart, he knew that he himself had the talent one day to outshine him.

Marlowe's plays are a very good place to start learning about verse. He became celebrated for his portraits of over-reaching men – characters who challenge the status quo, are briefly triumphant and then suffer a spectacular downfall. They all speak with a propulsive energy. They employ grand, luxuriant imagery. So the verse is thrilling to perform. It requires the actor to surf the wave; but, in technical terms, it is quite simple. Jonson, his younger contemporary, wrote of Marlowe's 'mighty line' and it's true that the inescapable beat has an hypnotic power. If you observe the regularity of the verse rhythm, then the writer will cast his spell and provide the necessary energy.

This relentless, hurtling quality is clearly evident in the characters of Tamburlaine and Faustus, two early Marlowe creations.

Edward II, a later play, is very slightly different. The verse is regular, but some of the flamboyance has gone. The narrative is more carefully controlled. When I was doing the play, I used to say that, if the early Marlowe plays are like battleships, then *Edward II* is like a dull grey submarine. It moves steadily and imperceptibly towards the terrible ending – Edward famously dies as a red-hot poker is pushed into his rectum. The language is, for the most part, deliberately workmanlike; and the characters are, every one of them, unattractive.

It all sounds rather unappealing, but Gerard had great theatrical flair and produced a show of unapologetic opulence. He was assisted in this by his designer, Sandy Powell, who has since gone on to win many awards, including several Oscars. We were all dressed in clothes that looked vaguely Elizabethan, but that were given a modern, industrial flavour. Sandy used metallic fabrics for many of us – gold for the king, a foul black-green for the villains of the piece, Mortimer and Queen Isabella. Edward's male lover and the focus of predictable discontent wore tailored leather jackets, one black and one white, that were covered in metal studs that glittered like jewels. Gerard created a court that was formal and strictly hierarchical. Members of the cast complained that they spent much of the play on their knees; but there was method in Gerard's madness. He wanted to set the play in a world that was simultaneously rigid and decadent, peopled by men and women who were both power hungry and self-indulgent.

At the centre of this world we see a king who is, in the eyes of those around him, dangerously irresponsible. Unfortunately, Edward, if asked, would find it difficult to define what his responsibilities are. It is important to understand that he has never known a time when he has been less than a crown prince. He was born to be king and thereby to exercise absolute power. So he doesn't see that his behaviour is foolish or that his demands are tactless. Before acceding to the crown, he enjoyed a close and loving relationship with a man called Gaveston. This latter, low-born character has been exiled by the old king and, as the play starts, the new King Edward has, to the horror of his courtiers, recalled him. The first half of the play deals with Gaveston's downfall and death.

It is reasonable for a modern audience to trust that the relationship between the king and his lover is passionate and genuine; and it is natural to judge the behaviour of those who seek to destroy it as homophobic. We need to believe that the two central characters are brave men who are treated unjustly. Derek Jarman's wonderful 1991 film of the play, which starred my old university friend Tilda Swinton, and which came out at about the same time as our production, does exactly that. It was a profoundly important piece of work, since we were, at the time, in the middle of the horrors of the AIDS epidemic and gay men were, quite literally, fighting for their lives. Homophobia was back and proud. There was a smattering of homophobes in the Swan audience. I think the vast majority of those who came to see the play were appreciative, but a tiny minority objected to our production and its unashamed exploration of homosexuality. The most memorable were a teacher who had brought a group of her girls and wrote to say that our distortion of the text was unforgivable; and a Dutch couple who were on their honeymoon with her parents – an interesting idea – and who walked out of the show. I can understand that they might have felt uncomfortable.

Marlowe complicates things, though. Even if the relationship between Edward and Gaveston is played as deep and genuine, Marlowe is not the sort of writer who is particularly strong on romantic, as opposed to sexual, love. *Edward II* is not *Romeo and Juliet*. Edward and Gaveston are not immediately attractive. In Marlowe's mind, they don't have to be. He is more interested in power; and more excited by the flouting of convention or the challenge to accepted authority than by a committed moral stand. To be honest, when Gaveston is murdered, Edward, after a momentary spasm of grief, seems to forget him pretty quickly. He certainly doesn't talk about him. Rather, he moves swiftly on to new favourites. The most impressive scene in the play is not about love, fulfilled or frustrated, but rather about the crown. It occurred to both Gerard and me that here is evidence of the most important relationship in Edward's life. Even if he himself has never thought about it, Edward's persona is absolutely defined by his being king; and, in losing the crown, his identity is threatened.

Shakespeare responded directly to this – as he was wont to do when it came to Marlowe. For instance, many think that *The Merchant of Venice* was inspired by Marlowe's grotesque and shamelessly antisemitic melodrama, *The Jew of Malta*. In reply to *Edward II*, Shakespeare gave us *Richard II*. I played Richard late in my career and, inevitably, memories of Edward came flooding back. There were many striking similarities, including a long scene in which Richard is forced to give up his crown. This scene was regarded as so inflammatory by his contemporaries that, apparently, Shakespeare decided to cut it out in some early performances. I don't suppose Queen Elizabeth, who once compared herself to Richard, would have been happy that her subjects were watching a scene of abdication on the London stage.

Perhaps, in writing *Edward II*, Marlowe encouraged Shakespeare to be braver, to challenge the political *status quo*. Equally, the more brutal elements of Marlowe's plays, the harsh judgement and easy prejudice, may have encouraged Shakespeare to trust his own more humane instincts. And so he gave us the incompetent and arrogant Richard II but also the proud and vulnerable Shylock.

I have never done another play by Marlowe. I would love to have tried my hand at Tamburlaine – the young shepherd who rises to rule a great empire – but that is no longer a possibility.

Perhaps I am still capable of playing Faustus. We'll see. However, there were other writers whom I first met at Stratford that have played a more prominent part in my life – particularly Anton Chekhov.

I have said many times over the years that, when Terry Hands offered me the part of Konstantin in *The Seagull*, it changed the course of my career. The Chekhov play was my last show in a season that had earlier included the Marlowe. I know that King Edward is a very serious role, but there is something heightened, even excessive, about him and his situation. Excess is Marlowe's speciality, after all. Konstantin, on the other hand, is ordinary, but he breaks your heart. He is a playwright, the son of a successful actress. He loves a young woman who shows little interest in him and leaves him, having fallen in love with an older, more successful writer, to begin a life on the stage. Konstantin finally shoots himself. His is a very sad story. Terry Hands's offer was a signal that he trusted me with writing that dug deeper than Marlowe ever could. He was effectively telling me, just as he had hinted a couple of years before, that he thought I might one day play parts like Hamlet or King Lear. Konstantin demanded from me a new methodology and an exploration of as yet uncharted emotional territory. That challenge was Terry's gift to me; as was the most beautiful show – a ravishing set by Johan Engels and an extraordinary cast of actors – that he directed impeccably. I don't think I have ever seen a better production of the play. I fell in love – with Anton Chekhov, with *The Seagull* and with Konstantin. He is one of the very few characters that I have worked on – perhaps the only one – about whom, for a period after the run had ended, I felt proprietorial. For years after, I found it difficult to watch other actors play him. A small part of me still thinks of him as mine.

I am not alone in falling so helplessly for Chekhov. Most British actors that I know feel the same way. He is the only playwright who, for us, can seriously stand alongside Shakespeare. I was once asked, at a meeting of the Shakespeare Society of New York, whom I thought was the greatest playwright in history and I replied, 'Chekhov'. I was being deliberately contrary, but I wasn't saying anything absurd; because Chekhov's plays are, quite simply, faultless.

As I began to rehearse *The Seagull*, I was struck by the fact that Chekhov gives his actors all the information that they need – and does it effortlessly. This sounds odd, I know – surely such information is the least we can expect from any great writer and, anyway, if information is not given then it can hardly be important, let alone necessary – but the picture is a little more complicated than that. So much of our work is about filling in the gaps, as it were. I've already mentioned a few moments in Shakespeare's plays when constructing a 'backstory' is absolutely necessary. Where is Lady Macbeth's child? What happens to Hamlet when he is banished from Denmark? Have Beatrice and Benedick had an affair before their stage-story starts? I don't believe it's possible to play Hamlet or Macbeth or Benedick without answers to these questions. Chekhov makes no such demands. This is not to say that learning about the world that he wrote about is not valuable. If you're about to do *The Seagull*, it's useful to ask about the lives of writers and actors in nineteenth-century Russia. Practical details are also helpful. It's surprising how many British actors know how to handle a samovar, for instance, or can tell you about the status and workload of ex-serfs; but the minutiae about the emotional lives of individual characters are all there in Chekhov's text. Perhaps this is because his vision, despite its focus on universally applicable states of mind such as love, envy and disappointment, is microscopic. Chekhov is Vermeer to Shakespeare's Rembrandt.

I can't claim this comparison as my own. I have stolen it from a passing remark by my old friend Philip Franks, who is not only an actor and director but also an artist. I once asked him to take me to the National Gallery in London and talk me through some of the pictures. I have never felt confident about looking at paintings or sculpture or other artworks. Some people would say that this doesn't really matter, that one need only feel what one feels. That always feels unsatisfactory to me. When it comes to art, I need guidance. Standing in front of a Rembrandt on the day of our visit, I asked Pip to explain why it was considered a great work. 'The thing is, Simon,' he replied, 'Rembrandt is our Shakespeare.' This made perfect sense. Rembrandt, like Shakespeare, is a master of the grand gesture – alongside deep psychological penetration. In technical terms, both are sometimes wild, apparently careless. Vermeer, like Chekhov, is precise and allusive – fascinated by the details of daily life.

Chekhov will not allow you to ignore his hidden instructions or stray too far from the story as he intended it. The line and history of each character are so clearly drawn that any deviation may result in a sort of acting paralysis. This certainly happened to me. Many years after *The Seagull*, in 2009, I played the merchant Lopakhin in *The Cherry Orchard*, Chekhov's last masterpiece. For me, who once lazily assumed that Chekhov always writes in pastel colours, as it were, this late play is a reminder that he can be brutal. The playwright is as humane as ever, but I found *The Cherry Orchard* to be a very bleak and unforgiving play. Almost everyone seems at best careless, at worst untrustworthy. Lopakhin is no exception. He is from a family of serfs who were, like all their fellow serfs, emancipated forty years previously. He is clearly an astute businessman, but admits to a sentimental attachment to the local landowning family – the family who own the cherry orchard of the title. This family once adopted a girl – now a young woman – called Varya. Everyone assumes that Lopakhin will marry Varya, but it seems that he is more interested in her mother, the beautiful, glamorous Madame Ranyevskaya. I felt, early in rehearsal, that the most important motor for Lopakhin's behaviour is this interest in Ranyevskaya. To me, it looked obsessive, all-consuming – so much so that my Lopakhin ignored Varya completely. Nothing wrong with that, I thought at the time. This is exactly the sort of predicament that makes a character interesting to watch. In my mind, Lopakhin had no interest in Varya, whatever her expectations might be.

However, towards the end of the play, Lopakhin tries finally to propose to Varya, not necessarily wholeheartedly, but with the best of intentions. During the run of performances, I started to feel that my early decision to ignore Varya, to concentrate solely on her mother and to ignore the other characters' expectations that Varya and Lopakhin might marry, appeared reductive. In fact, the proposal scene became rather difficult to play. In psychological terms, it seemed to come from nowhere. Chekhov, I began to think, had a more nuanced, less emphatic story in mind. Perhaps Lopakhin responds, in some way, to both women – mother and daughter – and if I were not to fall flat on my face I should respect that. Lopakhin genuinely likes and admires Varya. He doesn't ignore her – which is what I was playing at the beginning of the run. He is not surprised by her family's idea that they might end up together. But, when it comes to it, he can't, for many reasons, bring himself to propose marriage.

This is why Chekhov's accuracy – his demands, I suppose – are not a straitjacket. If he avoids unnecessary information, then it follows that he simply gives the actor what they need and no more. The writing is precise but not overwhelming. There are vast tracts of the emotional landscape that are left for the actor to explore. This allows for self-contradiction, something of which I became acutely aware in the other Chekhov play that I have been involved with – *Uncle Vanya*, in 2002. What intrigued me about playing Vanya was the impossibility of clarifying a simple subtext. At any one moment, whatever he might be saying, Vanya seems often to experience directly contradictory emotions simultaneously. The subtext is unsettled and multilayered. Sometimes, the contradictions are the stuff of cliché. Vanya declares his love for Yelena; but he also hates her. He wants to be with her and he wants to run away. But often, the contradictory feelings are more unexpected – at times he feels courageous and frightened, confident and insecure, happy and sad. Likewise, at the moment of the proposal to Varya, Lopakhin likes and dislikes her, is flattered and insulted by the assumption that they should marry, is aggressive and vulnerable.

This psychological landscape is, I think, quintessentially Chekhovian. He is a writer who seems unwilling to confine or limit the range of possible human responses; and, furthermore, he always avoids judgement of an individual character's behaviour. When we played *Uncle Vanya* in New York, one critic, who didn't like our production, wrote that we avoided confronting the evil in the play. 'Evil' is a big word – and, in this context, a limiting one. I honestly cannot see that there is any evidence of evil in *Uncle Vanya* or, indeed, in any of Chekhov's four great plays. There are plenty of other failings, including casual cruelty, but not evil. Chekhov wouldn't presume to judge. He is, quite simply, not that kind of writer.

At the end of *The Seagull*, just before Konstantin shoots himself, the playwright asks that he should remain on stage, alone, tidying up his desk, in silence. The script stipulates that this silence should last for 'several minutes' – a long, long time on any stage. Terry Hands was determined that we should follow Chekhov's instructions. Much to my surprise, he took out a stopwatch during one run of the last act and timed my silence. When I tried to do it that first time, Konstantin cleared his desk, ripped up his manuscripts and thought about breaking his pencils, but then decided that this was a futile and self-regarding gesture. I took off my spectacles and put them in my jacket pocket. (Mum had told me that, when she was training to be a doctor, she was taught that suicides who wear glasses remove them before they kill themselves.) After a minute, I ran out of things to do. So I just stood there; until, after at least a minute, perhaps more, had passed, Terry allowed me to go.

And that's how it stayed during the run. A long moment when the audience watched a motionless young man standing by himself, contemplating his own death. Or perhaps Konstantin was beyond thought. He wasn't thinking or feeling anything. He wasn't happy and he wasn't in pain. He wasn't good and he wasn't bad. Nobody was judging him. I hope Chekhov would have been pleased.

The Autocrats

Prospero

I returned to Stratford in 2016, after twenty-five years, to play Prospero in *The Tempest*. After our first night, I had a couple of beers, walked back to my house, switched on the radio and discovered that Donald Trump had been elected as president of the United States. As Yeats might have said, the centre hadn't held. The ceremony of innocence was drowned. Our last performance in Stratford coincided with Trump's inauguration in Washington. I mention this only because it is both curious and depressing.

The town felt and looked much the same as it had a quarter of a century earlier; but I was aware of some changes – often for the better. Much to my delight, it was now possible to get a decent coffee – in a small shop up by Shakespeare's birthplace. Most mornings, my colleague Jenny Rainsford, her little boy, Inigo, and I would race through the streets to grab a flat white and a delicious cinnamon toast to start our day – an unthinkable luxury in the old Stratford. The centre of town now boasted a big, modern bookshop. Perhaps most significantly and certainly more prominently, the theatres had been rebuilt. The facade of the main building and the foyer – which I always thought were rather chic – had been kept much as they had been; but the main auditorium was now a larger version of the Swan Theatre. The audience was seated on three sides of the stage and, unlike the barn that it replaced, the theatre, despite its capacity, felt intimate. The second house, the Swan, remained untouched. A couple of minutes' walk up the road, the Other Place was unrecognisable. To be honest, changes to this small theatre had begun before I left the company that first time; so the old tin hut was a very distant memory. In its place was a smooth red-brick complex – including a luxurious, light-filled rehearsal room, where we worked on *The Tempest*, and a café which served delicious cakes. It was all very clean and tidy.

The house that I had been allocated was small, but it was directly opposite the main theatre building. A few doors down was the place where I had lived when I was last in Stratford. This was a bigger building with three bedrooms and had now, I noticed, been converted into offices. Squatting behind this house was the wardrobe department, which, in the old days, I used to visit regularly. It was one of the most exciting places in town – packed with an extraordinary collection of tailors, milliners, corset makers, armourers, dyers, seamstresses. There was always a quiet hum of activity, because their work was never-ending. I didn't have the opportunity to drop in this time, but I know that they're still there, but now in a less decrepit building. The whole complex has been comprehensively reorganised. Apparently, it's the largest wardrobe department in the country; or so I was told by a guide recently when I visited the theatre to take in a show.

The backstage of the theatre – behind the main house – had been neatened up. All the dressing rooms were now identical. The four principal ones – with their French windows opening out on to small balconies overlooking the river – were gone. So were the beds. I was told that some non-theatrical expert had decided that, since this was a workplace, beds were unnecessary. They may have been right, I suppose; but they presumably hadn't ever done two performances of *Hamlet* in one day. If they had, they might have found they needed a bit of a lie down between shows. On the whole, though, every detail in the building had been carefully thought through and cleanly executed. Perhaps, I thought, it just needs time to look a little less pristine.

I suspect that I have always had a fondness for theatres that are a bit of a physical mess. There are limits, of course. Rodents in the dressing rooms are not really acceptable; nor are leaking roofs. But, on the whole, I like the backstage of a theatre to be chaotic – a contrast, I suppose, to the promise of skill and precision on stage. I have some sentimental notion in my head about a thing of beauty rising up out of the dirt. I'm tickled by the fact that a number of London's West End theatres – some of the grandest in the country – are right in the middle of the seediest part of town. It feels historically appropriate somehow. It's like a link to Burbage and Garrick and Siddons and all those great actors of a less hygienic past.

I'll admit that there was much that I missed in the new Stratford. I couldn't help feeling nostalgic, while recognising that nostalgia is a waste of time and effort. I realise, too, that things were bound to feel very different now that I was older. For instance, I couldn't party as hard or drink as much as I used to. When I had last been with the company, much of my time outside the theatre had been spent in the pub – though not, I hasten to add, during the day. Now, I restricted myself to a quick beer in the theatre bar after the show and then it was straight home to bed. I went to the famous pub – the Dirty Duck – only a couple of times during the whole length of the run.

And I really couldn't complain about the work itself. Our director was Greg Doran, one of the kindest, most equable men I've ever worked with. How he managed to retain such good humour and do his job as artistic director of the RSC, I will never know. He has devoted his working life to the company – as actor and as director. His love of Shakespeare is unwavering and, as he himself would admit, near-obsessive. He combines the skills of a great director and a very distinguished academic. His erudition is recognised as extraordinary. I noticed that, in rehearsal, he always gave Shakespeare the benefit of the doubt. That sounds odd, but what I mean is that, when we came up against something particularly difficult or obscure, whereas my instinct would always be to change or cut the offending passage, Greg would try everything he could to make it work.

An example of this occurred during rehearsals for a scene in *The Tempest* that is commonly known as 'the masque'. The First Folio version of the play – the only authoritative version we have – was printed from a copy written out by a scribe called Ralph Crane. Crane is an interesting figure in Shakespeare scholarship. He had a hand in the printed version of a clutch of Shakespeare's plays. His work is very distinctive. His punctuation, for instance, is idiosyncratic and immediately recognisable; and he includes elaborate stage directions. It seems that he is describing details of performance, rather than simply reproducing the playwright's presumably simpler instructions. Greg read both Shakespeare's text and Crane's stage directions with great care. He knew that *The Tempest* has always been a feast for the eye as much as the ear.

For instance, Prospero, at one point, organises this theatrical entertainment – the masque – which involves music, instrumental and vocal, three goddesses descending from the sky and a group of dancing countrymen. Crane describes all this in some detail. At one point, the rustics are asked by one of the goddesses to put on 'rye-straw hats'. Crane (if we presume it's him following Shakespeare's instructions) writes that they are 'properly habited' – which presumably includes the hats. For some reason, this proved to be tricky. I can't remember exactly why. Perhaps the hats were difficult to carry or to keep on while the men were dancing. More importantly, nobody really understood why they should be wearing hats in the first place. This sounds rather silly, I know, because it's such a minor detail. As I have said, my instinct would have been to cut the hats and, probably, the dancing peasants as well. But Greg worked hard to find a reason for them – and their hats – to be there. Shakespeare or his theatre company had included them and that had to be respected.

Oddly, when Greg and I first met in London to discuss my playing Prospero, we ended up talking about masques. These were lavish and hugely expensive court entertainments that were very popular in the Jacobean period. They often involved complicated special effects, the master of which was Inigo Jones. Even now, reading about what he managed to achieve and bearing in mind his simultaneous work as an architect, Jones's work seems, literally, unbelievable. The king and his courtiers were presented with and presumably delighted in, among other things, a globe that spun in the air without any visible support, dragons and other mythical beasts flying through the hall and – my personal favourite – hundreds of candles lighting simultaneously. In keeping with this magnificence, the words spoken by the performers, who were often courtiers, even royalty, were refined and elaborate.

Unlike his friend and rival, Ben Jonson, Shakespeare never wrote a masque. I suspect that he felt they were not his style; which is a relief for any Shakespeare fan because, frankly, masques can be a little wearying to read. Nevertheless, there is no question that *The Tempest* is steeped in the aesthetics of the masque; and Greg told me at our first meeting that he had been puzzling for some time about how to acknowledge this in his new production of the play. He wanted to find an equivalent of the work of Jacobean designers using the technical wizardry of the twenty-first century. He and his team had been in touch with, among others, an actor called Andy Serkis. Andy became famous for his wonderfully sad and scary portrayal of Gollum in the films of *The Lord of the Rings*. I think it was because of this life-changing experience that he decided to work on those techniques that allow an actor to transform themselves on screen in a way that had been impossible before the arrival of sophisticated computer technology. He founded a company called Imaginarium, where men and women could metamorphose into great apes or panthers or bears. It was real magic – like Prospero's. Without any apparent hesitation, Andy and his team of magicians offered their services to Greg.

A few weeks before rehearsals started, I was invited to the Imaginarium headquarters in the suburbs of London. I watched Mark Quartley, our Ariel, being fitted with small discs all over his body by a small army of very clever people. He was asked to repeat certain movements, which were then stored in some way and later reassembled as a three-dimensional avatar of Mark. Forgive me if I cannot explain the process more clearly, but I found the whole thing utterly baffling and remained baffled until the end of the run. All I know is that we ended up with many identical Ariels, all with a limitless set of skills.

The Ariel avatars and other technical tricks were incorporated into a design of luxurious beauty. There was nothing minimalist about this design. I remember being smothered in deep blues, bright turquoise and rich indigos. The play opens with a shipwreck and so Stephen Brimson Lewis, our chief designer, turned the theatre space into the hull of a great ship that swayed sickeningly from side to side. The individual thrills followed thick and fast – Ariel trapped inside the trunk of a tree or soaring up above the stage disguised as a flash of lightning or as a taloned harpy; a goddess rising from the floor wearing a huge skirt patterned with changing flowers; a final simple ring of light to trap Prospero's enemies.

And, of course, as befits a masque, there was lots of music. Our composer, Paul Englishby, had discovered that Mozart had once toyed with the idea of turning *The Tempest* into an opera; and so two of our goddesses sang a duet of dazzling pseudo-Classical coloratura. There were Ariel's haunting set of songs and strange sounds – a new music – as Prospero worked his final spells.

With such an abundance of options, there were many things to be sorted out. A vocabulary, or rather rules of engagement, had to be developed and defined. I'm not sure whether it was unexpected or predictable that we found that Ariel-as-avatar worked when he was performing his magic, but not when he was talking to his master. I certainly felt – and I know Greg and Mark agreed – that the relationship between Prospero and Ariel depended on human contact. We needed to talk eye to eye, face to face. There is a clear paradox in this. After all, Ariel is not human. Somehow his otherworldliness could be expressed only by a human being consciously ridding themselves of their humanity. But the actor playing Ariel also needed the freedom – as a human – to react spontaneously to his fellow performers. I have mentioned already the pivotal scene when Ariel advises his master to show compassion for his enemies. Every night my Prospero responded differently to his servant's words. He might accept them or dismiss them; he was often silent but he sometimes wept or roared with frustration. Mark would, almost imperceptibly, take what I gave him and modify, equally imperceptibly, his behaviour.

I found that the idea of long frustration became a key component of my Prospero. Early on, I mentioned to Greg that I had always thought of *The Tempest* as a cold play. Certainly, the previous production that I had been involved with, the one directed by Sam Mendes, had been, at least visually, cool and understated. The structure of the play – a series of strictly mirrored scenes – may contribute to a sense of emotional repression. The whole work is tightly controlled. Furthermore, the central character is not an attractive man; he's difficult to warm to. However, my judgement of the play changed as I worked on Prospero. Far from being cold, I discovered that *The Tempest* was fuelled by something close to fury.

Prospero is an aristocrat and a ruler. Many years before the play starts, he is deprived of his autocratic power as the Duke of Milan, exiled and sent to a remote island with only his infant daughter for company. He has not lost his despotic instincts and uses his considerable magical powers to subdue and control the indigenous population of his new, tiny kingdom. He discovers that a ship is passing close by the island. On board are those who had earlier orchestrated his downfall. With Ariel's help, he whips up a fierce storm, the ship is destroyed and Prospero's enemies are stranded on the island. The stage is set for revenge.

It is Prospero's brother who activated the original coup back in Milan. He, along with the brother of the King of Naples, who also finds himself stranded on the island, constitute the principal focus of Prospero's anger. I suspect that we are supposed to feel that Prospero has been unfairly treated. The usurpers, despite Shakespeare's much-lauded even-handedness, are portrayed unsympathetically. Indeed, their single, extended conversation in the play is like an echo of the Macbeths. The trouble is that, when he was Duke of Milan, Prospero clearly spent most of his time locked away in his rooms studying his magic. In other words, he probably, at least from his brother's perspective, was an ineffective and lazy ruler. He quite simply wasn't doing his job. I can't tell whether this complication is a deliberate ploy on the playwright's part. But at no point does anyone challenge Prospero about his time as Duke of Milan. Nobody says that his brother might have had good reason to seize power. On the contrary, the conspirators are portrayed as power hungry and brutish.

The only clue that I can find that Shakespeare might be challenging his own assumptions – and the assumptions of the other characters in the story – comes at the very end of the play. It's a tiny, but important, moment. Having taken Ariel's advice, Prospero decides to forgive his enemies – including his brother. This act of forgiveness is about as graceless as one could imagine:

> *'For you, most wicked sir, whom to call brother*
> *Would even infect my mouth, I do forgive*
> *Thy rankest fault – all of them . . .'*

His brother does not reply. Shakespeare's late plays are mightily exercised by the nature of forgiveness. I strongly believe that Hermione, although silent, forgives her repentant husband in *The Winter's Tale*. *Cymbeline* and *Pericles* end with a reconciliation between a father and his mistreated or unlucky daughter. Here, in *The Tempest*, there is something indistinct and unresolved about the outcome of the brothers' encounter. For a start, the offer of forgiveness is depressingly high-handed; and no hint of an apology is offered by Prospero. He seems to think that he has done nothing wrong. Shakespeare gives no real indication, beyond his silence, as to the brother's feelings at this moment. Perhaps, as in other examples I have talked about, the simplest option is to play a genuine resolution; but I always felt in performance that the brother is within his rights to turn down Prospero's offer. Who says that Prospero's talk of forgiveness – indeed, any talk of forgiveness – need necessarily be accepted?

Not that Prospero appears to notice or even care; he quickly moves on to other, more important business. My point is that there is a possibility that, in some ways, the great magician fails in the task he has set himself. He doesn't exact the revenge that he originally planned; and equally the alternative – forgiving his enemies – is rejected. He seems to take little pleasure in the retrieval of his dukedom or the future marriage of his daughter. There is no stability at the end of the play. So many people over the centuries have seen Prospero as Shakespeare's self-portrait – the playwright as a great magician who late in life gives up his creative powers. It seems unlikely to me that he thought this would be his last play – though, frankly, who knows? – but I do sense that there was in him a need to forgive and be forgiven and a recognition that this might not be easy or even possible. And so, in my mind, Prospero returns to Milan a disappointed and frustrated man. He is not visibly repentant and he has not been forgiven.

The Tempest features characters that are imprisoned – principally Ariel and Caliban. Both are eventually given their freedom. In contrast to the first version of the play that I did, I found that this time the parting of Ariel and his master was rather upsetting. It's curious how Shakespeare's plays can change if viewed from the perspectives of different characters. My Prospero, as one would expect, was very sad to see Ariel go; but Mark's Ariel seemed sad, too. After he was dismissed, he walked slowly and despondently off the stage. It was if he didn't know where precisely he was going or what precisely he would find there.

The last words of the play are from Prospero. He talks directly to the audience. It's a strange speech, because it's spoken simultaneously by the character and the actor. Some readers might hear it as spoken by the playwright. I had never noticed before that it ends with a plea:

> *'Let your indulgence set me free.'*

The figure in the play who feels most imprisoned – locked in by his memories, his anger, his desire for revenge – is Prospero himself. We can see evidence of this unhappiness at earlier points in the story. One of the most anthologised moments in the play is also one of the most beautiful passages that Shakespeare ever wrote. I'll write it out in full:

'Our revels now are ended; these our actors,
As I foretold you, were all spirits, and
Are melted into air, into thin air;
And like the baseless fabric of this vision,
The cloud-capped towers, the gorgeous palaces,
The solemn temples, the great globe itself,
Yea, all which it inherit, shall dissolve,
And like this insubstantial pageant faded
Leave not a rack behind. We are such stuff
As dreams are made on; and our little life
Is rounded with a sleep.'

This is miraculously beautiful. Many people have read it at funerals and memorial services because it seems to promise such calm and peace after death. I was once asked to join a group of very distinguished actors to perform passages from Shakespeare for a rather grand celebratory recital at Buckingham Palace. One of the performers was Sir John Gielgud. He must have been in his late eighties. The director asked him whether he would like to perform this passage from *The Tempest*. 'Oh God, no,' he said, 'I've done it so often recently. At all my friends' funerals.' Instead, he chose a scene from *The Merchant of Venice* – two young lovers, Lorenzo and Jessica, talking quietly together as they listen to music. On this occasion, Sir John's Jessica was the actor Samantha Bond. Sir John knew the whole scene by heart. At one point in the recital, it appeared that he had forgotten his lines. Samantha, who was holding the script, gently nudged it towards him. He equally gently brushed it away, took a few short moments to gather his thoughts and picked up where he had left off – as if nothing had happened. I presume he knew vast tracts of Shakespeare by heart. A few years before, I had played a very small part in a radio version of *King Lear* directed by Ken Branagh. Sir John played the king. He did the whole part – or at least the single scene I was involved with – without a script in sight.

Taken out of context (at a funeral, for instance), these marvellous words from *The Tempest* sound melancholic, perhaps, and lyrical. In the context of the play, I think it is a different matter. The next thing that Prospero tells us after this speech is that he is 'vexed'. In fact, it is the speech itself that seems in part to vex him. He has just provided a spectacular entertainment for his daughter, Miranda, and her new fiancé, Ferdinand. This masque ends with a dance. In our production, Jenny Rainsford and Danny Easton, who played the young lovers, span ecstatically around the stage. It was hugely energetic and essentially innocent; but their happiness, or rather the hint of sexual awakening, infuriated Prospero. He stops the show, the performers magically disappear and he turns to his future son-in-law. He then delivers the famous speech to him – not to his daughter or to the world at large, but specifically to him. For a young man, it must seem unnecessarily reductive and cruel. It is, in short, the worst father-of-the-bride speech ever made. Prospero finishes his rant and, by now rather shamefaced, dismisses the two youngsters.

My analysis may be crude; but I think it is important to register the fact that sometimes the narcotic beauty of Shakespeare's language can disguise what is actually being said. It happens a couple of times in *King Lear*; and the last moments of Othello's life are so magnificent that it can wipe away the horror of his wife's murder. Actually, in Othello's case, that may be what he, subconsciously, is trying to do. In Prospero's case, I couldn't shake off the thought that he is, in many ways, a lesser man than he thinks. He could have been great, but he missed his chance.

At the end of the play, having been 'set free', Prospero returns to Milan. He says that there he will wait for his own death. There's nothing else for him to do. It's an unsatisfactory, even miserable, end; and, if the play is some sort of farewell from the playwright, then I cannot escape the feeling that there is disappointment, even bitterness, in the mix.

Richard II

By the time I was offered *Richard II*, I was far, far too old. I always think of Richard, rightly or wrongly, as a young man. The Almeida Theatre in London asked me to play him just before the outbreak of the COVID pandemic – so very recently, in other words. I was enjoying the last gasp of middle age. It was an unexpected but interesting offer; and despite the fact that I was halfway through a long five-year period working almost exclusively on another project – a play called *The Lehman Trilogy*, about the history of the great banking dynasty – I accepted. We had just finished a run of the trilogy in London and were enjoying a prolonged gap before taking it on to other venues – including Broadway – so now I had a chance to explore a different play.

As it turned out, the pandemic struck New York not long after we arrived in town with *The Lehman Trilogy*. We managed just four performances in March 2020 before we were sent home. Like many others, it took time for me to appreciate the enormity of what was happening. On the day that our show was cancelled, I walked down to the theatre with Adam Godley – one of my two fellow actors – just to check that the information we had received was correct. We assumed that other shows in town must have been forced to cancel and, to be honest, we also wanted to soak up the atmosphere; because, at that stage, the situation was, for us, merely curious and rather fun. Discovering that our theatre was dark, we walked a couple of blocks to the street that houses all the famous theatrical bars and found that the place was packed with British actors and directors. The atmosphere was predictably festive – even though one show, a musical called *Six*, which was due to open that evening, had needed to postpone their celebratory first night indefinitely, which must have been very frustrating. I sat with Marianne Elliott, who was directing *Company*, and one of our writers, Ben Power, and proposed that all the shows whose casts were drinking around us – *Company*,

Hangmen, The Lehman Trilogy, Six – should pool their resources, hire a shed somewhere and play everything in rotation with a minimum of sets and props. Marianne and Ben looked wearily at me. They told me it was a ridiculous idea. I had a few more drinks and left early for home.

We had been told unofficially that we would be back on stage in three weeks. I thought I might use the time to travel around the USA. I could catch up with friends, even visit the southern states, which were unknown territory for me. However, the very next day after the cancellation, I got a phone call from the production office advising me to go straight back to London. This was probably wise, since there were now scary reports on the television that Manhattan was about to be cut off and the military sent in to keep order. It seemed that many, many people were falling ill, even dying. I got a late flight that evening out of JFK. It felt as if I was fleeing a war zone, although the terminal was eerily dark and quiet. On the plane, across the aisle, I spotted a famous opera singer who was escaping from the Met.

It was only when I got back to England that I realised how serious things were. There was absolutely no work in our business for anyone, anywhere. No medium – stage, screen, radio – was untouched. I had always assumed that, whatever might happen in the world, there would always be a place for live performance. After all, simple storytelling needs no more than storytellers and a willing audience. I had not taken pandemics into account. So we all – actors, directors, dressers, crew, stage-door keepers – had to sit quietly, avoid spending too much money and wait.

We put on *Richard II* before the disease struck – in the days of innocence. The story of the play is simple enough. A feckless king, Richard, is deposed by a group of political enemies led by a man called Bolingbroke. The king is killed and Bolingbroke takes the crown as Henry IV. It is the first in a sequence of eight plays that Shakespeare wrote about a devastating period of English history – the Wars of the Roses. The murder of Richard, an anointed king, is the single act that ignites a terrible and long-lasting conflict. It is, in Shakespeare's eyes, the original sin. He clearly disapproves of the chaos and violence that this abuse of the established order brings in its wake. More, the murder is a crime of such magnitude that it takes generations to find effective absolution. In his eyes, Henry, who ordered the murder of Richard, is a guilty and profoundly irresponsible man.

This is certainly how Henry himself sees it. He is one of the many unhappy characters in Shakespeare that has difficulty sleeping. He cannot shake off his guilt, however expert he might be as a ruler. He swears that, as penance, he will travel to Jerusalem, when he feels that his life is coming to an end, and die there. Shakespeare enjoys the irony that Henry never makes it to the Holy Land, but rather dies in a room – popularly known as the Jerusalem Chamber – attached to Westminster Abbey.

I have never played Henry IV. However, I was once asked to a hugely enjoyable dinner in the Jerusalem Chamber. I was to join a celebration of the anniversary of Henry's coronation. The food was apparently based on recipes of the period. Our host was the genial and hospitable Dean of Westminster, who had asked me to read passages from Shakespeare's play *Henry IV, Part II,* in which Henry's death is depicted. Geoffrey Streatfeild read Prince Hal, the son who would inherit the crown as Henry V. Before we ate, the dean explained the significance of holding the dinner in that particular room. He pointed out the fireplace in front of which the king is believed to have collapsed. He mentioned that the building had been commissioned by Richard II. Above us stretched magnificent beams across the roof – on all of which, at regular intervals, we could see the monogram of the builder-king. After the dean's speech, I stood up to do my piece. Towards the end, as Henry died, I looked up to the roof. It was a spontaneous gesture; but, of course, what I saw, and what the dying Henry must have seen if he had done the same, was an inescapable reminder of his crime – a seemingly endless line of Richard's repeated emblem. It took me and the audience completely by surprise. Up until that point, nobody had made the connection. It was, I think for all of us, a genuine and unsettling discovery – although nothing much was said about it at the time.

Henry must have died in physical and mental agony. I felt sure that I was not the only person in the Jerusalem Chamber to feel unnerved. A year later, a man stopped me outside Pimlico tube station in London to tell me that he, too, had been a guest at the anniversary dinner. What he remembered most clearly about the evening was not the grandeur of the occasion or the splendour of the feast, but the chilling reminder of Henry's deep-rooted guilt.

Richard II, in the original versions, is a very long play. Joe Hill-Gibbins, our director, had worked hard to deliver for us a much shorter version. It was a very skilful piece of editing. The show now lasted less than two hours and we played it straight through. Inevitably, the political shenanigans were simplified. The two central protagonists – Richard and Bolingbroke – were isolated. Around them, a small group of actors played everyone else. Various characters – some very famous ones, like John of Gaunt, who delivers the much-quoted speech about England as a 'sceptred isle' – came fleetingly into focus and then faded away again. For much of the time, the cast moved in a pack or like a shoal of fish, applying pressure or registering support to the king and the usurper, as and when the winds of war shifted.

The show was strictly choreographed. Joe has spent a good span of his career in Germany and he brought some of the techniques he had used on the continent into the rehearsal room. For me, a large part of the attraction of the project was the challenge of a new methodology – a more expressionist approach. At the time, I needed something that I would find hard to understand. As a result, I was uncharacteristically silent during the weeks of work, which I now know Joe found a little difficult, but this was because I was unsure of what questions to ask or what debates to initiate. I was confident that Joe knew what he was doing and it seemed that the best policy was to listen and keep quiet.

Our show was not pretty to look at – and nor was Richard. This was interesting. Almost all the Richards that I know about are unquestionably pretty. Ben Whishaw, in his marvellous Richard for the screen or David Tennant as an equally brilliant king for the RSC, both looked lovely. Their Richards wore very beautiful clothes and clearly had impeccable taste and a fastidious aversion to any hint of vulgarity. This feels appropriate. We all know, don't we, that Richard is the man who introduced the fork and the pocket handkerchief to England? So he knew about the finer things in life. More importantly, looking good – a carefully curated appearance – is an essential ingredient of Richard's self-regard. He's very skilled at creating a regal image – most spectacularly when, at one point in the play, he appears to a potentially hostile group of his enemies as a brilliant representation of the sun. Like Edward II in Marlowe's play, Richard was brought up to be king and so, I suppose, he would consider looking like a king to be an essential part of the job. It's also the only thing he's ever known. I think one can see this long-established sense of style in his portrait at Westminster Abbey or in the resplendent 'Wilton Diptych' at the National Gallery in London. Richard's vanity and his extravagance infuriate his nobles. They, unlike the king, see no use for it all – even as they, against their better judgement, find it seductive. It is no accident that the man they choose to succeed Richard is a very different type of king and has a very different, less glaringly theatrical, idea of kingship.

Joe eschewed all this. I was dressed by our designer, Ultz, in black jeans and a black T-shirt. Everyone else looked similar. The set, which had no doors for exits or entrances, was like a prison cell – dull grey metal sheets bolted together to cover walls and floor. This provided a clear metaphor, of course; but it had a literal meaning too. Richard, abused and humiliated, ends his life in prison. In our production, he had buckets of filthy water thrown in his face.

The effect of this brutalism was that Richard's vanity became internalised. When he condescends to meet Bolingbroke, he describes himself as 'like glist'ring Phaeton'. There was never a possibility that I might bear any resemblance to the son of Apollo; but, in that moment, I had to believe that I did and, equally importantly, I had to convince others. Bolingbroke himself describes Richard at this point as 'the blushing discontented sun'. It felt like a shared delusion – a symptom of 'groupthink'. In some ways, Joe and Ultz's vision simplified and clarified the central debate. Richard's extravagant behaviour was not really the issue. Most of his interaction with his favourites had been cut; as had his high-handed demands for money. The central question for the discontented nobility was whether they had the right to overthrow a king chosen by God, anointed by His bishops and, above all, validated by their own support.

Shakespeare's own political beliefs are closely hidden behind the words he wrote and will always remain impossible to retrieve and define. He does not often refer directly to contemporary events. One of the few figures of his time whom he mentions in his plays is the Earl of Essex. Essex was a powerful, glamorous and popular figure. Queen Elizabeth was, at the time, not popular and, significantly, without a direct heir. There were rumblings in court that she should be replaced. For many, Essex was the obvious choice for monarch. In *Henry V*, Shakespeare compares the king's triumphant return to England, after his successes in France, to the Earl of Essex's eagerly anticipated appearance in London after his campaigns in Ireland. One can, I suppose, extrapolate from this that the playwright admired the earl – but we cannot be absolutely certain of this. As it happens, we do know that contemporary politics played a part in the early performance history of *Richard II*. Firstly, the long abdication scene was cut by censors. Secondly, scholars believe that a special performance of the play was commissioned by a group of Essex's supporters. They clearly felt that it would resonate with those who shared their confidence in the earl and their doubts about the queen. The show went ahead. Some of Shakespeare's colleagues were hauled before the authorities to explain themselves. They managed to escape without severe punishment, presumably by pleading their innocence of any ulterior motive on the part of the men who paid for the performance. Whether this was strictly accurate or not, the idea of the deposition of an absolute monarch was clearly in the air.

Just as with Edward II, the major trauma of Richard's life is losing his crown. That is self-evident. But there are differences between the two men. Edward seems almost taken by surprise when he is asked to abdicate. It's as if the idea never occurred to him. Richard's keen sense of victimhood means that, from very early in his story, he is acutely aware of the forces ranged against him and the price he might be asked to pay for both his unpopularity and for his deeply embedded conception of his political role. He both believes and mistrusts the communal fantasy of kingship in which he has to play the central part. When he is asked to step down, he unconsciously blames those around him who are complicit in the myth of kingship. But he expects to suffer. Shakespeare also borrows the template of the abdication scenes from Marlowe, but enriches the psychological texture. Edward is distressed by the loss of his crown; Richard is distressed by the loss of his crown and by the loss of his identity; but he is most disturbed by the shattering of the political consensus. These multiple layers are a characteristic of Shakespeare's writing. So many of his plays – from *The Comedy of Errors* on – explore questions of identity; but in *Richard II* this exploration is extended and enriched. What some see as Richard's compulsive and unattractive need to self-dramatise, his habit of looking at himself from the outside, as it were, is, everyone would agree, a sign of his insecurity. But I found this profoundly sad, not irritating, partly because Richard's identity is so closely bound up with his understanding of his political function. At one point, he bemoans the loss of his name, which, while not strictly true – he can still call himself Richard, I presume – encapsulates his distress. Only in his last moments, when he urges his soul, the soul of an anointed king, to 'mount' and, leaving 'gross flesh' behind, to take its proper place in heaven, is he confident enough in his self-worth, his royal birthright, his God-given status, and finally at peace.

I wanted to avoid being camp when I played Richard II. It is a role that encourages self-conscious theatricality and, to be honest, I find camp easy. Many of my performances have, over the years, been described as camp. There's nothing wrong with that, of course, but I would like to think I'm a little more protean than this would imply. It's a bit like my always being described as 'chubby' or 'stout'. Playing Restoration fops for a year at the RSC probably didn't help the ubiquity of the 'camp' label. After the first night of *The Man of Mode* in Stratford, I went to have dinner with Terry Hands in the local pub. Pam, the landlady, used to entertain a group of critics in the dining room after press nights. Part of the ritual was walking past them to another table, trying to gauge from their expressions the response to the show. They never gave anything away. When I joined Terry that night, he asked me how things had gone and how I had coped with the inevitable first-night nerves. I told him that, while in the bath that morning, I had heard, on the radio, an interview with the actress Evelyn Laye. Miss Laye was a performer famous, in the old days, for light West End comedies. In the interview, she said that she dealt with her nerves by repeating very softly, 'I am Evelyn Laye, I am Evelyn Laye, I am Evelyn Laye.' I told Terry that I had, that night, used the same technique, whispering to myself, 'I am Simon Russell Beale, I am Simon Russell Beale, I am Simon Russell

Beale.' 'How interesting,' Terry replied. 'From what I saw of your performance, it looked as if you were saying, "I am Evelyn Laye, I am Evelyn Laye, I am Evelyn Laye."'

9

Not long after I left the RSC, the National Theatre in London made me an offer. It was to play another fop. I can't remember in which play. To be frank, it wasn't a very exciting idea. There was nothing wrong with the project itself, of course; it was simply that I didn't want to continue doing the sort of work I had done in Stratford. The National clearly felt that I had earned my fop credentials, passed my fop proficiency exams, as it were, and was now sufficiently experienced to continue in the same sort of roles at their more senior theatre. My agent rang the casting department and asked if there was another part in another show that I could do alongside the fop. She was reminded that this was not how the National worked. They cast each play separately. In other words, the rules they worked by were different from those followed by the RSC. I didn't take the part. I was disappointed, of course. The National was, at the time, the most exciting theatre in the country. Throughout my whole time with the RSC, I was aware and envious of the wonderful work that one could see on the South Bank of the Thames. I had seen much of it myself. But the National was, for me, a foreign country. As an outsider, even the theatre building looked both blank and forbidding – a hulking, impregnable mass of concrete lowering over the water.

In 1995, not long after this first, foiled attempt at breaking through the barriers, the director Matthew Warchus invited me to join him at the National in his production of *Volpone* by Ben Jonson. He asked me to play, not a fop, but a nasty little man called Mosca, a servant of the titular character. I accepted without a second thought. I had no idea then how it would change my life. For the next twenty-five years, the National Theatre was my professional home. I love and admire the institution – and the building – without qualification. I left a small part of my heart in Stratford, of course, but, for a long time, I was not away from the National for more than a year at a stretch. A couple of decades after my first performance in the Olivier Theatre – the largest auditorium in the National complex – I read an irritable letter in one of the daily papers. The writer complained that, as far as he could see, all the shows that the National were doing involved either Alan Bennett or Simon Russell Beale; and he wasn't happy about this. It was clearly an exaggeration; but I concede that he had a point. I did a lot of work at the National. I was very, very lucky.

I still get a quiet and self-aggrandising thrill when I walk down the north bank of the Thames and see, across the river, the full splendour of the theatre building. There's my theatre in its glory, I always think. For a long time now, when night falls, the exterior has been flooded with light, so that it glows magenta or emerald or violet. When it first opened, a custom was established that, on every opening night, a firework would be let loose into the sky in celebration – and, presumably, as an advertisement that exciting things were happening inside the building. It was called 'Ralph's Rocket', after the great actor Sir Ralph Richardson. The ceremony fell into abeyance long ago; it's probably seen as a shameless waste of money and no doubt it's dangerous. I would love to see it back.

Whatever some critics say, the National Theatre is housed in a wonderful building. I think it's beautiful – a proud, fearless work of art – and, equally importantly, it does the job for which it was built. The rehearsal rooms, for instance, are very large and blank, full of light and air. Many of the offices on the highest floors of the building have access to balconies over the river and, in consequence, splendid views of the West End. The location is incomparable. If audience members approach the theatre over Waterloo Bridge from the north side, they can enjoy the best view in London – the Palace of Westminster to the right, St Paul's to the left. There are oddities, of course. I have no idea why the rubbish used to be dumped daily next to the main entrance on the river side. I was told that the original plan assumed that the public facade of the theatre would face away from the Thames rather than towards it. God knows why. But clearly, when the plans changed, some of the more basic functions of the theatre that should have remained hidden were suddenly visible. All the time that I was there, the backstage was dour and unloved. The paint was chipped and, outside the dressing rooms, there were always clusters of wires strung along the ceiling. Photographs of past productions were hung on the corridor walls in a valiant attempt to cheer up the workers. It was, frankly, a mess; and perfect.

The dressing rooms are arranged in a large square formation in the heart of the building. The windows of all four floors face inwards; if you feel so inclined, you can wave or shout across to colleagues. Since there are three individual theatres, there are usually three independent companies crammed together at any one time. A first-night ceremony began to develop while I was there and is now firmly established. When the actors of a particular show are called to the stage for their press-night performance – the 'first night' – members of the two other companies rush to the windows and bang the glass repeatedly for a minute or two. I confess to finding this show of solidarity rather moving. It's an acknowledgement of the stress that our fellow performers might be going through, a sign of community, of course, but it's also a gesture that is for actors only and nobody else. Very few other people who work in the building are welcome in the dressing rooms before the shows – not directors or designers or crew members. So the banging of the windows is an ovation by actors for actors.

When the National Theatre celebrated its fiftieth birthday, Nick Hytner invited a host of performers – including some very grand names – to present a show on the Olivier stage. It was televised and broadcast live. Nick knew about the customary banging on the windows. Now I think of it, he'd probably never seen it in the flesh. He asked the stage managers to ensure that all the performers were in their dressing rooms when 'beginners' was called; and he positioned photographers on each side of the square to capture the moment of the ovation. All went ahead as Nick had planned and, a couple of weeks later, the actors were sent prints of the photographs. I have them framed and hung above my desk. The figures standing at each window are too small to make out clearly, but I know, if took out a magnifying glass, I could probably identify Judi and Maggie and Derek and Ralph and Benedict and many, many more.

It takes some time to find one's way around the interior maze of the National. I must now have seen every inch. I was up on the highest roof when London experienced a solar eclipse. All across the city, I could see groups of people who had had the same idea as I had and were standing at the most elevated point they could reach, staring up at the sky. It looked like a movie about the Second Coming. I have been taken down to the very lowest level of the building, where water from the Thames laps just beneath one's feet. It's as if the huge concrete structure is floating on the mud.

And then there's the green-room bar – buried away far from members of the public. Years ago, it used to keep pub hours; now it's open only in the evenings. It's pretty basic. There are old, peeling posters pasted on three sides and the fourth opens on to a narrow concrete balcony that overlooks a side road and the large neighbouring building. There's a television screen on one wall, where fans can catch up with major sporting events. For a couple of horrifying days, it carried non-stop coverage of the 9/11 attacks on the World Trade Center, until someone decided that the endless repetition of the same terrible images had become unbearable. For most of the time, during the day, the bar is almost empty. Occasionally, one can spot actors sitting there, waiting quietly for upcoming auditions but, otherwise, it's very quiet. However, in the evening, after the shows have come down, it's crammed with actors and their guests. In rather limited theatrical terms, it is – or, at least, it used to be – one of the most exciting places in London. All the greatest theatre actors in the country have spent some time there. On my first visit – as a friend of one of the performers – I stood there gawping at all the famous faces. I think I was still a student at the time; or had just started out as a professional actor. In the corner, I spotted Ian Charleson. There, in front of me, was the man who had been so beguiling in *Chariots of Fire* and so sexy in the National's production of *Guys and Dolls*. He would go on to give a legendary performance as Hamlet, though I wasn't to know that at the time. We were fleetingly introduced. I never met him again.

The production of *Volpone* was dominated by our leading actor, Michael Gambon. He was a large man – or rather he gave the impression of great substance. His personality filled the room. He had elegant hands with long fingers and a barrel chest. He once told me that anyone who wanted to become a great stage actor needed a big chest. I suspect that, having looked me up and down, he was just being kind; or, more probably, he was teasing. He moved like a dancer. As all those who worked with him will tell you, Michael was mischievous. In the grand tradition of theatrical raconteurs, he could spin a great anecdote; but he quite obviously left it unclear as to whether any of his stories were true or not. Perhaps this ability to bamboozle a listener was part of what made him a great artist; and there is no doubt that, as Volpone, he gave a monumental performance. He always did, of course. When we first met, for a read-through of the play, he apologised in advance for the poor quality of his first attempts at the principal role. He found it difficult to read aloud in front of a group of strangers, he said. When he opened his mouth – Volpone begins the play with a grandiloquent speech – his voice shook the room. There was no hint of hesitancy or weakness. I think he might have been having me on.

I did two plays by Ben Jonson during my time at the National. They were very different productions. *Volpone* was shamelessly lush, a gorgeous-looking critique of the lives of the very wealthy in Renaissance Venice. It reeked of decay. My second Jonson play, *The Alchemist*, was directed by Nick Hytner and was set in contemporary London. It was a very seedy, small world, with no hint of Venetian splendour. However, the text of both plays posed the same problems and provided the same satisfactions. Jonson sounds odd to many modern ears. His writing is similar enough to Shakespeare's for us to assume that, after only a few minutes of playing, it will become relatively easy to understand. But, whether we are aware of it or not, Shakespeare's words are part of our aural environment and Jonson's are not. It takes time to get used to them. I think many of the actors in both companies had a sense that audiences found it difficult to relax. There may be a more complex set of reasons for this than unfamiliarity. Jonson's work is stuffed with strange words and Latin tags, and that is difficult enough. But it is also sharp-edged and severe in its judgements. The characters that people his plays are, for the most part, either stupid or venal; and, despite his satirical purpose, the writer ensures that the good end happily and the bad unhappily. Jonson adheres to a very strict moral code. There is no evidence of Shakespeare's fluid humanity.

My Italian friend, Mimmo, came to *The Alchemist*. He was not convinced by Jonson. When asked, by a client in his hairdressing salon, what the play was about, he replied, in his lightly accented English, 'What's it all about? I don't know. It's all about rubbish.' Mind you, Mimmo has his doubts about Shakespeare, too. 'Everyone takes twenty minutes to say they're leaving the stage,' he once told me. 'They all wear black and die at the end.' But he has loyally attended every show that I have done, bless him.

Jonson might not display Shakespeare's breadth of interest, but the plays are riotously funny; and the construction of the plots – especially in *The Alchemist* – is astonishing. The playwright doesn't put a foot wrong. He must have sat down with a big piece of paper spread over his writing desk on which he charted the movements of each character minute by minute. It's the closest a Jacobean got to writing farce. Someone, I can't remember whom, has compared Jonson, accurately, to a watchmaker. It's no wonder that he was exasperated by Shakespeare's more lackadaisical approach. And, as for his evident brilliance, I remember Terry Hands saying to me that, in a just universe, the government would long ago have established a Royal Jonson Company.

I have never played a classic farce. But I know that they are notoriously difficult – and often miserable – to rehearse. After the hundredth run-through of a particular routine, it's sometimes difficult to remember that a farce is supposed to be funny. *The Alchemist* was not a miserable experience by any means, but it was hard, technical work. With farce or farce-like plays, so much time is spent working out which door to come through or hide behind or which prop to pick up or, in the case of the Jonson play, which disguise to adopt. Actors are also required to run around a great deal; so endless energy is an unavoidable requirement. I remember Alex Jennings muttering under his breath to Lesley Manville and me – fellow conspirators in the play – as we were racing up and down the multiple layers of the set, all three of us spouting endless Jonsonian verse, 'Christ, these fucking stairs . . .'

The National introduced me to many new forms of drama and many new writers – Shaw, Stoppard, Pinter, Gorky. My first artistic director was Richard Eyre, but I never really got to know him while I was employed at his theatre. I was far too junior. It was only later, when I worked for him on a film adaptation of the *Henry IV* plays, that I discovered what a wonderful man and what a prodigiously skilled director he is. And generous, too. Of all the attributes necessary for a successful artistic director, generosity must be one of the most important and, I would guess, one of the most difficult to maintain. The ability to recognise talent even when the results on the stage are not to your liking is a sign of great confidence. Richard has that ability; and so, clearly, does Nick Hytner. The result is that, as is well known, both of them enjoyed reigns at the National Theatre that were periods of triumphant achievement.

Richard was succeeded by Trevor Nunn, for whom I had worked at the RSC. One of the first things that Trevor did was to establish a repertory company of actors – the same group performing a series of plays – not unlike the model that was followed up in Stratford. He was responsible for one of the few near-perfect productions I have been involved with – *Summerfolk* by Maxim Gorky, in 1999. The play is a long and detailed study of Russian holidaymakers enjoying the last days of summer, far from the city, in their rural dachas. Revolution is not far over the horizon. It feels like a response, or, rather, a sequel, to Chekhov's *The Cherry Orchard*. I was asked to play the tiny part of an overworked doctor, who was called Dudakov. Dudakov was happily married with a brood of young children, all of whom appeared on stage. As with Chekhov, the writing was funny, sardonic and rueful, but with a sharper satirical edge. Like Chekhov, it was glorious to play.

Trevor knew exactly what he wanted. He seemed to have a detailed picture of the production in his head. At least, that's how it looked to me, but then I was in the rehearsal room very little. He must sometimes have had to improvise. In fact, there was a moment when, unintentionally, I contributed to a small change in the script. It was a result of my anxiety. The trouble with small roles is that, because there is so little to do and there are so few words to say, there is a danger of tying oneself in knots with the effort of getting it all absolutely right. At least with a part like Hamlet, there is time to warm up, to get into your stride. In the last act of *Summerfolk*, Dudakov, exhausted from work and from helping to look after a host of children, had to rush on stage to examine a young man who had unsuccessfully attempted suicide. The man, played by Jasper Britton, had tried to shoot himself. In one of our final rehearsals, the doctor put on his glasses, peered at the wound and confidently announced to the assembled company that his diagnosis was a slight wound 'to the right shoulder'. The doctor – or, rather, I – was wrong. Jasper immediately corrected me. 'Left,' he muttered weakly. 'Left,' Dudakov repeated. This was not in the script, but it was too good to let go. Despite not being a part of the Gorky original, Trevor kept it in.

In the same year, Trevor was also responsible for my first experience of a full-blown musical. He asked his close friend and colleague John Caird, whom I was later to work with on *Hamlet*, to direct a production of Bernstein's *Candide* – a show with a rather troubled history. The score is, as one would expect, magnificent, an *homage* to the great Western European musical tradition that Bernstein loved so much. The overture is dazzling, the final chorus is overwhelming and in between is a riotous exploration of every type of classical music you can think of, from chorale to serialism to nineteenth-century opera. However, the book – the script that carries the story – is a mess. So many writers – distinguished writers, too – have contributed to *Candide* since its first outing that it's almost impossible to locate any narrative coherence. This may be partly due to the fact that *Candide* is a satirical work and the targets of satire have kept changing over the years – and the team of writers responded to this. John wanted to start again. He announced at an early rehearsal that he aimed to keep all Bernstein's music and that, between us, our job was to build up a new script; and that new script would be based on the original source material – the eighteenth-century novella by Voltaire. It was a clever and simple idea. Any satire would be Voltaire's, not somebody else's; and it became clear that Voltaire's contempt for hypocrisy and complacency is as relevant now as it was when he was writing.

I was given the responsibility of narrating the whole thing, while the multi-talented Daniel Evans – now a very important theatre director – played the title role. Despite Bernstein's demand for a lush, symphonic sound, the orchestra was pared right down and the *tempi* were very fast indeed. The result was sharp and aggressive. The set consisted of a large black circle ringed by a gold, metallic band. Each member of the company played many different parts. Someone told me that during our chaotic final dress rehearsal, the backstage felt like a village jumble sale – with costumes piled knee-high or flying through the air as actors raced around trying to complete multiple quick changes. In time, over the run, things thankfully calmed down and the production was well received by audience and critics. In line with John's instructions, we managed to include nearly all of the original score. There was only one number that we had to leave out; we just couldn't find a place for it. And, for the most part, the lyrics remained unchanged. We had to alter the words of one song. They happened to have been written by Stephen Sondheim; so we, rather hesitantly, got in touch with him and asked his advice. He graciously rewrote them.

John stormed into rehearsals one day and said, 'We've got it all wrong. We keep talking about Bernstein's *Candide*. But it's not Bernstein's *Candide*, it's Voltaire's *Candide*.' This blunt statement reinforced the aims that John had articulated during the first working days – that we should go back to the original source material – but it also led to his staging a rather strange opening to the show. I thought it was great; others didn't. It certainly wasn't how a musical usually begins. Essentially, we started with the writer rather than the composer. As the audience came in, they saw a large trunk set in the centre of the stage. When the lights began to dim, Voltaire walked down the central aisle of the auditorium, crossed the empty space and sat on the trunk. Silence fell and, for a long moment, Voltaire remained motionless. He then looked up, as if a thought had come into his head, and the famous overture began. The writer had summoned up the music. Later in the same overture, Voltaire got off the trunk, opened the lid, and all the other characters climbed out one by one from beneath the stage. Now the story could begin in earnest.

Since I was playing Voltaire, it's predictable that I would find this thrilling, even if some critics felt that it was a weak beginning to the evening. But I saw it as a statement of intent; the show started as it meant to go on. *Candide* was primarily Voltaire's creation. He never left the stage. Although I had very little to sing, I had a great deal to speak – long passages of Voltaire's prose. As it happens, it was during one of these passages that I fell off the stage – the only time I've ever done so. I was walking backwards around the far circumference of the playing space, trying to give an impression of cool control. I could see very little, since a fierce spotlight was following me and there was dry ice everywhere. I was wearing a pair of heeled, eighteenth-century shoes and, of course, I was talking and talking. According to a friend who happened to be watching the show, I unaccountably disappeared out of the light and then, almost immediately, reappeared – like, he said, one of those wobbly toys you see in the back of minicabs. Fortunately, the stage was not much higher than the floor of the auditorium but I landed in the lap of some poor, unsuspecting woman. Having got back into the spotlight, I had to stand there while another member of the company sang a number. When it ended and before I started the next piece of narration, I bent down to apologise to the woman and to check that she wasn't injured. She looked surprised – more surprised, in fact, than she had done after the original collision – and assured me in a whisper that she was fine. I sensed that she was not telling the whole truth. It must, in all honesty, have really hurt.

I was asked to perform some new work at the National. I joined Charlotte Jones for her rewriting of *Hamlet* – a play called *Humble Boy* – and acted Stalin in John Hodge's *Collaborators,* a marvellous exploration of the relationship between the Soviet dictator and a terrified Bulgakov – the writer embodied in a performance of great delicacy by Alex Jennings. But I wasn't to do another musical until, in 2005, I went to Broadway to join the company of *Spamalot.* Based on a Monty Python film, this was, perhaps, a less refined work than *Candide,* but it was joyous to play. It was also my only experience of a musical in the city where the musical is king – New York.

Losing Your Mind

Timon of Athens

Timon of Athens is, quite simply, the oddest play in the canon. There are so many things about it that don't look right. It's a muddle. For a start, its printing history is very curious indeed. This history links two plays together – *Timon* and *Troilus and Cressida.* The editors of the First Folio, as they scrabbled around for copies of the forty-odd plays that their friend had left behind, naturally assumed that they would get to include *Troilus and Cressida* in Shakespeare's book and, understandably, left space for it. They then found that they had great difficulty in obtaining the rights for the play. A number of publishers in London owned the rights to print many of Shakespeare's plays and their permission had to be obtained before those same works could be included in the new collection. Without *Troilus and Cressida*, there was a danger that the Folio would be left with an embarrassing and unsightly clutch of blank pages. Some early printings of the book are, indeed, missing *Troilus and Cressida*. It is thought that, in desperation, the editors looked through their friend's back catalogue and found, in a bottom drawer, a version of *Timon of Athens*. The gap was rapidly filled.

Frankly, I'm not sure that the playwright would have wanted to include it. No doubt, there are people who would disagree with me, but, to my eyes, it looks unfinished – no more than a late, almost-performable, sketch. What is certain is that it is one of Shakespeare's collaborative efforts. For *Timon*, he joined up with the younger Thomas Middleton. The latter wrote sections of the *Macbeth* that we have inherited and may also have helped with *Measure for Measure*; so the two writers presumably got on well enough. It still comes as a surprise to many that Shakespeare collaborated at all; but it was in the nature of how the theatrical environment worked at the time that co-writing was common – even for a genius. I guess that the fiercely competitive group of London writers who wrote for ever-hungry theatres had to produce such a great volume of words so regularly and so consistently that there was no time to stand on one's dignity. Work was work, after all.

It's fun to speculate how Shakespeare and Middleton might have approached *Timon*. The plot, as it stands, is very simple. This is unsurprising, since the source material is a very brief story included in Plutarch's *Lives of the Noble Grecians and Romans*. Timon – the central figure – is a very rich Athenian. We have no idea how he made his money. He's just very rich. That's all the playwrights think we need to know. He is also very generous. He holds marvellous parties and is forever presenting his friends with extravagant gifts. He is a lavish patron of the arts. Inevitably, his compulsive spending lands him in trouble and he loses all his money. Again, we don't really know the details of this crash. His friends, far from offering him their support, disown him. Hurt and furious, Timon leaves Athens and starts a new life as a hermit in the surrounding countryside. People visit him on occasion, but his company is so unpleasant – he can't stop railing against the world – that they never stay for long. At one moment, as he is digging around for something to eat, he finds, buried in the ground, an impossibly large amount of gold. This feels like a plot device from an old fable. The Athenians hear of Timon's good fortune and rush out to befriend him again. He rejects them and, ignoring the gold, wanders off the stage to die.

The first half of the play is probably written by Middleton, although, no doubt, Shakespeare looked it over and proffered the occasional thought. As a solo writer, Middleton was responsible, among other things, for a series of bouncy city comedies. The early dialogue of *Timon* reflects this. The writing has a spring in its step; it's fluid and easy enough to perform. Then Shakespeare takes over in the second half and the verse becomes gnarled, tortured and much harder to deliver. Since Timon is by now a very disturbed character, this volte-face in terms of the style of writing is, though jarring, appropriate. It's inevitable that each playwright would have his own interests and employ his own individual techniques. Shakespeare never wrote a city comedy, but, needless to say, he knew a thing or two about extreme unhappiness. The two writers must surely have agreed that each should play to their strengths. But perhaps if they had had the time or inclination to work more intensively on the play, *Timon* would have finished up as a smoother and more coherent product. As it stands, there is a perceptible shift in tone halfway through the story; and it is up to the modern theatre practitioner to decide whether this shift is something worth exploiting.

Did Middleton and Shakespeare scribble down ideas about each other's work, sending messages back and forth across London? I presume they must have done. One of the more puzzling parts of the play deals with a subplot, which springs up out of the blue and then is barely developed. It concerns a character called Alcibiades, an Athenian rebel who, at the end of the play, takes over the government of the city. I can imagine Shakespeare and his younger colleague agreeing that this secondary storyline had potential and that they would come back to it later. But they never did. In fact, I think they probably decided that the whole thing was, on balance, unworkable. Many scholars believe that it was never performed – which tells you something.

Of course, it is precisely these problems that make the challenge of staging *Timon* so fascinating. It seems that those who decide to present the play fall into two distinct groups. The first take the script as we read it in the Folio and, without changing a word and giving the playwrights the benefit of the doubt, trust that, in performance, it will make sense. The second group, which includes Nick Hytner and me, are more ruthless and change everything that we deem, perhaps foolishly, to be weak or ill-written. Nick decided to do a production of *Timon* at the National Theatre in 2012, the year that London was hosting the Olympics. The city – one of the world's great financial markets – was basking in self-confidence. On every street corner, there were volunteers wearing purple shirts who acted as kindly hosts to the many international visitors – and, rather charmingly, to residents such as myself. It felt good to be a Londoner. Given that *Timon* is one of the most aggressive and unattractive plays that Shakespeare wrote and given that it highlights the greed and self-interest of the very rich, it was, frankly, a mischievous choice – compounded by Nick's early decision that we should set the production in London rather than in Athens. It quite clearly was not going to be a feel-good evening for our local audience. In fact, there was a more serious reason for this relocation than mischief. So many of the plays from the Elizabethan and Jacobean periods, even if they are set elsewhere, feel as if they are about Londoners – or, at least, English men and women. As I remember, Nick's original choice for the city's Olympic year was more celebratory – *A Midsummer Night's Dream*. That idea must have faded in his mind, because, one day, ringing me just before boarding a plane, he asked whether I knew *Timon*. I replied that I must have read it at university, but hadn't looked at it since and knew very little about it. He offered me the title role and, trusting in his judgement that it would be worth doing, I accepted.

As it happens, Nick was to direct *A Midsummer Night's Dream* a few years later at his new playhouse opposite the Tower of London – the Bridge Theatre. Sadly, I played no part in it. I think of it as one of the most successful and enjoyable things he has ever done. He played fast and loose with the authoritative text. Titania's words were spoken by Oberon – so it was the king rather than the queen of the fairies who fell in love with Bottom. The rude mechanicals, who spend their time rehearsing and performing a play for the duke, personified all the most irritating and pretentious traits of modern theatre culture; and Puck grew so cavalier with his spraying of the magic potion that everyone, at one point or another, seemed to fall in love with everyone else. It was a promenade production, which meant that the performers mingled freely among the audience. At the end, loud music played and the whole theatre danced together. It was as if a greater power – Shakespeare, God, Nick Hytner – was saying, 'For God's sake, stop worrying. And stop judging. Just keep loving.'

Having decided that *Timon* would be our offering for the Olympic year, a small group of us met to go through the text. One of the team was Ben Power, whom I would later join up with on his version of *The Lehman Trilogy*. We worked intensively for a couple of days, huddled over multiple editions of the play. The Alcibiades subplot went almost immediately. It disappeared because, quite simply, it didn't make much sense. It was neither prepared nor resolved convincingly. Alcibiades still had a role to play, of course, but it was more tightly woven into Timon's story. He was transformed, in our contemporary version, into the leader of a countercultural movement that bore a distinct similarity to the Occupy protesters who, at that time, were crowded around the steps of St Paul's Cathedral in London. Our Alcibiades was different from the original aristocratic and ambitious figure that Shakespeare had imagined, but nevertheless fulfilled the same function – as the man who would head the Athenian state after the play is over. I had observed Nick, in his famous modern-dress productions of classical plays, using this technique of finding an equivalent in our world for characters and situations devised centuries earlier. I think, for him, it was part of the fun – to develop, in this way, a witty and incisive commentary on the original text.

Among many other things that we discovered in our first reading together, it was interesting to note that, for the second half of the play, Timon doesn't get a proper break. To me, this was a further indication that the work is unfinished. Shakespeare tends to give his leading characters time to rest for a few minutes as the pressure of the latter half of their story grows more and more intense. This is certainly true of Hamlet, Leontes, Macbeth and King Lear. Richard III is an exception – although there are a few short minutes when the king is off-stage – but maybe that's because it's an early work. I imagine one of the actors telling the young playwright that sometimes less is more and that conserving your leading actor's energy might be a wise idea. I imagine, too, Shakespeare taking this advice on board. Timon, however, spends a disproportionate and unusual amount of time on stage; and this is exacerbated if the feeble subplot is discarded, as it was in our production. Timon is also relentless and monomaniacal in his analysis of the world around him. He doesn't stop – which is tiring for both actor and audience. One critic, despite admiring much in the show, described the evening as like being repeatedly hit over the head with the First Folio. He may have had a point.

After our brain-storming session, Nick went off to prepare a working script. Weeks later, he came into the rehearsal room, on our first day, clutching copies of his edition. He explained that he had felt the need to add a few lines from other Shakespeare plays – principally from *Coriolanus*. No audience member seemed to notice these interpolations – or, at least, they never mentioned them – except Ralph Fiennes, who, when he came to the show, clocked them immediately. Of course, he had just completed a monumental film of the play, which he had directed and in which he also played Coriolanus; so perhaps it was to be expected that he would recognise the odd, strangely familiar line here and there. Still, I was impressed. Much later in the rehearsal process, Nick discovered that it was difficult to settle on a fitting ending for the play. He needed to find a couple of lines that had a more effective sense of finality or flourish than were in the original. He asked the stage manager to collate all the Shakespearean lines that she could find that contained the words 'peace' and 'liberty'. He felt that, at the end of the story, Athens deserved to look forward to a happier future. After half-an-hour on her laptop, the stage manager presented Nick with a substantial selection. He chose a line from *As You Like It*. It was a line spoken by a character called Celia, the ever-loyal friend of the central figure, Rosalind, just as they are both about to flee from an oppressive life at court into the Forest of Arden. Again, when it came to the performances, nobody seemed to recognise it. So, Shakespeare's virulent and unforgiving diatribe against the evils of greed and self-interest ended with a passage from one of his most delicate and witty comedies. The incongruity tickled me.

The play opens with a scene in which Timon appears at his most expansive and generous. In the original script, he is pestered by a string of artists clamouring for his attention and, of course, his money. Nick set these encounters in an environment with which, as director of a major national theatre, he confessed to being very familiar. Timon was guest-of-honour at the opening of an art gallery – named after him, of course – which was attended by all the richest and most influential people in the city. A gaggle of good-looking waiters, of both sexes, floated through the throng of guests, carrying rectangles of slate piled with elaborate canapés. Everyone was drinking expensive champagne. The first half of the evening continued in the same vein. In Tim Hatley's glorious design, characters appeared in luxurious offices that enjoyed breathtaking views of London, sat down to fabulous dinners and, at one point, were entertained with a private performance by senior dancers from the Royal Ballet. This sequence was something of a coup – a short work by the much-admired dancer, Edward Watson, performed every night by bona fide members of the national ballet company.

And then everything collapses. The second half of the play was set in the wasteland of a failed building site. Timon, now homeless, lived among a forest of concrete stumps – grim evidence of some bankrupted architectural project. He kept his few belongings in a shopping trolley and scrabbled for food in black binbags that spilled their rotting contents over the stage. It was here, bizarrely, that he discovered the gold. Nick admitted that he found this moment difficult to stage. As I said earlier, it has the quality of a myth or legend; and it seemed that the only way to deal with such an unlikely dramatic twist was to embrace its absurdity. In our version, Timon found, not a couple of coins or even a heavy purse, but enough gold to serve as the reserve of a small country. From below the stage, as golden light flooded through a trapdoor, I dug out a number of heavy ingots and piled them high. After a moment of sardonic delight, Timon hid them away and, for the rest of his story, ignored his newfound wealth.

I admit that it didn't really work; but then Shakespeare's writing hadn't helped. One of the things that I most admire about Nick Hytner's productions is his concern with the minutiae of narrative logic. When I worked with the director Katie Mitchell, in the early years of her career, she displayed the same formidable rigour – the school of super-realism, I suppose. I have spent many pleasurable hours with Nick in the rehearsal room talking through tiny details that would appear to any outside observer to be irrelevant, but which are cumulatively significant. I think the moment with the gold bugged him, because it seemed an example of careless or lazy writing. Why is the gold there in the first place? Who buried it? Why is there so much of it? These questions remained unanswered; and that, understandably, was unsatisfying.

Other textual difficulties, however, opened up interesting possibilities – Timon's isolation, for instance. He has no family – no wife, no children, no parents. The only relationship we witness that has any emotional component is with his loyal steward – played magnificently, in our production, by Deborah Findlay. She loves and admires him; but he takes her love for granted. He remains absolutely and happily alone. It's a small psychological step from this observation to the definition of the reasons for Timon's compulsive generosity. Quite simply, he buys friendship just as he buys beautiful houses, *objets d'art*, thoroughbred horses and magnificent greyhounds. In this way, he remains detached and thinks of himself as secure. I decided, too, that Timon had inherited his wealth from long-dead parents and therefore could not be expected to have any conception of his own vulnerability. It seems doubtful that he has a complex inner life; he neither loves nor is willing to accept the love of others. His wealth defines him; and, as with Richard II and his crown, when he loses his money, he also loses himself.

In fact, more accurately, Timon loses his role and his sense of self-worth and, unlike Richard, feels compelled to redefine himself. Many would argue that his new personality is an improvement on the old. At least, they would say, he ends his life as a man who is honest about himself and the world around him. Whether this enlightenment makes him happy is another matter. I cannot put it any better than to say that, despite the power of his righteous anger, Timon dies somehow incomplete as a man – ironically, rather like the play.

These thoughts tied in with another peculiar feature of the text. Timon dies offstage. His death is reported twice – another oddity. It appears that he has drowned; or, at least, a monument has been hastily erected at the sea's edge. I don't know of any other tragic hero by Shakespeare who dies offstage. In the normal run of things, the central character in a tragedy dies bang in the centre of the playing space, bathed in light, surrounded by a gaggle of distressed spectators. It seems only right and proper. Timon creeps off to die like a stray dog. This may have been something that Shakespeare would have changed as he continued his work on the play; but it's actually a powerful idea that he may very well have retained. I found it useful as it stood. There was something unbearably moving about a man fading away, gradually losing definition, disappearing silently into the water. His self-regard is so minimal by the end of his story that he can't muster up the interest or the energy for an impressive death scene. At the end of the play, what we see, or rather what we hear about, is the ultimate personal (and theatrical) nihilism.

I wondered, at one point in rehearsal, whether, in the final moments of the story, we should flood the stage with water. I liked the idea of the whole horror, the profound disappointment, being swallowed and washed clean by the sea. It would be expensive and tough for the technical team, of course, but it would certainly be impressive. Nick, predictably, looked unconvinced.

Halfway through the run, I fell on stage and broke a finger. It was during the fourth act, when Timon is at the full height of his fury. I slipped on an old plastic binbag. I knew immediately that it was a bad fall – there was an audible crunch – but I continued talking for a few more lines. Some of the papers reported, flatteringly, that I kept going for a couple of minutes; but, sadly, that is not true. After a few seconds, I looked at my hand and one of my fingers had been bent into the shape of a Z. My fellow actor, Hilton McRae, whispered that I should probably leave the stage and get to a hospital. So I explained to the audience that I had injured myself and walked off. Poor Hilton was left to entertain the audience by himself. Apparently, he was marvellous.

I tell this story not so much for the gory details as for the fact that what happened next showed how smoothly the National can run when it needs to – like a Rolls-Royce. When I reached the wings, various cast and crew members said how sorry they were, even as they were stripping me of bits of my costume. My understudy, Paul Dodds, who was about to make his entrance as another character, was speedily dressed as Timon and, within seconds, walked on stage. He took up from where I had left off, raging violently against the rooted iniquity that Timon could see all around him. I think Paul's first line was 'I am sick of this false world' and it was downhill – or uphill – from then on. Under tremendous pressure, he delivered, I believe, a faultless performance, without a single textual mistake. Before I had reached my dressing room, the show was back up and running. It was as if nothing untoward had happened.

The theatre nurse and Jo, my dresser, bundled me into a cab and I was driven to St Thomas' Hospital, where another nurse introduced me to the delights of gas-and-air and pulled my finger back into shape. I had insisted on showering before I left the theatre, which my dresser and the nurse said was unnecessary and foolish; but, remembering that my grandmother advised me always to wear clean underpants in case I was unexpectedly run over by a bus, I thought it was better to appear in the casualty department as clean and as neat as possible. Not that the staff at the hospital would have cared, but I didn't want to look like Timon at his most desperate.

The next day I was back at work, albeit with a bandaged hand. As I arrived, Paul Dodds was standing in front of the stage door, having his picture taken for a national newspaper. I stood and watched and then, when the photographer was satisfied, Paul and I walked together back to our dressing rooms – to do the show that night in its original version.

King Lear

Timon's age is indeterminate. Towards the end of the play, out of nowhere, one of the Athenian bigwigs reminds him of his earlier success as a general. So, presumably, he is a mature man; although I suspect that a citizen in ancient Greece could probably attain the rank of general quite early in their career. Notoriously, we have difficulty pinning down how old Hamlet is. The playwright implies that he must be in his thirties; but, before the play starts, he is a student at a university in Germany, which might make a modern audience member think he is younger than that. He certainly behaves, at times, like a teenager. In both cases, it's not really that important and it clearly didn't bother the playwright. King Lear, on the other hand, is unquestionably an old man. He says that he is eighty; and the play is, in large part, a study of old age. I was quite young – in my fifties – when I played him professionally, but at least I wasn't seventeen, as I was when I tackled the part at school. Some friends and colleagues thought that, as a middle-aged man, I was too young to play Lear and that I should wait a few more years. They may have been right; and I would certainly like to play him again – when I am closer to the right age. Theatrical lore links King Lear with Juliet. If the latter part is given to a performer in their early teens – Juliet's age in the play – then there is a risk that the demands of the role might be beyond them. Likewise, there is a similar risk in giving Lear, a massively demanding part, to an actor in their later, feebler years.

In fact, I wasn't alone in playing Lear when I was still relatively young; many had done the same before me. And, of course, I was following in the venerable footsteps of the actors for whom Shakespeare first wrote his plays. I recall a fascinating conversation on the balcony of the National Theatre bar with my friend, the writer and academic, James Shapiro, when the subject of actors' ages came up. He promised that, having read all the comments about my playing Lear in my fifties, he would go back home to New York and do a bit of light research about Shakespeare's company, the King's Men. Unsurprisingly, it turns out that a career in the theatre in those days was a young man's game. Richard Burbage, the company's leading actor, and many of his fellow performers must have grown used to playing old men and women. It was an unexceptional component of their bag of tricks. And, by the way, at the same time, alongside the senior actors, the playwright must have employed the talents of an extraordinary stable of very young men – the female impersonators. They must have enjoyed great talent and fearsome training. How else could Shakespeare have written such complex women's roles as Rosalind, Lady Macbeth and Cleopatra?

As his story progresses, Lear loses his mind – just like a handful of other Shakespearean characters, of course. But, re-reading the play before the start of rehearsals in 2013, I was struck by the details of the king's descent into madness. Because this descent is charted over a relatively long period, all the different elements of his insanity are very clearly delineated. Here are sudden bursts of rage, perhaps even physical violence. Here are the mood swings, the emotional lability, the lapses of memory, the sexually charged language, even the hallucinations. It was as if Shakespeare had observed, at close quarters, a man succumbing to the horrors of senile dementia, or had even read a medical textbook. Lear is mad in quite specific ways; and the play is, in large part, the study of a deteriorating mind, just as *Romeo and Juliet*, for instance, is a study of first love. I know that, throughout his career, Shakespeare recorded the behaviour of kings and queens, courtiers and soldiers, men and women of all types and conditions. He's famous for his breadth of interest. But here, in *King Lear*, the specificity was striking. Shakespeare seemed to be reporting as much as inventing. This prompted me to look outside the limits of the text – an approach that I had never before employed with a play by Shakespeare. I turned, of course, to the medics in my family.

I was sitting in the garden of my sister's house, talking with my nephew Ben, who, at that time, was training to be a doctor. We began to talk about dementia. I wondered aloud whether any psychiatric specialist had analysed Lear's behaviour. It's the sort of parlour game that seems popular among some medical professionals. Years ago, my father sent me an article about Ophelia's madness that he had seen in a well-respected medical journal. So I felt sure that someone somewhere must have written about Lear. Ben went away to trawl the internet and came back very promptly to tell me that a senior doctor had, after looking at the evidence, decided that Lear suffers from a condition called Lewy body dementia; and, indeed, the symptoms described by the doctor matched those of the old king. The only problem with using this information as a guide to performance is that nobody recovers from dementia and it seems that Lear does, in some ways, get better. But that statement is itself debatable and, anyway, Shakespeare is writing a play rather than an academic paper and has other, broader aims in mind than strict scientific accuracy. So I decided, even with some caveats in mind, to use Lewy body dementia as a template for my version of Lear.

My brother Andy, a senior consultant at a large regional hospital, offered to introduce me to a work colleague who specialised in geriatrics. She kindly agreed to meet and show me around her department – in particular, the dementia wing. She had a large, generous smile and an aura of imperturbable, amused detachment. This was a necessary protective strategy, I presume. Many of those in her care were, of course, very ill. There was a circular walkway in the largest room of the ward; patients, if they felt the need to walk, could start on their travels and, unaware that they were going round in circles, would never get lost. I found this both ingenious and depressing; as was the fake bus stop located just outside the building, where no buses ever stopped, but which patients, if they managed to escape the confines of the hospital, always seemed to locate. There they could wait safely – and fruitlessly – for transport to take them home.

I took notes, which felt a little callous. After all, I was aware of a great deal of unhappiness around me. I noticed, too, that all the patients were physically tiny, as if they had shrunk through their illness. Like most of us, I've watched people grow progressively older over time and I assume this shrinkage is to be expected. Peter Hall was a man of colossal presence and great power. It could be argued that he created, almost from scratch, our nationally subsidised theatre culture. He suffered from dementia in the last years of his life. The last time I saw him, before his death in 2017, he had metamorphosed into a very small, frail figure. He was also shy and benign rather than imposing, as he had been in his prime. I mimicked him directly in *King Lear,* though it is arguable whether benignity is ever much in evidence in the old king. Through the length of the show, I tried to shrink, just as Peter had. The first thing that his daughter, Rebecca, said to me, when she came to see the show, was that I must have based a great deal of my performance on her father. She was right.

The most evocative features of the dementia ward, though, were the circular walkway and the fake bus stop. They struck me as a mundane and pathetic representation of Lear's predicament. The king's story starts with his announcement to family and friends that he wishes to abdicate. He will give up any practical political responsibility. He divides his kingdom between two of his daughters. He then foolishly insists that he is, despite his renunciation of power, to be treated with the same respect as before and to enjoy similar benefits – including a retinue of a hundred knights. Having no home of his own, he and his attendants will travel around the country staying with accommodating relatives. In other words, he wants to have his cake and eat it. I suppose he thinks that this is the least he deserves; but, of course, it proves to be a disaster, in both national and personal terms. In a very short time, internecine struggles turn into full-scale civil war; and, mirroring this, the old king, without the support of his children, is left on the sidelines, raging impotently and slowly losing his sanity.

Being sidelined and homeless is not something that the king appreciates. The legendary director Peter Brook once made a wonderful movie of *King Lear*. He employed an abiding image of wagons carrying people from castle to castle all over the country. Clearly, Brook seems to be saying, there is an urgent need both to cement new alliances and to neutralise the residual power of the former leader. People have to keep moving in order to keep safe – and alive. It's the sort of thing one can't really present realistically on stage, but it works wonderfully on film. The sight of the speeding carriages thundering through the gathering storm sums up the nationwide discombobulation that has resulted from Lear's actions. All the figures in the story are unsettled, quite literally – Lear most of all. One of the most heart-stopping moments in the story is played out by the king and his ever-loyal court jester when, looking for a bed for the night, we see them pausing together in transit between the houses of his two daughters – just like old people waiting at the bus stop for a bus that will never come. Without warning, Lear, for the first time, articulates his fear that he might lose his mind:

> *'O let me not be mad, not mad, sweet heaven. I would*
> *not be mad.*
> *Keep me in temper, I would not be mad.'*

It seems clear that, for Lear, the possibility of madness is not new; and, of course, it provides the simplest explanation for his behaviour in the opening scene. I decided, as many actors have done before me, that the king's abdication is a pre-emptive gesture. He feels he has to retire before his dementia kicks in. What is distressing for his family is that he doesn't suddenly turn into a kindly old man. In fact, he is rude, aggressive, even vitriolic. His attack on his eldest daughter – in which he expresses a wish that she remain childless – is one of the most unpleasant passages that Shakespeare ever wrote. His attempt to divide and rule his daughters, although childish and ultimately futile, is simply malicious. It's a familiar story for many people, I know. Illness does not miraculously make a nasty person nice.

It's sometimes easy to forget this; or, rather, the pain that the king suffers later somehow wipes away his early cruelties. He is so often described as magnificent or tortured or vulnerable that his appalling behaviour seems, on balance, excusable. This is, after all, what Lear himself believes. In his own words, he is, until very late in the day, 'a man more sinned against than sinning'. The self-pity is astonishing and unpleasant. But is it also a symptom of the mental decay of old age and therefore forgivable? Many, many people have come up against this conundrum in their own lives. Dealing with aggression and cruelty from those whom you love and admire is a moral test that is supremely difficult to navigate. I'm sure that one of the reasons that *King Lear* is judged by some as the greatest play ever written is that Shakespeare digs deep into this problem of sympathy for a damaged and dangerous human being; and follows that with the necessary questions of forgiveness and redemption. As with Hamlet, so, in a different way, with Lear; we all know or will know exactly what Shakespeare is talking about.

Towards the end of the play, Cordelia, Lear's youngest daughter, visits her father. They have been estranged since the very beginning of their story and have not seen each other since the king banished and disowned his daughter in a grotesque display of cruelty and rage. Now he is weak and ill. In our production, Lear lay in a hospital bed, wearing ill-fitting pyjamas with a drip attached to his arm. Cordelia came into the ward, just as any daughter today would come in, to see a man, whom she had last seen at the height of his power and authority, looking desperately vulnerable. Again, it is a situation familiar to many of us. It's never easy seeing a parent lying ill in bed. Lear is aware that he has behaved badly, but, in his distress, his language becomes almost hallucinatory. The writing is simply lovely and, because of its beauty, holds out the promise of reconciliation and healing. At the end of the scene, as, in our version, the king struggled to get out of bed, Cordelia says this:

> *'Will't please your highness walk?'*

To which her father replies:

> *'You must bear with me. Pray you now, forget and*
> *forgive; I am old and foolish.'*

I found this moment very upsetting to play – precisely because Cordelia's suggestion of a walk is so ordinary. It's the sort of thing that any child talking to their elderly and hospitalised parent might suggest. There is too much to talk about, too many problems for father and daughter to resolve, for anything to be sorted out in a quick bedside chat. There are, no doubt, many long walks ahead. In other words, even if the possibility of forgiveness has, by now, been raised, it marks the beginning of a process, not the end.

And, of course, the promised end is never reached. This is part of the reason why *King Lear* is such a profoundly bleak play. When we next meet Lear and Cordelia, now both prisoners-of-war, the king spins out a passage of great, lyrical beauty, in which he imagines happily spending the rest of his life in captivity with only his daughter for company. Cordelia, significantly, does not respond; because, however tantalising Lear's vision might be, it's nonsense. This is Shakespeare at his very best, enchanting the listener so successfully that their own judgement – let alone the judgement of other characters on the stage – becomes muddied. But, as with the last moments of *Othello* and many other plays by Shakespeare, the writer is challenging us not to fall for his seductive skills. Beware, he seems to be saying, beware of being bamboozled.

Finally, shockingly, Cordelia is murdered. Reconciliation between father and daughter is now impossible. Lear, howling with grief, carries the corpse of Cordelia on to the stage and then dies himself. There are two distinct versions of this famous scene – one from the quarto edition, the other from the First Folio. When I played Lear, I was asked to present a television programme about the making of Shakespeare's Folio. One afternoon, an academic called Sonia Massai, who specialises in the history of Shakespeare editions, showed me a copy of Lear's death scene as it appears in the Folio. The old king's final words were as follows:

> *'Look on her: look, her lips,*
> *Look there, look there!'*

The quarto version is not nearly as interesting as this and, consequently, for Lear's last moments, the Folio is normally used. At the National Theatre, we followed the accepted tradition. I was brought up, from my time at school, to read this short passage as indicative of a transitory flash of hope on Lear's part. Perhaps because of the focus on his daughter's lips, I was taught that the king may believe momentarily that Cordelia is breathing. He may be delirious or deluded, but he dies happy. He thinks that his daughter is, after all the horror that he has witnessed, alive. This is how I was playing it in our production at the time of my meeting Sonia. It was a sentimental, but effective choice. However, looking at the text that afternoon in the library, debating the issues raised by textual variants, I thought that there might be other options for delivering these lines from the Folio. That night, on the spur of the moment, I delivered the command to 'look there' with the intense anger of a man showing the corpse of his beloved daughter to the uncaring spectators gathered around him. It was as if Lear was, quite rationally, saying that this is what his life, and, by extension, the lives of other human beings, amounted to – an impotent, old man staring at the dead body of his child. As another character in the play says, the gods torture us as schoolboys torture flies.

I played around with different readings quite often during the run of *King Lear.* My fellow actors didn't seem to mind; or, at least, they were kind enough not to mention it. For all I know, they may have hated my lack of discipline. When I started out as an actor, I was more rigid, I think. I kept strictly to the decisions that were made in the rehearsal room. I followed the rules I had set myself; I improvised very little. But things have changed as I've got older. In *King Lear,* I and all my fellow actors tried many different things with a confidence that can only come from assured and generous direction. Sam Mendes certainly allowed the space for spontaneous experimentation – as in Lear's death scene.

The design by Anthony Ward was both simple and spectacular. We were given an empty, circular space, which we filled with the bare essentials for each scene – a large conference table for the opening moment of Lear's abdication, for instance. This was a technique that Sam used often. Starting with nothing in the rehearsal room, he would try various different stagings of each scene – with different readings, different choreography, different props – and then, late in the process, plump for the version he liked best. He would also simplify as rehearsals drew to a close, leaving his cast with only the barest essentials. So it was with *King Lear*. There were, however, a few, grander features that were designed or decided upon early on, before rehearsals started. As the storm which dominates the middle of the play began to brew, the stage rotated and a narrow walkway rose at an angle from the floor. Lear and the Fool climbed up it and, from the very top, suspended high in the air, as it were, they roared against the thunder and the lightning that surrounded them. Another early decision required the employment of a number of actors to play Lear's attendants. At the beginning of the story, the old king was supported by about forty soldiers – young men who represented the 'hundred knights' who, over the course of the evening, either desert him or are dismissed by Lear's daughters. These actors had to be cast before the first day of rehearsal. They made a great, surprising impact. The group became a single, new character – a threatening, untrustworthy power behind the throne, which slowly fades away to nothing.

One of these knights was played by an actor called John Hastings – a keen Shakespearean. At every performance, he would learn a passage of verse – a new one each day – and whisper it in my ear before we walked on stage. It was a prodigious feat of memory and technical skill. It also provided a precious moment of quiet before we embarked on the long journey ahead. When the run ended, John gave me a book in which he had written out all the verse that he had performed for me – an unexpected and much-appreciated gift.

The empty space had to serve, at one point, as a refuge for Lear and a small group of his supporters. It's a desolate and intriguing scene. The storm is dying and Lear is slipping into insanity. He has stripped off most of his clothes and is soaked to the skin. He hallucinates – he sees three dogs who bark at him. He acts out a mock trial of his two older daughters. Although he is hyperactive, his friends can see that he is physically and mentally exhausted. In our version, we used an old bathtub, a solitary lavatory bowl, a creaking bench and the discarded detritus that one might find in a builder's workshop. It was as if this was the only accommodation that could be found for an old, fragile and powerless man.

Among many other things, this scene is memorable for the fact that it is the last time that we see the Fool on stage. At this point, he disappears from the story. He is not seen again. The playwright gives no indication of what happens to him – until the very end. Nobody else on stage seems to notice his absence – which is odd, given that, up to this point, he has never left the king's side. The Fool simply fades away. For years, this has intrigued academics and theatre practitioners alike. Some have developed a theory that, since the Fool and Cordelia never appear together, both parts may have been played by the same actor. Cordelia is such a dominant figure in the latter half of the play that, so the argument goes, one actor could not be expected to continue with the Fool at the same time. So he had to disappear. This doubling seems to me to be unlikely. The demands of the two roles are so different; playing a fool and playing a woman were both specialist tasks in Shakespeare's theatre. This theory of multitasking is, however, strengthened by a single line in Lear's last scene. As he gazes at the dead Cordelia, the king says that 'his poor fool is hanged'. He doesn't elaborate further; but the line resonates in provocative ways. Is Shakespeare conflating Cordelia and the Fool? Is he acknowledging, with a sort of metatheatrical witticism, that the two parts were acted by the same person?

To be honest, I'm not convinced. In any case, it is much more affecting that the king, in his last moments, when his mind is elsewhere, should suddenly remember his loyal companion; and that this memory should not be complicated by any tangential reference to his daughter or, indeed, to casting policy in Shakespeare's company. Furthermore, the idea that the Fool might have hanged himself is very powerful. As he witnesses his master's decline, the Fool seems to lose hope – just as he loses his influence over the king. It makes sense that he might want to die. This is why many productions stage the Fool's suicide. Sam decided to do something different. In our production, Lear killed the Fool – which horrified some members of the audience. The king took a length of lead piping and battered his old friend to death. The fool breathed his last lying in the abandoned bathtub. Lear, by this stage, has no conception of what he is doing and, later, he appears to have forgotten all about it. I felt that this gave the king's sudden recollection of the Fool as he himself prepares to die – and his misremembering of how the Fool met his death – a greater and more distressing weight.

One night, during the third preview, the actor who was playing Edmund had to leave the stage. He was suddenly taken ill and couldn't continue. These things happen, of course, and, luckily, he was back after a short spell of convalescence at home; but it meant that his understudy had to go on halfway through the performance. There is a series of unspoken rules about the duties of understudies. For a start, it is assumed that they need to have learned their lines – at the very least – by the time the show officially opens. During the preview period, before the press night, the workload is so heavy, especially for those actors who are playing principal roles and covering others, that any understudy would be forgiven for not having their secondary part securely under their belt. At some time after the official opening there is often an 'understudy run' when all those who are covering other parts get together to stumble, as best they can, through the play. When our Edmund had to leave the stage, it was very early in the life of our show and so we had no confidence that his cover would be ready to take over. The understudy was playing the Duke of Burgundy, a tiny role that features only in the first scene. The actor's name was Paapa Essiedu. He stepped in after the interval and, showing no sign of nerves or insecurity, gave a perfect performance. It was a lesson in cool self-control.

I like to believe that, as in a vintage Hollywood movie, this was the moment when a star was born; but I'm afraid that this wouldn't be accurate. The truth is that Paapa was always destined to be a major actor and needed no help from our production of *King Lear*. Soon after, he went on to play Hamlet in Stratford and has since enjoyed a dazzling career on stage and film. But I like to cling to the fantasy that it was his unexpected appearance as Edmund that thrust him into the spotlight. I hope Paapa will forgive me.

10

It sometimes seems that I have spent half my adult life in America – particularly in New York. I hesitate to say that the Big Apple is my second home; but now, when I land at JFK airport and take a cab into Manhattan, it feels unexceptional and familiar. It's inevitable, I suppose, that I will never experience again the thrill of my first sight of that extraordinary skyline as I and my fellow cast members were driven, crammed into a coach, across the Brooklyn Bridge. In those days, the towers of the World Trade Center were still standing, proud and apparently indestructible. We stayed in a hotel nearby. The hotel may very well have been destroyed on that dreadful day in 2001. I have never felt any desire to walk down and check.

On that first visit, I might have slept in downtown Manhattan, but I spent most of my days just across the East River at the Brooklyn Academy of Music – fondly known as BAM. The theatre economy in the US is very different from that found in the UK, the most obvious difference being the latter's reliance on state-subsidised theatre. Despite the weight and influence wielded by the West End in London, for instance, the city's theatre culture, at least when it comes to straight plays, is fired, in many cases, by work coming out of powerhouses such as the National Theatre and the Almeida in Islington and provincial repertory theatres. BAM seemed to me like an American equivalent of those subsidised companies; and, from the minute we first walked into the building in 1998 with the National Theatre's production of *Othello,* I and my colleagues felt at home. It became, for some time, my professional base in New York. Over the years, I performed many shows at BAM – all by Shakespeare or Chekhov. Broadway – and the very different world of commercial theatre – would come later.

There were two theatre spaces at BAM, a large and a small. I performed most of the time in the smaller space, a gorgeous building whose interior had been designed, some time before, by Peter Brook. When he arrived at the site, it was a run-down opera house with, inside, a conventional arrangement of stalls and circle. Peter rebuilt the interior so that a single bank of seats rose up from the stage. I was told that airguns had been fired at the brick walls to achieve a rather chic, distressed surface similar to that in Peter's Parisian theatre. Whether or not that is true – and I really hope it is, partly because I would have liked to have been involved – the result was rough-edged, elegant and, most importantly, intimate. The theatre building would become over time an integral component of the work that visitors saw in front of them. It was easy to imagine how a production like Brook's famous *Mahabharata* would have fully filled the space and embraced the audience.

I played the larger theatre only once. In 2001, I was touring the USA with *Hamlet* – Phoenix, Tucson, Boston, Minneapolis – and the invitation from New York came as a surprise. BAM unexpectedly asked us to visit at very short notice for just one week – as a companion-piece to Peter Brook's own production of the play, which starred Adrian Lester as a gentle, effortlessly aristocratic prince. Perhaps the authorities at the theatre were amused by the idea of hosting two very different versions of the same play at almost the same time. I wouldn't know. Adrian and his team played the small theatre and we were asked to move into the larger auditorium, a huge barn of a building that could seat thousands of spectators. To be honest, it was a major physical effort for all of us – similar to acting in the great Greek amphitheatre at Epidaurus. Our voices were not amplified and so we were required to shout unaided for over three hours. It was also our last date on a long tour and we were tired.

Fortunately, the show was judged to be a success. On the morning the reviews came out, I had to sit for an interview with a journalist. He came to the meeting clutching a copy of the *New York Times*. On the first page of the arts section was a picture of my face. The journalist pointed out that this photograph was large enough to go 'over the fold'. I had never heard this phrase before. I didn't ask for an explanation, but the journalist clearly thought it was significant. I presume 'the fold' in question was the crease halfway down the page, which meant that the picture was of some considerable size and very dominant. At one point during our talk, he asked me whether I had plans to see any other shows during my short stay. I replied that the only free day I had was the following Sunday and that I would have loved to have seen the matinee performance of the much-lauded version of *The Producers* with Matthew Broderick and Nathan Lane. Unfortunately, it was sold out. I had heard that some very grand people had been unable to get tickets. In addition, the Tony Awards ceremony was to be held that same Sunday evening. *The Producers* had been nominated for a huge, record-breaking number of awards. So, presumably, the demand for tickets that afternoon would be even fiercer than usual. After some tentative enquiries, I had given up on the idea.

The journalist told me that, since a large photograph of me was in a very important newspaper that day, I should try again. After all, he said, I had some leverage now. I can't remember whether it was he himself or someone in our production office who managed it, but, magically, a day later, I was sent two tickets. It felt illicit and very 'New York'.

The Producers was a wonderful show – everything one could have hoped for from a classic Broadway musical. I took our company manager, Trish, as my guest. After the curtain came down, we dropped hastily scribbled notes at the stage door for the two leading actors, neither of whom we knew, and then left them to sail off to the Tony Awards. *The Producers* enjoyed a triumphant evening – Tonys were awarded them in double figures.

Over the years, I have been invited to a couple of Tony Awards ceremonies. The first time was in 2004 when I was playing in my first Broadway show – a transfer from London of Tom Stoppard's *Jumpers*. The second was during the run of Sam Mendes's dazzling production of *The Lehman Trilogy*. The Tonys are very grand occasions, not so much for the splendour of the event itself but for the excitement that is generated outside the building. Streets are closed off, large crowds gather, pundits air their opinions, stars are interviewed on the red carpet and television crews record all the details for the local news channels. It feels important, a celebration of an essential component of New York life, of the city's image and its economy.

When I started out as an actor, the London annual theatre award ceremonies were rather more low key than those in New York. We were all rather shamefaced about the whole thing, which I guess didn't really matter, were it not that this diffidence reinforced the judgement of many that theatre was irrelevant, even silly. It certainly couldn't compare with the movies. That has always, predictably, infuriated me, but I sense things have changed since then. I've not been to a London theatre award ceremony for twenty years now, but I'm aware that their profile has been raised and sharpened. That, in my eyes, can only be a good thing.

A sense of febrile glamour is part of life on Broadway; or, at least, it is assumed that glamour is always on offer should you want it. The theatres themselves – at least backstage – are often crumbling and run down; and nobody would argue that

Times Square, the centre of theatrical Broadway, is, for all the sensory overload it provides, exactly elegant. But, in contrast, the auditoria are usually ravishing. There is a well-established tradition that famous people will come backstage after a show to pay their respects – even if they have never before met the performers. It's a gesture of old-fashioned courtesy and much appreciated. This is not the case in London. So the New York custom can sometimes take you by surprise. There is little you can do to prepare for the sight of Paul Newman standing unexpectedly in your dressing room as you are beginning to wind down after a show. On that occasion, he had come to *Jumpers* with his wife, Joanne. Both were charming, of course. Paul was quiet, shy and beautiful. I have fond memories of discussing Lorca and the state of Andalusian theatre with Antonio Banderas as Lauren Bacall sat on the dressing-room couch. Dustin Hoffman, Tom Hanks, Al Pacino and Harvey Keitel have all dropped by at one time or another – all American actors, of course.

Needless to say, none of these great artists became friends – except Lauren Bacall. She was different. I first met her at a dinner party hosted by Barbara Walters. It was common at that time for guests at these sort of gatherings to stand up at the end of the meal, as coffee was being served, and talk about their work. That evening we heard about US policy in the Middle East and changes in New York secondary education. I didn't concentrate on what was being said. I was performing *Uncle Vanya* at the time and spent the evening paralysed by the thought that I might be asked to share my ideas about Chekhov with my fellow diners. To my immense relief, I wasn't called to speak.

It was a memorable evening. On the table were huge bottles of a superb claret and the food was predictably splendid. My hostess decided, after the meal, to show me her jewellery collection – including pieces by an American designer called JAR, whom I admire hugely. And I was sat next to Lauren Bacall.

Miss Bacall – or Betty, as she was known – was, quite simply, magnificent. She could be fierce and certainly demanded the highest standards from her professional colleagues, but she was kind, attentive and worked hard to keep informed about the latest cultural and political developments. When I first met her, I felt it would be inappropriate to quiz her about her extraordinary life, but, as it turned out, she talked openly about Bogart and Sinatra and the Kennedys. We would meet for coffee or dinner, go together to the theatre or hang out in her apartment on Central Park West, once sharing a Chinese takeaway while watching a George Clooney film. Later in our friendship, I would meet up with her when she came to London and we would go to eat oysters at the Wolseley restaurant on Piccadilly. When Betty died in 2014, I was in England. I could not get to her funeral – a very great and lasting regret.

Despite all these excitements, life as a visiting actor in New York, especially over a long period, could be very lonely. There were days that, having seen all the sights, some many times over, I found it hard to find stimulating things to do or people to hang out with. I had met a great number of famous and powerful people in the city, but I didn't exactly have the confidence to ring them up and ask them to join me for a quick beer. I have twice spent Christmas in New York and I can't pretend that I found that easy. This would be the case in any major city, I know; and I learned quickly that one solution was to get out of town on those days when I wasn't working. I enjoyed a melancholic but satisfying stay at a nineteenth-century hotel in a small whaling port on Long Island and, on one occasion, as I've mentioned, I dropped into the Folger Shakespeare Library in Washington to look at their gobsmacking collection of Shakespeare folios.

And then there was Boston, a city that I got to know quite well and that I love – although I wonder that this might be because the centre of town feels rather European. I had played *Hamlet* there as part of our world tour. After one Sunday matinee, Dustin Hoffman called round. He was filming nearby, I think. He had managed to catch only half of the show and promised to return on the following Sunday to see the remainder. I didn't expect him to be able to keep his promise, but he did. This latter show was our last in Boston and, as the cast were bundled on to a coach that would take us to the airport and our flight to Minneapolis, Mr Hoffman pressed a hundred-dollar bill into my hand and told me to buy a drink for the team before we boarded the plane. He then stood on the sidewalk and, as the coach drove away, waved us goodbye.

A day in Boston would often include a trip to Cambridge – and to the campus of Harvard University. I would wander through the streets, surrounded by ravishing architecture, visit the Coop bookstore or sit by the Charles River – all an indulgence of my academic pretensions. I could, for a short while, imagine I held some impressive professorial post. In fact, I was once invited to join a class that was led by Stephen Greenblatt – a very prominent academic who writes superb books about Shakespeare that are often provocative and always eminently readable. I decided to talk about characters in the plays who speak less than one might expect: Cicero in *Julius Caesar,* for example, or, my favourite, Menelaus in *Troilus and Cressida,* who, despite his wife's abduction being the first and major cause of the Trojan War, barely opens his mouth. I found this fascinating, though I'm not sure that the students were particularly impressed.

My work has kept me pretty well confined to the two opposing coasts of America. I have promised myself that, one day, I will visit the vast plains of the Midwest or the glories of the South. I would love to spend some time in New Orleans. I am aware, too, that my experience of the States has been limited principally to frantic urban environments. It would be good to spend some time in the mountains – though my friends will laugh at my saying this. I suspect that they think of me as someone who is comfortable only in big cities. I might have to go exploring under my own steam, but maybe I'll be offered a show in Atlanta or a film in the wilds of North Dakota. Either way, I want to see much more.

After *Jumpers*, my second experience of Broadway was with a very different beast – the musical *Spamalot*. Despite its inspiration being the British film *Monty Python and the Holy Grail*, and despite its being devised by Eric Idle, this was the most purely American production I've ever done. Indeed, part of the show's appeal lay in its being a near-parodic version of a classic Broadway musical. On my first night, I stood anxiously in the wings, listening to the overture, and I noticed that the piece revelled in every convention of the genre. It also served as an unnerving reminder of my *chutzpah*. What did I think I was doing, pretending to be a proper song-and-dance man – and in New York, of all places?

I had been invited to take over from Tim Curry as King Arthur and I was the only British actor in the company – just as Tim had been. I was surrounded by big players such as David Hyde Pierce, Hank Azaria and Chris Sieber, all three of whom were playing Arthurian knights. A constellation of much-lauded Broadway stars, they were the engine of the show. The director of *Spamalot* was the unquestionably great Mike Nichols. I didn't see much of Mike during the rehearsal period – there was really no need – and, although he came intermittently to check how I was doing, I got to know him properly only after I had opened in the show, when we would enjoy the occasional meal together. As one would expect of a man of such limitless creative energy, he was extremely good company. And the show he directed was a riot.

Ironically, although I was the solitary British actor, I knew far less about Monty Python than anyone else on the team. The phenomenon seemed to have somehow passed me by. I think the original programmes were first broadcast when I was a teenager and, in that period of my life, I watched very little television. At school, it was frowned upon – except on Saturday afternoons, when the coverage was mostly of sport; and, since my holidays were spent in West Germany, my viewing then was limited to the British Forces Broadcasting Service – at that time, a single channel of conservative taste, as I remember. My American colleagues, on the other hand, seemed to know Monty Python well – as did the New York audience. The latter recognised every joke and greeted every routine as an old friend. I suspect they would often join in. I would often hear a suspicious soft murmur from the stalls. Predictably, fans would arrive at the theatre dressed up as knights and, on a couple of occasions, we heard reports of men dressed as King Arthur galloping down to see the show through the streets of Manhattan. Inevitably, these kings would be accompanied by a friend, clapping coconut shells together to imitate the sound of a trotting horse, just as in our show.

A conceit that a few journalists employed in writing about my joining the team of *Spamalot* was the incongruity of a Shakespearean playing King Arthur in a Broadway musical. They professed to be surprised and unsure that my previous experiences would be of any use. I don't think they really believed what they were saying. I'll admit that the dance routines were tricky to learn, but I felt secure enough about singing on stage. Talking to one of the journalists, I pointed out that, when it came to the acting, most performers tend to use similar techniques, to ask the same sort of questions, whatever the project that they're involved in. For instance, with King Arthur, I felt that a central element of his psychological make-up was the fact that, unacknowledged and hidden far in the back of his mind, he knew that he didn't really have a horse. That uncertainty gave him a bit of depth.

I danced and sang very little in the show – at least compared to the rest of the cast. My job was to stand on the sidelines, either smiling benignly or looking bemused. I would watch open-mouthed as Lauren Kennedy, our Lady of the Lake, belted out a series of impossibly difficult numbers or as Hank Azaria, at one point playing a French soldier with a preposterous accent, threw an inflatable cow over the battlements of his besieged castle. Most extraordinary was David Hyde Pierce, a delightful man, who, every night, interrupted a big routine to sit and play the piano for a few minutes. In narrative terms, there was no rational explanation for this. It was introduced simply to amuse the audience and David's fellow cast members. He was a very brilliant pianist (and could also play the organ). He told me once that he had originally wanted to become a professional musician. Each night, he would take an event of the day – the anniversary of Chopin's death, say, or Mexican Independence Day – and improvise around it. After each show, he would challenge me to guess what the day's theme had been. Most times I failed – I had never heard the Mexican national anthem before, for instance – but his performance was always glorious to listen to.

On the day I left the show, I hosted an English tea party in the theatre – between the matinee and the evening show. I couldn't afford to give separate presents to each company member – which seemed to be the custom. So I thought we'd have a party. We had scones, jam and cream, cucumber sandwiches and treacle tart. There was even a separate table for hardcore gourmets, which served bread, butter and Marmite. Only a few brave souls were tempted by that; but I hope the company realised how grateful I was for their generosity and warmth in welcoming me into their strange world.

The Lehman Trilogy, my third Broadway show, was a very weighty project indeed. Like *Jumpers* so many years earlier, it was an import from the National Theatre in London. Sam Mendes, who spends a great deal of time on the lookout for fresh ideas, read in the newspaper about a show that had originated in Italy and that told the story of the Lehman Brothers bank. This story began with the arrival of three young men in the United States during the middle years of the nineteenth century and ended inevitably with the collapse of 2008. Between those two events, we visit a small shop in Alabama, and follow the boys as they begin to trade in cotton. We move to New York and watch them help to finance massive building projects – such as the railways that crossed the American continent and the Panama Canal that cut it in two. We move on to the crash of the early twentieth century and the final years of the bank, by which time their trading had become an almost abstract game of manipulating very large numbers. In other words, it was a huge story – essentially a short history of capitalism; and it had to be crammed into one evening in the theatre. The original production, which toured the Continent, was very long and used a wide range of theatrical techniques.

Intrigued by what he had read in the newspaper, Sam asked if he could look at the script. It was in Italian and, on the page, looked like a long poem. A literal translation into English was commissioned and then Ben Power, whom I had first met on *Timon of Athens*, agreed to help turn it into a play. It was arranged that a group of actors would meet at the National Theatre and, over a couple of days, see if this bulky work could be transformed into something manageable. I was invited to join this group.

It really was the most extraordinary piece of writing – hardly a conventional play at all. At that first workshop, it was not yet properly divided between individual speakers. It had an incantatory quality, like a prayer. Phrases were repeated over and over, and the Jewish heritage of the three brothers was highlighted. Jewish prayers such as the Kaddish and the Shema were threaded through the work. I found it mesmerising but knew, if Sam decided to put it on stage, that it would be a significant challenge. Later, when Sam chose to direct the show, which would have its premiere at the National in the summer of 2018, and cast me as the eldest brother, we had a long chat over the phone. He warned me that the project would stretch me. I pointed out that it would stretch him too.

We needed to find a new theatrical vocabulary. We realised early on that, in our version, a large cast was not needed. After much thought, we ended up with just three actors – each playing one of the brothers – who would then present every other character in the story. So it was that Ben Miles, Adam Godley and I, wearing black nineteenth-century frock coats that never changed, impersonated a series of children, ancient rabbis, flirtatious young women, brutal traders, *femmes fatales*, smooth financiers and even, at one point, a tightrope walker. A pianist played, sitting in the auditorium – the fourth member of the cast. The music never stopped; so there was in the air a flavour of the world of silent cinema. The four of us, three actors and one musician, did not leave the performance space for three hours.

Es Devlin designed a set on an epic scale: a large rotating glass box in front of a huge cyclorama. On to this was thrown a series of black-and-white images – of cityscapes, burning cotton fields, a horse-racing track. The box was, in essence, a large office in some anonymous major city. It was monochrome and ineffably chic. When we began rehearsals, Sam filled this office with everything one might expect to find there – a coffee machine, a water cooler, a whiteboard, marker pens; but it gradually became clear to him that, as with the size of the cast, less might very well be more. All small props were scrapped, except for the odd pen. Ben, Adam and I used only a number of boxes – like those in which, at the moment of the bank's collapse, employees who had lost their jobs had packed their belongings – and with these built, quite literally, a number of different environments. The final result was an idiosyncratic mixture of technical virtuosity and what used to be known as 'poor theatre' – performances that use only the minimum of extraneous material.

Playing *The Lehman Trilogy* was an unusual, almost unique,

experience for all four of us. It required absolute, sustained concentration over a long period. It was, consequently, very tiring. But, unlike *King Lear* or *Hamlet*, it required no emotional expenditure at all. It was a purely intellectual or technical exercise – and no less thrilling or intense for that. I don't think any of the performers can remember the first public showing of the play with any clarity. The whole thing moved so fast that, for us, it became a question of holding on as best we could. Over the years of the run, we would talk in rueful tones of a bottle of champagne, which was hiding in a fridge somewhere, one that we would drink together after the first performance we considered faultless – with no verbal slips, in other words. We never drank it. In fact, I don't think it existed. We knew that the perfect performance would never happen. But I suppose the quest kept us on our toes.

Facing Death

Falstaff (On Film)

I have spent most of my professional life on stage. I guess that my career is, in a sense, an extension of what I did for fun at school and university. My hobby became my work. Since it was something that I grew up with, I have always felt at home in the theatre. Film work came later. This delay wasn't planned; it's just the way it happened. The downside of coming to it relatively late, though, is that it took some time for me to feel comfortable in front of the camera. It's easier now, but it still feels a little odd.

This is not to say that I haven't enjoyed some memorable experiences making movies and TV. As I write this, I'm in the middle of shooting season two of *House of the Dragon* – a prequel to the hugely popular *Game of Thrones* – which is proving to be great fun to make. I'll admit to watching the addictive first series in one week-long binge, so I had to do minimal research before taking the job. It also feels oddly familiar in other ways. The bloody power politics on display recall the equally bloody internecine struggles of Shakespeare's history plays. The cast is predictably friendly and hugely skilled – as is the team of four directors. Apart from anything else, though, the range of technical skills on display is stupendous – just as it was on other blockbuster projects with which I've been involved. Every day there is yet another miracle of construction or design or computerised prowess to gasp at. The huge sets seem to spring up overnight like mushrooms; and there is always an exquisite new costume or elegant piece of weaponry to admire. This surprised me at first, since, at least when it came to the sets we work in, I had assumed that most of it would be computer-generated. But, to my delight, on the very first day, I was given a tour of my own castle by one of the team – like some fantasy estate agent.

Pride of place in my small list of films must go to a 2017 movie directed by Armando Iannucci called *The Death of Stalin*. I first met Armando, who is not only brilliant but also courteous and kind, in a small Italian restaurant not far from the headquarters of the BBC in central London. We had a drink and talked about his new project. He didn't make me an offer then and there, but, of course, I hadn't expected him to do so. I left after an hour and, halfway home, realised that I hadn't offered to pay my share of the bill. I frantically rang my agent and asked if they could contact Armando to apologise for my rudeness. She told me not to be ridiculous; but I so wanted a part in the film that I couldn't bear the thought that I might lose it because the director thought I was tight-fisted. It was ludicrous, I know, but I was anxious. I don't think my agent made the call, though she might have done; and I'm pretty confident that my spending habits never crossed Armando's mind.

A few days later, I was crossing Blackfriars Bridge when my phone rang. It was a call from my agent to tell me that I had been offered the part of Lavrenti Beria – Stalin's last chief of police and a member of the Politburo. Needless to say, I was thrilled and, later, proud that I was asked to play a part in one of the most idiosyncratic British films of the last twenty years. Armando created something extraordinary – both funny and deeply serious. It is, tonally, unlike anything that was doing the rounds at the time. Part of its appeal – and a risk that I think Armando knew he was taking – lies in the heterogeneity of the group of actors that were gathered together. We came, not only from different countries, but also from different acting traditions. Among the performers, there were experts in improvisation, in comedy sketch writing and in 'classical' theatre. We each spoke in our own voice – and with our own native accent. Coherence was achieved by the extremity of the situation in which all the characters found themselves – the struggle for power after the death of an autocrat. In fact, the impact of the film lies in its picture of political chaos. Everyone in the story is improvising; and Armando's open-armed direction reflected this instability.

Of course, in reality, the work was minutely choreographed. The script was altered and refined every day. As I arrived in the early morning, new pages for future scenes would be thrust into my hand. I kept – and learned – all the different versions as a sort of insurance policy, my master copy becoming thicker and heavier as the shoot continued. I don't feel confident about improvisation – it wasn't really part of my training – and I thought that if I had several versions of each scene in my head, I could fall back on those if necessary. When it came to it, though, Armando didn't require extensive improvisation. It was more a case of changing the odd word or phrase here and there. He required playfulness rather than wholesale invention. Once he had got what he needed, he would often ask us to replay a particular scene just for the fun of it, but with no pressure to produce anything new. He made me feel relaxed and comfortable – for which I am profoundly grateful.

Armando managed all this – all this effervescence – while telling a story that was grim and genuinely frightening. That's what made the result so extraordinary. He should, in my eyes, have won every award going; but sadly that was not to be.

Another major movie event for me was playing Falstaff on film for the great Richard Eyre in 2012. This was not the first time I had been cast in a cinematic version of a Shakespeare play – I had played a small part in Kenneth Branagh's *Hamlet* – but, in terms of complexity and profile, you can't really compare Falstaff and the Second Gravedigger. I played Falstaff in two films, which conflated both parts of Shakespeare's *Henry IV*, as part of *The Hollow Crown* series. As with the blockbusters, the design was miraculous – especially, in this case, the costumes and the make-up. Whatever the project, these two departments always seem to be peopled with perfectionists who have an almost obsessive concern for the tiniest details. They are primed to spot a single stray hair or a wayward pleat or a loose button. Rupert Simon, my brilliant make-up artist, created Falstaff's look with just that type of care; and the result was both seedy and magnificent – a man concerned for his dignity while weighed down by his increasing physical decrepitude.

I enjoyed this, because, in my mind, Falstaff must be aware, especially in the latter moments of the story, that he is coming to the end of his life. The big question is whether he acknowledges this or dismisses it. In a way, Falstaff is a mirror image of the other dying man in the two plays – the king, Henry IV, himself. The latter spends his time assessing the value of his achievements and the weight of his sins. He does this consciously and deliberately and, although Falstaff may not dig as deep as the king, such self-analysis cannot be far below the surface of his mind. Does he successfully repress these anxieties? Perhaps he doesn't care about his imminent death. The two older men also both enjoy their most intense relationship with a much younger figure, Prince Hal, who will later succeed to the throne as Henry V. He, of course, assumes, as young people do, that he will live for ever. That is part of his attraction. In his company, the possibility of decay barely registers.

A fear of death seems a gloomy place to start when thinking about Falstaff. Surely, one might think, he is known principally for having a good time – not for pondering his own death. And, after all, he was one of the most popular characters of the Elizabethan stage. Presumably, the audience loved, above all, his lust for life. There is a story – probably untrue – that Queen Elizabeth herself commissioned a play from Shakespeare that would show Falstaff in love and the playwright came up with *The Merry Wives of Windsor*. The queen had demanded yet more fun; and so that is what Shakespeare gave her. It's interesting that the Falstaff in this later play seems a fundamentally different man from the Falstaff of *Henry IV*. Whatever Her Majesty might have thought, I'm not sure that the earlier Falstaff is interested in romantic love, although he seems fond of Doll Tearsheet, a prostitute who works in the pub where he spends most of his time. Falstaff can presumably pay – or promise to pay – for sex when he needs to; so that's not really an issue. He doesn't seem to be looking for love. He wants respect and assumes that Prince Hal is fond of him. He is proud of his status as a knight. He likes drinking. That's about it.

I once had lunch in New York with the famous literary critic Harold Bloom. He was a large man with firm, unshakeable opinions. As we ate, he tried to convince me to take on Falstaff as soon as possible. I was playing Hamlet at the time. However marvellous Hamlet is, Harold said, I should quickly move on to Falstaff, because Falstaff is the greatest character that Shakespeare ever wrote. It was imperative that I should play him. It would do me good. It was no accident, of course, that Harold, at least on first acquaintance, shared many characteristics with the Fat Knight; but his enthusiasm – and the enthusiasm of the Elizabethan playgoers – is curious. Isn't Falstaff the sort of person you would try to avoid if he frequented your local pub? He might be witty, but he's rather self-important and a bit of a bore. He's also untrustworthy. Isn't he, fundamentally, a shit?

The answer to each of these questions is yes and no; and that is why there is something generous about the contemporary Elizabethan affection for Falstaff. They understood that, for all his faults, Falstaff asks very little from life. He's not simply witty, he's funny – at least, at a distance. Despite his friendship with a prince, he has no genuine interest in power. He just wants enough money to enjoy the basic pleasures of eating and drinking. He's lazy and can abuse his status as a knight and as a friend of a prince, but he's not hugely demanding. Above all, he loves his pub – and there's something very ordinary and English about that. It happened over time that Falstaff became representative of a type of Englishness – up there with John Bull and even, given his career as a small-time thief, Robin Hood; but there's nothing remotely heroic about Falstaff. Like many of us, he wants to be left alone to enjoy small, quotidian pleasures. If, as Harold Bloom believed, he deserves his status as one of Shakespeare's greatest creations, it is precisely because he does *not* contemplate death like Hamlet or experience acute human pain like King Lear. Rather, he either avoids or refuses to wrestle with that sort of thing – like many of us, I suspect.

There is one fleeting moment when Falstaff comes close to recognising the inevitability of his own death. He is in the country, far from the familiarity of London, and he is staying with a friend. After dinner, they talk of old times; or, more precisely, the friend talks. Falstaff is bored and irritable. Inevitably, most of the people that the friend mentions during his long string of reminiscence are now old, or maybe dead. As the evening's subdued entertainment is winding down, and the friend implies that they have both come to the end of their lives, Falstaff is forced to agree that they 'have heard the chimes at midnight' – a melancholic and beautiful line. It's the sort of thought that Falstaff would not normally entertain. He doesn't linger long over it. To be frank, it's been a dreary and depressing visit. Falstaff leaves the countryside and returns to the city as soon as he can.

When Hal becomes king, he terminates his association with Falstaff. The dismissal is brutal and no appeal is possible. The 'old man', as Hal calls him, is, naturally, surprised and hurt. As with Malvolio in *Twelfth Night*, I used to think about how Falstaff's life would develop after the end of the play. I was certain that my Malvolio would find some way to exact revenge on his aristocratic employers; but, in contrast, I felt that, in Falstaff's case, nothing fundamental would change. He's Shakespeare's great survivor. Most importantly, he would never think, however it might look from the outside, that his life has been wasted. That would never occur to him – except in fleeting and easily suppressed moments of doubt.

In time, Falstaff dies, but in different play – *Henry V*. This is, of course, a sequel to the two earlier plays in which the Fat Knight plays such an important part. His death is reported by another character, the pub landlady, Mistress Quickly. This is intriguing. It is assumed that Shakespeare would have wanted to keep a character as popular as Falstaff alive as long as possible; but it seems that the actor who had triumphed in the role was not available. Perhaps this actor was the clown, Will Kemp, who had left the company and then had decided to dance to Norwich. We don't know; but clearly and, presumably, to the playgoers' huge disappointment, Falstaff had to be killed off by his creator. Furthermore, since he couldn't be there in person, he had to die offstage.

Mistress Quickly's description of his last moments is extensive and detailed. She says, marvellously, that, as he was dying, his nose was reduced to a sharp point – a common occurrence, I've been told, with those near death. There is one puzzling moment in the speech – at least from a textual perspective. Falstaff is described as 'babbling of green fields'. The present participle in this phrase is not Shakespeare's. The authoritative text is corrupt at this point and makes no sense. 'Babbling' is a later conjecture that has been accepted by most subsequent editors. What intrigues me is not so much the textual puzzle as the idea that Falstaff should be thinking of green fields – the rolling English countryside – in the first place. It's as if Shakespeare is trying to expand the image of Falstaff as representative of an essential Englishness by including something bucolic. But there's nothing bucolic about Falstaff. Babbling sounds gentle – or, at least, unaggressive. Perhaps he should be screaming or cursing the green fields of England. That, it seems to me, is closer to the Falstaff we've come to know. He lives and dies in a city pub – without a green field in sight.

I would like to play Falstaff again – on stage. My version on screen was darker than I had intended. He wasn't very funny; and so an essential ingredient was missing. Comedy on film is a mystery to me. I find it easier to judge whether something is funny or not when an audience is there in the flesh and I can hear their response. Maybe in the theatre I can produce a version of Falstaff that is more concerned with life than with death.

For a few years, from 2008, most of the work I did on film didn't involve acting – or Shakespeare. Some time ago, the BBC asked me, unexpectedly, to present *Sacred Music*, a documentary series about the development of religious music over time. I suppose their thinking was that, since I had trained as a child in a cathedral choir, I would be a good choice to present a history of the sacred repertoire. I had sung a great deal of it, after all. So that was the story they asked me to tell. But the truth was that, for years, I had shied away from listening to the pieces that I had grown up with. My interests had moved on to a more secular tradition. I still needed to hear J. S. Bach every so often, but, as an adult, I rediscovered, among others, Beethoven and Schubert and became fascinated by twentieth-century music. As a result, the new documentary series was an education for me – however knowledgeable I tried to look on screen.

We were a very small team – four or five people. Most of the time, we would race around Europe in a small van – the director, an assistant, the cameraman and me. I sat in the back, frantically trying to learn vast tracts of script that I was expected to deliver to camera at our destination. Sometimes, rarely, we would take the train. Given the nature of the story we were telling, we spent weeks in east Germany and Austria – parts of the world that were new to me. The country was as beautiful as one would expect – large expanses of groomed farmland, a series of picture-perfect towns clustered round cavernous churches or looming castles; but what struck me most forcefully was the sense of an epicentre of European culture that, in England, is now almost forgotten – or, at least unvisited. The reasons for this neglect are obvious – two world wars, political isolation, the Holocaust, for a start – but it was an extraordinary and salutary experience to travel through Weimar and Wittenberg and Leipzig. We visited Goethe's house in Weimar and, in the same city, filmed in front of the theatre for which Schiller wrote his plays. We toured the palace where, for a short period, Liszt was in charge of the music. I sat in a prison cell in Wartburg Castle and tried to imagine Luther hunched over a desk as he translated the Bible into German. I did a piece to camera outside the church from which he launched the Reformation. I played Bach's organ in Leipzig, with his successor perched on the bench by my side.

And much of the music I heard was new to me. In a church near Notre Dame in Paris, I joined three other singers to perform early examples of polyphony from the twelfth century. This was unexplored territory. The most difficult parts were taken by members of the Sixteen, the choir who provided all the music for the series. Harry Christophers, their director, thought it would be fun if I joined them on this occasion, but wisely decided that I should sing the drone – a long, sustained note above which the other performers delivered their dance-like fireworks. I could just about manage it. The sound of the four voices filled the church – a perfect match of music and architecture.

I was asked to interview a long line of experts – academics, singers and, for the programme that focused on contemporary music, composers. In Estonia, I met Arvo Pärt and talked to him in the radio studio where he had worked before he fled the Soviet Union. He was known to be shy, even private, so the interview felt like some sort of journalistic coup. As it happens, in conversation, he was wry and seemed quietly amused by the whole thing. I chatted to John Tavener not long before he died in 2013. He showed me a small chapel that he had built next to his house. A serious and gentle James MacMillan and an avuncular John Rutter gave up their time to answer my questions. I had to learn various techniques, which were handed on to me by staff at the BBC – like nodding encouragingly when an interviewee is talking and keeping absolutely silent during an answer so that editing is easier. The best advice was more general: during the long period of a documentary shoot, never stand when you can sit (or sit when you can lie down) – and wear comfortable shoes.

The series on sacred music was followed, a couple of years later, by a similar history of the symphony. The itinerary was just as stimulating and demanding as the previous project, and included Russia and the USA. The most exciting moments, though, were in the recording studio. There I could listen, ostensibly alone, to great orchestras performing the most exciting work in the repertoire. I suppose it was a reminder of how powerful live music is. That's obvious to everyone, I hope. More immediately, it felt as if they were playing just for me – a very seductive delusion.

One day, I would like to make a series about the history of the concerto. People will say that my interest must lie in the inherent theatricality of the form – the battle or the love affair between soloist and orchestra. But, actually, I would like to look at the way instruments – the piano, the violin – have developed over the centuries; and how that has affected both composers and players. I haven't managed to persuade anyone else that it's a fascinating story. But, you never know, someone might bite.

Afterword

When I was about ten years old, my mother and I spent a week together in Great Ormond Street Hospital, the world-famous centre for paediatric medicine in central London. We were there with my sister Lucy, who was very, very ill. I was still a working choirboy at the time, but I guess that I must have been given a few days off from school – a half-term exeat, possibly. Mum and Lucy were essentially alone in the city, with only me for company; the rest of my family were in Singapore. We had very little contact with them – at least, as far as I could judge. In those days, making a telephone call from England to the Far East was very difficult. A specific time had to be arranged, which took a great effort and required some planning, and, furthermore, the call was very expensive. Mum clearly missed talking to Dad and, despite support from the extended family, she must have felt very isolated. She and I spent every day sitting with Lucy, a tiny, barely conscious figure lying in a large plastic oxygen tent. I was probably unaware of how unwell my sister was. I think, during that time, she nearly died.

Mum and I stayed in a hostel that was run by the Salvation Army. It was just around the corner from the hospital. I think it might still be there, continuing its admirable work of looking after patients' relatives. It wasn't luxurious, of course. For breakfast, they served very hard boiled eggs, I remember. I used to mix the yolks with butter to make them look runny. I can't recall what we did for lunch or supper – a hurried sandwich in the hospital, I presume.

Mum and I had our evenings free. She must have felt that I needed a treat after hours on the ward and she decided, on two occasions, to take me to the opera house in Covent Garden to see the ballet. We attended, in quick succession, *Giselle* and *La Fille Mal Gardée*. The idea of ballet was not new to me. I had read about it and devoured pictures of beautiful, delicate women and gorgeous, heroic men in assorted books and, above all, in the *Princess Tina* annual, a copy of which my mother bought for me one year. I knew about Fonteyn and Nureyev. I might even have heard of Balanchine. I taught myself the five basic positions that every dancer has to master; though given my size, it must have looked odd when I went through them. On the other hand, perhaps it was endearing.

I had, however, never sat through a flesh-and-blood, full-length performance of a ballet. Needless to say, I was bowled over. My mother told me later that I cried during *Giselle*, though this might have been because I was tired and sad about other things – Lucy's health and Mum's anxiety, above all. Those two nights marked the beginning of a lifelong interest; although. inevitably, as I grew older and the possibility of my becoming a dancer became increasingly remote – not that this was ever a serious option – ballet was superseded in my head by music and drama.

I never, in a million years, would have thought that, one day, I might appear as a real, grown-up dancer in a real, grown-up ballet on the stage of Covent Garden. But, astonishingly, when I was in middle age, that's exactly what happened. In 2010, I was performing at the National Theatre in *London Assurance* by Dion Boucicault – one of the silliest plays ever written. On the first day of rehearsal, Nick Hytner, our director, told the cast very firmly that the production had to be funny. Otherwise, he said, the whole venture would be a waste of time. Fortunately, it did turn out to be very funny, in large part because the writer Richard Bean provided us with a brilliant update of the play, with an abundance of genuinely funny jokes. Towards the end of the show, my character, a man of imperturbable idiocy, was asked to dance. He elected to show off his meagre balletic skills – a leap or two, a half-hearted attempt at an *arabesque*, an *entrechat*. It was ridiculous and, on his part, delusional. One night, Nick's friend, the choreographer Christopher Wheeldon, came to see the play. He rang me not long after and told me that he was planning a version of *Alice's Adventures in Wonderland* and wondered whether I would be interested in playing the part of the duchess. I pointed out that I really wasn't a dancer – and certainly not a ballet dancer – but Christopher insisted. He believed that, with enough training and a great deal of hard work, I would be able to pull it off. However doubtful I felt, it was something that I couldn't refuse; and so I accepted the offer.

A few months later, I found myself walking into the Royal Opera House on my first day as a member of the ballet company. I was given a card with my name on it and, underneath, written confirmation that I was now, officially, a member of the Royal Ballet. I still have the card. That day was the start of an exhilarating six months. Up on the top floor of the building, I joined a group of the fittest, most hard-working and committed performers I have ever met. They didn't stop. They kept dancing from the first moments of morning class up to late in the evening. I couldn't maintain their schedule – I would have died within the first week – but I was given a lighter version to follow. Every morning, I would start with my own individual class under the watchful eye of the *prima ballerina*, Marguerite Porter; and then I would join the others for rehearsal. Christopher had insisted, at the beginning of the process, that I and my teachers should aim to turn me into a dancer, rather than an actor who happened to be dancing. I never fulfilled that promise, but it was a worthy ambition. In fact, it was not until the first public showing that I managed to perform all the right moves in the right order and at the right time. I think, by then, Christopher had given up hope and was, consequently, rather surprised.

Unexpectedly, the thing I found most difficult was not the steps themselves, but acting through the steps. I had never relied on my body alone to express anger or fear or amusement or whatever. There had always been words to help me with that. Dance uses a different vocabulary, which I had to learn and use with confidence.

A few weeks ago, I went back to the opera house to sit in the wings and watch a performance of *The Sleeping Beauty*. I was a guest of two of the dancers, Kristen McNally and Christina Arestis, who had become friends during my time on *Alice*. In fact, Kristen, poor thing, had had to dance a long and complicated scene with me and, through the weeks of rehearsal, showed herself to be a model of almost superhuman patience. In *The Sleeping Beauty*, she danced the role of the countess and Christina played the queen – unencumbered this time by my contribution. It was beautiful to see.

In narrative terms, *The Sleeping Beauty* makes no sense; but that doesn't really matter. The details of the story are less important than the display of physical beauty and technical skill. There is a famous moment in the ballet called the Rose Adagio. The Princess Aurora is asked to dance with four men who are all bidding for her hand in marriage. Balanced on one foot, on point, in *arabesque*, she offers her hand to one of her partners, who holds it for a short moment. She then lets go of his hand and, without changing her position and still precariously balanced on one foot, she offers her hand to the second man. She repeats this three times. It's a display of supreme control and every ballerina that I've talked to tells me that they dread it. Many in the audience who know something about the ballet wait eagerly for this moment and the expectant silence as they watch – will the ballerina make it through or will she stumble? – is all enveloping. One dancer told me that, when she performed the Rose Adagio, the only thing that she was aware of was the fierce, burning pain running down her supporting leg.

It's a profoundly impressive sight; not only because of the extreme physical skills that are demanded or the precision and beauty of the final result, but also because the dancer is, in a sense, stepping beyond herself, beyond her own thoughts and feelings. She is not aiming to tell us, the audience, about her own understanding of anger or pain or, even, given the fictional situation, love. She is not turning inwards – despite the pain in her leg – and then articulating what she finds there. This supremely technical moment in *The Sleeping Beauty* is not about self-expression, but, rather, about the expression of universal human potential. In other words, it's aspirational. However strange and bewildering the traditions of classical ballet may be, the pursuit of perfection is something that we can all understand.

Given the demands and constraints of classical dance and music, it is, perhaps, easier to achieve this abstract quality in those art forms than in drama. Actors, especially those who are asked to deal with great texts, are bound by the requirement to use words that, by their nature, are about the minutiae of human thought and emotion. Words are also slippery. That is part of the thrill of analysing Shakespeare, after all. But there are times when actors can achieve something like a universal impersonality. It's rare, but I have seen it. The greatest sustained display of acting power that I ever saw was in a play at the National starring Paul Scofield. It was a production of *John Gabriel Borkman* by Henrik Ibsen. It's a great play, but difficult for a contemporary audience. It tells the story of a banker – the son of a miner – who is imprisoned for fraud. The reason that Borkman gives for his criminal behaviour is that he has a dream of creating wealth – not merely personal wealth, but national too – from extracting the huge mineral resources buried deep in the Norwegian mountains. Ibsen sees this as a grand vision, I think, although we now could read it as environmentally abusive. In the final moments of the story – just before Borkman dies – the playwright writes his titular character a grand series of hallucinogenic speeches. This sequence is a curious mix of the power-crazed and the messianic. Borkman is humbled by the natural world around him, but wants to dominate or, in some way, embody it. He wants to excavate more iron ore than his father ever did. In the production that I saw in 1996 at the National Theatre, directed by Richard Eyre, it was at this point that Scofield began to stretch himself. I flatter myself that I had followed his every step up to this point; but now I lost him. I couldn't see how he was doing what he was doing. It was genuinely mysterious, almost magical.

Whether Paul Scofield was aware of his achievement I will never know. Curiously, a director who worked with him told me years later that this great actor seemed to be less concerned with charting a psychological journey than with the careful manipulation of his voice. He would work on his voice as the ballerina works on her body. He aimed to produce something of beauty – however one defines that beauty. Perhaps he felt that if he produced the right sounds the rest would take care of itself. Perhaps he felt that since he couldn't determine the details of an audience's response, then he would leave as much as possible unexplored and unsettled.

I did *John Gabriel Borkman* myself many years later, playing the title role. Part of the challenge that I set myself was to see if I could achieve the same transcendence that Scofield had. I failed. I fell short in those last moments. I probably tried too hard; and, anyway, our thoughts about the environment – and particularly about mining – have changed since the National production. There's little romance left in digging up the earth for profit – however fine the intentions behind it might be.

Shakespeare, like Ibsen, allows his actors to soar. Our work as theatre practitioners is often about looking inwards. The famous method developed by Stanislavsky is based on rigorous self-examination. Many performers joke that they use acting as a type of therapy. I have done so myself. Furthermore, theatre should examine contemporary political and social issues. And it should sometimes make us laugh. But there are grander possibilities, especially when we have the privilege to work with a great writer. Nick Hytner once said to me, perhaps after witnessing a disappointing production, that if one walks out of a Shakespeare play with the thought that there is nothing in the story that could not be sorted out with a decent course of light psychotherapy, then that production has probably failed. Nick's observation applies to Shakespeare's more serious work, of course, but I think it probably works with the comedies too. Shakespeare offers us the possibility of stretching higher, of digging deeper than any other writer that I know.

One night, many years ago, I came home after a performance and turned on the radio. As I prepared dinner, I listened to a chat show in which a quartet of pundits talked about recent events in the arts. One of the four was telling us how he hated live theatre – often a display, he said, of people behaving as no human being has ever behaved and speaking as no human being has ever spoken. I thought he rather missed the point. Great writers might very well hold the mirror up to nature, but, at its best, theatre alchemises ordinary experience into extraordinary gold. We actors almost always fail to produce something as great as Shakespeare's writing, we will almost always fall short, but that shouldn't stop us trying.

Acknowledgements

About twenty-five years ago, at some point during the year that I was playing Hamlet, my friend, Tony Holden, introduced me to Ursula McKenzie, a very important publisher. The three of us had lunch together at a rather splendid restaurant in Bath. Ursula asked me if I would consider writing a book. I replied very firmly that that would never happen and the subject was tactfully dropped.

A few years later, Ursula and I were enjoying another lunch. We had, by this time, become friends. I began to complain that I was rather short of money – I was still working in subsidised theatre, so this was hardly surprising. Ursula pointed out that if I promised to write a book, and, of course, signed a contract, then my temporary cash-flow difficulties could be resolved. I agreed, added my signature to a closely typed piece of paper and forgot all about.

Recently, it occurred to me that I ought to write the book or return the money. I chose the former option. So I have to thank Ursula for her friendship, her patience and her unshakeable confidence that, one day, a book would finally appear. I hope she is pleased. I'm sure she is surprised.

I don't know how any actor can function without a good agent. I have been very lucky. I have, over the years, enjoyed the company, help and advice of Meg, Rebecca, Simon, Dan, Vicki, Bea and Eugenie. I cannot imagine how chaotic things would have been without them.

May I mention the teachers who have helped and encouraged me? Some are dead now, so, for them, my thanks feel a little ineffective. But I wouldn't have fallen in love with Shakespeare or enjoyed such an intense relationship with classical music without John Llewelyn, Brian Worthington, Eric Griffiths, David Pettit and John Marsh.

Finally, I have worked with too many extraordinary people to list them all by name. They – and my family – have my undying thanks and, yes, my love.

Index